CHASING THE RODEO

ALSO BY W. K. STRATTON

Backyard Brawl

W. K. STRATTON

CHASING THE RODEO

On Wild Rides and Big Dreams, Broken Hearts and Broken Bones, and One Man's Search for the West

HARCOURT, INC.

Orlando   Austin   New York   San Diego   Toronto   London

www.HarcourtBooks.com

Library of Congress Cataloging-in-Publication Data
Stratton, W. K.
Chasing the rodeo: on wild rides and big dreams, broken hearts and broken bones,
and one man's search for the West/W. K. Stratton.
p.   cm.
Includes index.
1. Rodeos—West (U.S.)   I. Title.
GV1834.55.W47S87   2005
791.8'4'0978—dc22   2004023119
ISBN-13: 978-0151-01072-1
ISBN-10: 0-15-101072-2

Text set in Fournier
Designed by Linda Lockowitz

Printed in the United States of America

First edition
A C E G I K J H F D B

For Kenny Walter
and
the late Harry Ebeling:
great teachers, great friends

❧ Contents ☙

1. ESSENTIAL TRAVEL · 1
The National Finals Rodeo
Oklahoma City, Oklahoma—December 1967

2. LOOKING FOR JUNIOR BONNER · 22
The World's Oldest Rodeo
Prescott, Arizona—July 2003

3. RANGING OUT · 81
The Daddy of 'Em All
Cheyenne, Wyoming—July 2003

4. A LOT OF FLOURISH · 152
Bullnanza
Oklahoma City, Oklahoma—August 2003

5. LETTIN' 'ER BUCK · 205
Pendleton Round-Up
Pendleton, Oregon—September 2003

6. CODA: THE LAST RODEO · 280
Leakey, Texas—July 2004

The National Finals Rodeo
Las Vegas, Nevada—December 2003

Author's Note · 300
Acknowledgments · 303
Bibliography · 307
Index · 311

CHASING THE RODEO

⇥ 1. ESSENTIAL TRAVEL ⇤

The National Finals Rodeo
Oklahoma City, Oklahoma—December 1967

HERE'S A rodeo story for you.

The National Finals Rodeo kicked off its 1967 run in Oklahoma City on December 1, and I distinctly remember that day. It was one of those days when the wind sliced right through you, the sky was the color of fresh concrete, and the sleet-encrusted roads were, in the words of my next-door neighbor Paul Fey, "slicker than greased owl shit." Voices on radio and television discouraged all travel that wasn't essential.

I was twelve years old and living in Guthrie, Oklahoma, thirty miles north of Oklahoma City. I heard those warnings and sighed. It's not that I minded that school was closed down that Friday. But the highways too icy for travel? That was another matter. We had tickets for the National Finals, and I considered the drive to "The City" for the rodeo to be *essential* travel. Mom would consider it essential, too, but I wasn't sure about Dad. He'd be doing the driving. It would kill me if he agreed with the voices on radio and TV and decided we should stay home.

Mom had bought NFR tickets from the Guthrie Roundup Club back in the summer and had been guarding them as zealously as she guarded the milk bottle filled with real silver dollars she kept hidden in her closet. Since the inception of the NFR in the 1950s as rodeo's equivalent of the World Series, the event had struggled through tough times in Los Angeles and Dallas before relocating to the State Fairgrounds Arena in The City three years earlier. Ensuring the NFR's success in Oklahoma had become a matter of state pride. Buying a ticket gave you a chance to see the best rodeo cowboys in the world, but it also meant that you were doing something good for Oklahoma, a state that ached for anything that could generate some revenue or could raise its profile in the eyes of the rest of the country. (Even in the 1960s, Oklahoma reeled from its Dust Bowl image as a no-account place filled with ignorant Okies; many of the state's public libraries still banned copies of *The Grapes of Wrath*.) The NFR brought Oklahoma just the sort of national attention it craved. So good Oklahomans bought their tickets. *And* they turned out to fill the seats. Never mind a little ice storm.

We lived on five acres on the far-east side of Guthrie. On one corner of the property sat Dad's auto repair shop. From there, our small frame house was a half block up Pine Street. From my parents' bedroom window, I watched Dad trudge against the wind and sleet that night. It seemed to take him a lot longer than usual to make it from the north door of the shop to the front door of the house. I knew his face would be numb. I knew he'd be hearing the crunch of the frozen grass beneath his boots, the whistle of the wind, the pop from the leafless limbs of the Chinese elms in the front yard as they struggled with their load of ice. I knew he would be glancing up at Noble Avenue to see if any traffic was moving.

Dad stomped his boots clean on the front porch and came inside. Mom met him in the living room with fists planted on her hips. They went to the kitchen to talk. I cut through the Hollywood bathroom that separated my bedroom from theirs and plopped down on my Western-style bunk bed with a wagon-wheel footboard and cowboys and Indians on the bedspread. Ice on the inside of the windowpane next to my bed cinched my dark mood: I was certain that Dad would decide we should stay home.

A few minutes later, Mom came into the room. "Do you want to brave the storm and go to the rodeo tonight?" she asked.

Of course I ached to go, but it was important that I veil my enthusiasm. After all, I'd been twelve for a month and was practically a teenager. I'd already smoked my first cigarettes (stolen from my mother) and drank my first beer (from a six-pack of Falstaff supplied by a shirttail cousin). I knew about the Rolling Stones and Bob Dylan, and I even owned a copy of the Doors' first album. It wouldn't do for me to jump up and down like some *kid* and shout, "Are you nuts? Of course I want to go!"

"Yeah," I said. "I *guess* so. If you guys really want to. I mean, if Dad thinks it's safe."

She looked perplexed by my lack of excitement. That wasn't unusual. She often looked perplexed after talking to me in those days.

A few minutes later I heard Dad leave the house. Through the ice on the bedroom window, I saw our Chevy Impala station wagon pull up to the main door of the shop. Dad got out— still in his coveralls—and opened the door so he could drive the car inside. I didn't take that to be a good sign. I figured he was putting the car up for the night to keep it out of the sleet. I sighed and turned away from the window. But just then, Mom stuck her head in my bedroom and said, "Get ready. Dad's going to put the chains on the car."

I leaped up smiling, but only after she'd left.

I CAN'T REMEMBER the first time I went to a rodeo. I know I went to an amateur rodeo outside Guthrie, in utero, just days before I made my grand entrance on an unseasonably chilly Will Rogers's birthday, back when Eisenhower was president. (I always took that to be a good sign, being an Oklahoma kid who shared a birthday with Will Rogers, the great cowboy comedian.) I'm sure I was still in diapers when I first saw a rodeo with open eyes. Maybe at the Guthrie High School football field. Maybe at the Roundup Club grounds, which were sandwiched between Mineral Wells Park and the Logan County Fairgrounds. Maybe somewhere out of town. I do know rodeo's been a part of my life, in one way or another, for as long as I've been around.

I'm looking now at a photograph recently uncovered in the basement of my family's old house on Pine Street. It is Christmas morning, and I am four years old. On my head is a black Western hat. On my feet are shiny new black cowboy boots with fancy red and white stitching. My jeans are tucked into my boots. A two-gun belt, also black, rides low on my nonexistent hips, the holsters holding silver cap pistols. I have black leather gloves on my hands (movie foolishness, mostly inspired by Jack Palance in *Shane;* no real Western gunfighters—such as they were—engaged in such nonsense as wearing gloves while shooting). And there is a toy badge pinned to my shirt. I look like one bad tiny hombre.

The boots, hat, gun belt, gloves, and badge are Christmas presents. I can't remember them, and there's nothing really special about them. Any number of kids all over America probably got the same presents that year. Looking carefully, I see I'm wearing a brown belt through the loops of my jeans. This belt I do remember. It is a hand-tooled Western belt, and on the back is my middle name, Kip, the name I've always gone by. I wore this belt every day. Just as I wore miniature cowboy boots every day.

I'm not exaggerating when I say I wore cowboy boots every day. A couple of years later, I flunked shoe tying in kindergarten because I never wore shoes that tied. To this day people who watch me knot my sneakers say I do it backwards.

I came by my hand-tooled belt and boots honestly. My mother was a rodeo girl. From her teens into her early twenties, rodeo was her passion. As a senior, she chose for her Guthrie High School yearbook inscription the title of a famous Patsy Montana song, "I Want to Be a Cowboy's Sweetheart." Every weekend, she and her girlfriends loaded up whatever car they could borrow and roared off to the nearest rodeo. Maybe one of the Guthrie Roundup Club's rodeos. Or maybe the indoor collegiate rodeos at Oklahoma A&M (now Oklahoma State University) in Stillwater. Or maybe the jackpot rodeos at the Thedford Ranch near the tiny community of Orlando about twenty miles north of Guthrie. Or maybe the biggest rodeo in the county, the annual Eighty-Niners' Day Rodeo at Jelsma Stadium in Guthrie. They learned the intricacies of the sport. Undoubtedly, they flirted like all get-out with the cowboys. Mom told me she and her friends used to go to dances with the cowboys they'd met, sometimes impromptu dances at one of the girls' houses, where they'd play records, and two-step, and maybe play some dominoes and cards. You'd be naive not to believe that some serious business occurred after the dominoes were back in their box and the lights were turned down low.

So it's not surprising that Mom dressed me in boots and jeans and a Western. But there's more.

Here's another photograph. In this one I am maybe three years old, sitting in front of the couch in the trailer house we lived in before we moved to the acreage on Pine Street. To the right of me are my brothers, Elden and Dale. I'm the youngest of the three, but I stick out in other ways. For one thing, I'm wearing my cowboy boots, and my brothers are in black slip-on shoes. My hair is light and downy; theirs, dark and thick. My complexion is not as fair as theirs. I have a jutting jaw and high cheekbones; their faces are broader, rounder. It is obvious we are not blood relations. Although I call them my brothers, they are my stepbrothers.

And Dad's name appears nowhere on my birth certificate. I've accorded Dad the respect of a father since I was three years old; I've called him Dad for as long as I can remember, but the man listed on the certificate is Don Carlos Stratton Jr., a bull-riding cowboy from Denver whom my mom met one year during an Eighty-Niners' Day Rodeo in Guthrie. Their romance was brief and star-crossed, but it lasted long enough to create me. A rodeo girl and a cowboy. No wonder my boots felt comfortable. And no wonder the annual run of the National Finals Rodeo in Oklahoma City became a high point in my life.

OUR IMPALA station wagon crawled down the all but abandoned Interstate 35, the chains slapping the packed ice and snow on the roadway. A drive to the northwest section of The City that normally took just over thirty minutes consumed more than an hour, but the drive there wasn't nearly as bad as the walk from the parking lot to the State Fairgrounds Arena. My ears ached, and my fingers and my cheeks had turned to cardboard by the time Dad, Mom, and I made it inside the building.

If I fly into Oklahoma City these days, I leave Will Rogers World Airport by way of a freeway that takes me past the fairgrounds. Seeing the arena, I marvel at how small it is, an oversized checker of a building set against the long, narrow stock barns and other buildings that house Oklahoma's state fair. As a kid, I was sure it had to be the largest building in America. The top rows of seats seemed so high that I wondered if you might have trouble breathing at that altitude.

Now I know it was a cozy venue for watching a major sporting event (or rock concert: I saw Bob Dylan and the Rolling Thunder Revue give a memorable performance there in the mid-1970s). No seat was very far from the action on the arena floor, and the building was set up to give you freedom to wander. My hairstylist grew up in Oklahoma City, and her dad took her to the NFR every year. The high point for her came when her father led her back to the holding pens behind the chutes so she could watch the horses and the bulls. By the 1990s, most rodeos restricted access to these areas, mostly to protect themselves from accident liability. But back then, fans could go almost everywhere the cowboys went.

After we found our seats, Mom left Dad and me to find the restroom. She came back glowing. "I just ran smack-dab into Larry Mahan on the way to the restroom!" she said as she plopped down in her chair.

Within the world of rodeo in the mid- to late 1960s, running into Larry Mahan was akin to running into Elvis. Born in Oregon, he joined the Rodeo Cowboys Association (now the Professional Rodeo Cowboys Association, or PRCA) in 1963 after winning the Arizona High School Rodeo all-around cowboy title the previous year. By the time he'd won the high school title, he was already an experienced hand. He was awarded his first trophy buckle and prize money (six dollars) when he was twelve years old. He'd won the world saddle bronc riding title in 1965. In 1966 he claimed rodeo's most prized award: the all-around cowboy title at the National Finals Rodeo. But the way he did it astonished rodeo fans: He placed in the top six in all three "rough-stock" events—saddle bronc, bareback, and bull riding. In 1967 he would do even better. He'd win bull riding, place third in saddle bronc, and place fourth in bareback. And he'd claim his second consecutive all-around cowboy trophy. Even people who had watched the great Jim Shoulders in his prime shook their heads at Mahan's amazing accomplishments. Mahan was handsome, articulate, savvy. He became a pilot and flew from rodeo to rodeo, giving him a greater chance at prize money than cowboys who stuck to the highways. Journalists doted on him, as did businessmen who wanted him to pitch their products. Not surprisingly, Hollywood kept an eye on him as a potential box office draw (and indeed, he would end up appearing in films and made-for-TV movies). He knew what making himself available to the fans could do for his career. He didn't stay secluded somewhere behind the chutes at the NFR. He was always out "struttin' around the crowd," as Mom would say. It was smart strutting. Running into Mahan on the way to the restroom gave Mom something to talk about for years, thus boosting his image to everyone she told.

THE HOUSE LIGHTS went down on a sold-out arena with many empty seats; not all ticket holders had had the dedication to battle the ice storm. But this hardly diminished the excitement of the crowd. Multicolored spotlights positioned on catwalks far above us began to dance across the grandstand and the floor of the arena as the grand entry got under way. Music boomed over speakers hanging from the ceiling, followed by the voice of Pete Logan, smooth as whiskey and honey, welcoming us to the National Finals Rodeo.

The previous two years, the great Cy Taillon and Oklahoma's own Clem McSpadden were the NFR announcers. Throughout its history, the NFR has featured the very best in rodeo—the top cowboys and barrel racers, of course (based on their earnings through the season), but also the best livestock (based on the animals' performance over the season as judged by the contestants), the best pickup men, the best hands behind the chutes, the best clowns, the best announcers. To my mind, Taillon, Logan, and McSpadden form a sort of holy trinity of rodeo announcers, unsurpassed in the business then and now. The 1960 Finals at the Texas State Fairgrounds in Dallas must have been a wonder on the ears because all three took part in calling it. In 1967 Taillon was absent and McSpadden had begun his seventeen-year run (a record) as the rodeo's general manager. So Logan stood behind the microphone, with the formidable Chuck Parkison of North Hollywood, California, in the booth to complement him.

The grand entry unrolled as a swirl of lights, flags, horses, cowboys, and rodeo sweethearts. This may have been the year of Sgt. Pepper and the Doors and the Summer of Love in the Haight-Ashbury section of San Francisco, but none of that was evident there that night. The opening ceremony included a tip of the Resistol to "our brave fighting men in Vietnam and around the world"—something you heard at nearly all rodeos. Huge applause. To be sure, this was a crowd largely composed of what Richard Nixon would call the "Silent Majority"—and pity the longhair foolish enough to come around here with a protest or a love-in in mind. The faces of the men in the stands and on the arena floor bore no whiskers. Their hair was trimmed well above their ears and collars, and, by god, they expected yours to be, too. The women wore their hair shellacked and piled up in beehives. This atmosphere may have challenged my budding allegiance to America's youth culture, but I didn't care. This was a rodeo crowd, my people. And I loved them.

The rodeo moved through the timed events: calf roping, team roping, steer wrestling, barrel racing. Then, as now, I found the roping a little tedious. Barrel racing, interesting. Steer wrestling (or bulldogging, as we most often called it), intriguing—the event I could most see myself doing.

But bareback, saddle bronc, and bull riding were something else. I wanted to jump out of my seat each time a bucking chute gate snapped open, and I'd get so excited that I had a hard time breathing. Bull riding was best of all. It was not for nothing that the event traditionally ended rodeos. Hard to think of a better grand finale.

You could argue that the greatest moment in the history of rodeo occurred during the bull riding on that frigid night in Oklahoma City. You could argue that, and I'd agree with you.

FRECKLES BROWN was a small, unimposing man who had no freckles. Ask him about his nickname, and the corners of his eyes would crinkle as he'd answer in a deadpan voice that, yeah, he once had freckles, but years of riding bulls had shaken them all off. After shooting you a wry smile, he'd tell you the story about how when he was a kid he went to work milking cows for a man who owned a dairy: "He asked me my name, and I said 'Warren.' He said he couldn't call anyone *Warren*, so he started calling me *Freckles*." The name stuck. He had a lot of years riding bulls. Just a month shy of forty-seven, he was twice as old as Mahan, and he'd first climbed on the back of a Brahma at a 1937 rodeo in Willcox, Arizona, before Mahan was even born. Four years later, he won his first bull-riding title at the Stampede in Cody, Wyoming.

From the 1941 Cody Stampede until the 1967 National Finals, Freckles suffered more bad luck, bad draws, and bad injuries than most people can fathom. A bull rider's prime riding years are his early to mid-twenties. Freckles spent his prime years in the army and the Office of Strategic Services (Wild Bill Donovan's forerunner to the CIA) in China. Yes, he rodeoed some in China. Maybe he took part in the first rodeos ever held in that vast country, riding bucking mules and horses. But that didn't count for much back in the States. When he came back from the war, he and his young wife, Edith, settled in Lawton, Oklahoma, where he'd first met her while in basic training at Fort Sill. (Later the Browns moved to the Kelly Bend Ranch on the Muddy Boggy River outside Soper, Oklahoma, in the old Choctaw Nation.) A hand on his dad's sugar beet and potato farm in Wyoming, a cow milker in Arizona, a ranch hand on a spread adjacent to Yellowstone National Park, a rodeo cowboy with experience riding bucking mules in China—these were the skills that Freckles could fall back on as an ex-GI. He could get work on a ranch in southwestern Oklahoma, maybe. Something like that. But ranch-hand wages were pitiful. He and Edith figured out he could make more money out on the professional rodeo circuit, even if it meant that he take a job as a stock hand working behind the chutes to help cover the cost of his entry fees. His star never rose like those of his contemporaries Jim Shoulders and Casey Tibbs. But Freckles would tell you with some pride that he was known for being among "the ten or twelve sure-enough tough hands on the circuit." As the years slipped past, other rodeo cowboys held him in awe, even if his name wasn't well known outside the arena. Freckles had a rodeo soul.

For one thing, there was his whole approach to bull riding. *Studied* is a good way to put it. He watched rodeo bulls throughout the country and memorized their moves as they came out of the chute, bucking and spinning. Bull riders consider bucking bulls athletes. Like all athletes, bulls have certain routines they follow, just like baseball pitchers and batters do. Learn their moves, and you can get a competitive advantage. So there was Freckles, watching bull after bull, remembering all he could about them and about what the cowboys on them did right and wrong. And remembering everything possible there was to remember about every bull he himself rode.

The 1950s is often considered a kind of golden age for rodeo. But the 1950s were also wild and crazy on the rodeo circuit, and the macho measure of a man, often as not, involved how much drinking, gambling, and womanizing he could squeeze into the hours between shows. A rider who rode brilliantly one day might arrive the next day broke, drunk, and nursing a knife wound from a dance-hall fight over a woman.

When Freckles showed up for a rodeo, however, his mind was on the rodeo. Not that he was antisocial. He'd stop in at poker games to say hello, and everyone brightened up seeing him.

"Hey Freck," the famed trick rider Cecil Cornish always said when he saw him. "You remember that rodeo dance we went to over in Arkansas in the thirties?"

"Yes, I do," Freckles replied. "None of them girls wore shoes."

The other cowboys loved him. And they respected the veritable notebook he kept in his head about all those bulls. So when it came time to get serious about the bulls in the alleyway, they'd come to Freckles to pick his brain about how they should handle their draw. He was the man in the know.

Freckles was also one tough son of a gun, no matter how you measured it. "It seems like I'd just get to riding good and placing good," he said. "Then—*wham!*—I'd break my leg." The catalog of Freckles's injuries was stunning: right leg broken four times, left leg broken twice; left ankle once, right ankle twice. And so on. Journalist W. C. Heinz notes:

> He had had his left foot smashed a couple of times, and his neck broken twice. There was a piece of tendon from his upper left leg tied to the tendon in his left ankle, and the severed tendon in his right arm had been retied. There was a metal screw in his left ankle, and his neck was held in place by a plug made out of a piece of his hip bone. He had had ruptured blood vessels in his right thigh, and pulled muscles and ruptured vessels in his groin. He had suffered three concussions, and there is a scar over his upper right lip where it was hooked by a horn.

Heinz considered Freck the world's leading expert on doctors and hospitals.

Chances were, Freckles would ride even though his leg was broken. But not as well as he'd ride if he were healthy. So he didn't collect a pile of world champion belt buckles like his contemporary and friend Jim Shoulders. The one world title he did win came in 1962. That year he also suffered his worst injury when a bull named Black Smoke threw him, breaking Freckles's neck and leaving him paralyzed for a while. He was already past forty, long overdue for retirement from this most physically destructive of sports, when the two busted vertebrae confined him to bed. People thought they'd never see him climb into a chute to wrap a bull rope around his hand again. *Hell of a thing that's happened to Freckles—but at least he got his world title before retiring.*

Retiring? Freckles hadn't even begun to show his stuff.

Like the other cowboys, Freckles had a tough time just getting to Oklahoma City for the National Finals in 1967 because of the weather. He finally made it, though. And learned that for all the trouble he had navigating treacherous roads, his draw for the opening night was Tornado. For other bull riders, that would not have been good news.

For Freckles, it was an answered prayer.

A rodeo cowboy from the mid-1960s once told me that drawing Tornado made suicide look like an intelligent alternative. The bull's reputation was unmatched in the history of rodeo. He was held in awe by the cowboys he propelled off his back in spectacular style. The fans who had seen him were hardly less awestruck.

Tornado was now eleven years old and had been breaking bones and shattering egos at rodeos since the early 1960s. In fact, Tornado had made two hundred twenty cowboys bite arena dust before the eight-second whistle had sounded. That no one stayed on him was damned good for a bull that had been sickly and skinny when he was young; a lot of people had had no hope of his ever turning out to be much more than potential hamburger. But not his owner, Jim Shoulders. Shoulders became a stock contractor and a rodeo school proprietor as his own career as a bull and bronc rider wound down, and he saw potential that most people missed in the young Brahma-Hereford cross. Shoulders patiently built Tornado up to an eighteen-hundred-pound bucking wonder, which he then set loose to wreak havoc on the pro rodeo circuit. Tornado forever changed the way stock contractors looked at bulls. They sought bulls with his power, his bucking and spinning ability. Tornado became the prototype for bulls to come like Mr. T and Bodacious.

Not surprisingly, Tornado fascinated Freckles. Going all the way back to when he started riding in the 1930s, Freckles had never come across anything like Tornado. Every chance he got, he studied Tornado in the pens behind the arena. He never missed an opportunity to watch Tornado come out of the chute. For a long time, he gave people who asked his simple assessment: "I'm not sure that bull can be ridden." A lot of cowboys agreed with Freckles. They would rather forgo the ride than risk climbing on Tornado.

Unridable, yet not exactly rank,* either. Maybe. Freckles noticed that as bulls went, Tornado didn't seem to have much interest in hurting cowboys once they were thrown. He was not, as the line goes, one mean hooking son of a bitch. Instead, once he rocketed the bull rider from his back, Tornado usually responded to the cues from the clowns (called bullfighters these days) and headed toward the exit gate. At least that's how

---

*_Rank_ is sometimes used to describe any bull that is difficult to ride. But a more precise definition is a bull that's vicious, that will try to attack a thrown rider.

Freckles saw him. Others held different opinions. Once Mahan told me good-naturedly: "Yeah, that's about like that Freckles, make that son of a bitch Tornado sound like some kinda white mouse. That bull made the rest of us look like idiots." Whether he was mean or not, Tornado did offer a bull rider the chance to rack up a heavenly score—if he could just stay on board for eight seconds.

Through all those years of studying Tornado, Freckles never drew him. But finally he had his chance.

MOM GREW more and more excited as the rodeo progressed that frigid December night. Bull riding was her favorite event, and she knew more about the bull riders than any of the other contestants. She never met Freckles during her own rodeo days, yet she knew all about him—the tough luck, the comebacks. He was at the top of her list of favorite cowboys. When Logan announced that Freckles had drawn Tornado, she turned to me and said, "My goodness, wouldn't it be *something* if old Freckles rode that bull!"

Sure, that would be *something*. But I remember thinking that it was not possible. Even Mahan couldn't ride Tornado. Yet people all around us were springing to their feet to see what would happen in this contest between Freckles and Tornado. And I was standing, too, before the gate even opened.

Freckles pursued the perfect ride the way the Zen master seeks satori. It was as much a feel for everything being just right as anything else. Usually he didn't quite achieve it. But that night, everything seemed to have the right feel.

For a bull rider to have a chance at a high score (in the 80s or 90s), his ride should begin with the bull exploding out of the chute. Tornado always exploded. I've never seen a bull more impressive coming out of the chute than Tornado was that night. He came out with the power of a gigantic whale leaping from the sea. All four hooves flew impossibly high above the ground. A long trail of slobber whipped from his mouth. His front hooves slammed into the dirt while he simultaneously tucked his head low and kicked his rear feet so high that his body seemed almost perpendicular to the arena floor. He executed a sharp turn and began his spin with so much power that it astonished people who had never seen him perform. A *Daily Oklahoman* reporter observed from behind the chutes that Tornado had "enough energy to tear down any of the gates which loomed in front of him at almost every turn."

Freckles had his shoulders squared to the bull's body and maintained his form throughout the mayhem. And he put his mind in a place where it seemed impossible for it to go. He wasn't concentrating or remembering or planning. Instead, he became one with the bull.

Meanwhile, the standing crowd shouted and gasped with each maneuver Tornado made. On the one hand, you realized you were witnessing a wonderful thing. But on the other hand, all the experience you had watching rodeo told you that it was entirely possible for a rider having the ride of his career to slip down into "the well"* abruptly or to be corkscrewed off in the other direction just a second or two before the eight-second whistle sounded. So you were thinking, *maybe. Maybe. Maybe!* MA*Ybe! MAYBE! MAYBE!*

Then the whistle.

During the ride, Freckles was oblivious to the crowd noise. Oblivious even to the whistle. Freckles had no idea he had successfully ridden Tornado until he saw the clowns leading the

---

*Bull riders call the inside of a bull's spinning maneuver "the well." Being thrown into the well is treacherous for the rider, who is then particularly vulnerable to being stomped or butted by the bull.

great bull toward the exit gate. Then he looked up and saw the crowd on its feet.

And he knew.

Suddenly Jim Shoulders leaped into the arena, the first of scores of people to congratulate Freckles, even though it was in Shoulders's best financial interest to have the mighty Tornado continue its unridden streak. Shoulders didn't care; he knew greatness when he saw it. So did all the chute hands and livestock workers who were waving their hats and shouting. Then there was the crowd.

I looked around at the turmoil surrounding me. A middle-aged man with a blond flattop danced a jig in an aisle. A woman in a dress stood on her seat and bellowed. Some people had tears streaming down their cheeks.

"I stood out there in the middle of the arena with my hat off for the longest time," Freckles told me many years later. "But the applause didn't die down. It just kept going and going. And it wasn't just the fans. Even the rodeo cowboys were clapping and yelling. I finally walked off, but it didn't let up any." Freckles wasn't sure what to do. He peered around until he spotted Clem McSpadden. McSpadden motioned to him to go back into the arena. "So I did. And it started all over again."

I TALKED TO McSpadden about Freckles and Tornado after "The Ride" had settled into the stuff of myth, and he termed it the greatest legend-making incident in the history of rodeo. "I don't mean to take anything away from Freckles," he said, "but the bull was at a point in its career where it was fit to be ridden. But Tornado had such a reputation that most cowboys were thrown before they ever got on him. Freckles quite possibly was the only cowboy who could have ridden him because he just wouldn't think about the reputation. Freckles got on him and bore down and ended up riding him pretty easy."

But then McSpadden pondered it and thought he might be underselling what his old friend achieved that night.

To understand how great an accomplishment this ride was, you have to keep in mind Freckles's age at the time. He was thirty-eight when the National Finals Rodeo began in 1959. In my opinion, he was a better rider at forty-six than he was at thirty-eight. That in itself is something. Still, considering the physical demands of bull riding, Freckles's ride of Tornado at age forty-six would be like a man at age sixty being an outstanding major league baseball player. He was definitely a father figure to a lot of those younger cowboys. At the same time, though, he was able to compete with the best of 'em.

And on that night, beat the best of 'em.

But the age factor wasn't the important thing. McSpadden believed it was his character that made Freckles's accomplishment so appealing to the rodeo world. "Everyone was pulling for Freckles. You see, he was the most genuine, most humble, nicest man I've ever known. If the world was full of Freckles Browns, you wouldn't need locks on any of your doors. All he ever knew his whole life was hard work, so you had to hope something good would happen for him."

So GROWN MEN and women danced jigs, and cried, and shouted, and the ovation went on by some accounts for more than ten minutes, all without the aid of a JumboTron telling the crowd that it should continue cheering.

The news spread into the icy night, through the honky-tonks along Reno Avenue down into Packing Town, where Oklahoma City's stockyard and processing plants were located. McSpadden stayed up late that night and was up long before dawn the next morning. In addition to being a renowned rodeo announcer, McSpadden was also one of the most powerful politicians in Oklahoma (president pro tempore of the state Senate and later a member of Congress) and a blood relative of Will Rogers to boot. His face appeared in the newspapers and on television regularly, so he was recognizable on the streets. As he left his hotel in the predawn hours, winos came up to him to ask about Freckles and Tornado. They'd already heard the story and wanted to know more.

Soon the word traveled beyond wino gossip to a national audience. Even the dean of American sportswriters, Red Smith, weighed in on the matter of Freckles Brown in his column: "The next best thing to a lie, Joe Palmer wrote, is a true story nobody will believe, and anybody who would believe the story of Freckles Brown ought to report himself." W. C. Heinz, an influential magazine writer, devoted a chapter to Freckles in his book *Once They Heard the Cheers*. Red Steagall had a minor country hit with a song about Freckles. Some people thought The Ride should become a movie.

Even Tornado got his due. When Tornado died a few years later, the great bull was buried ceremoniously on the grounds of the National Cowboy Hall of Fame in Oklahoma City, just a few miles from the arena where The Ride had taken place. It was a singular honor for a rodeo animal.

IN THE DARK CAVERN of the backseat of the station wagon, I sat with my heart thumping as Dad slowly drove us back to Guthrie. I was still stunned by what I'd seen, enough so that I had nothing to say. I turned my cheek against the frozen vinyl of the back of the seat, closed my eyes, and replayed Freckles and Tornado in my mind.

Eventually, though, my thoughts turned away from the great ride. I pondered about the faces of the men I'd seen that night—mostly thin, mostly weathered in the shade of their

Western hats. I did this every time I went to a rodeo, cataloging face after face and wondering: *Could one of them belong to my real father?* Maybe. I'd never seen him, had never even seen a picture of him. I had no idea where he lived. In fact, I had no idea if he was even alive. For all I knew, he and Freckles Brown could have been best friends. Or he might have jerked the rope to open the chute for Tornado.

I've never suffered mysteries well, always feeling a tug to get to the bottom of things. Perhaps that's why I became a newspaper reporter while still a teenager. No reflection on Dad, who did the best he could to be a father to me and who treated me no differently than he did his own flesh-and-blood sons, but it bugged me that I knew virtually nothing about the man whose name I carried. It bugged me when I was a kid. It bugged me through most of my adult life.

Tonight it is clear and dry in Central Texas, nothing at all like it was that night in Oklahoma City more than thirty years ago. I stand on the porch and see stars above my house in the suburbs, not far from where one of the great cattle trails once ran, though you could never tell that from all the housing additions and shopping centers around here. From Interstate 35, I hear the rattle and roar of the semitrailers heading to and coming from Mexico. I feel the soles of my feet grow itchy. It occurs to me that I am now the age that Freckles was when he rode Tornado. Mentally tabulating my various physical maladies, I wonder how in the world a man my age could ever have climbed on that bull and ridden him so well.

I am also thinking about Cowboy Don, the name I coined for my long-lost father. Over the last half dozen years, I've demystified the enigma that was Cowboy Don. Or at least a lot of it. Because of what I've learned about him, and in turn about myself, I know I'm going to have to go out on the rodeo circuit for a while. A part of me is out there in the rodeo arenas and surrounding hoopla—the glitter and the dirt, cow shit and cotton candy, broken hearts and broken bones. It's time for me to come to grips with it. I listen to the trucks and peer at the stars and think, *I need to get rolling.*

It is essential travel.

⚔ 2. LOOKING FOR JUNIOR BONNER ⚔

The World's Oldest Rodeo
Prescott, Arizona—July 2003

I COULD HAVE PICKED a lot worse place to start than Prescott, Arizona.

It is the week of Independence Day, and Phoenix is roasting when the flight from Austin touches down, even though it is only nine in the morning. Downtown is a painful glare of office building windows and parking lot windshields encircled by dingy yellow smog, and I want nothing more than to escape to higher ground, much higher ground. So my wife and I hit Interstate 17 on a straight shot north out of downtown, happy that only remnants of rush hour traffic remain to slow us down. I push the speedometer up over seventy.

When we escape the suburbs, we begin a steady ascent toward the mountains, leaving behind us the depressing images of plastic grocery bag–draped saguaros in the interstate median. Phoenix sits at an elevation of about eleven hundred feet; Prescott is a mile-high city. After climbing more than four thousand feet over the hundred miles of highway between Phoenix and Prescott, you feel like you've entered not only a different region but also a time warp—and blessedly so. Old-timers tell you that development is ruining the area, but it's still easy enough for a newcomer to overlook the trailer houses, convenience stores, and housing developments and be overwhelmed by the natural setting. This is butte and mesa country, ponderosa pine country. Big country. The Western landscape is exactly as Hollywood mythmakers have trained us to believe. It is hard to imagine a better site for a rodeo, especially the self-proclaimed "world's oldest rodeo," Prescott's Frontier Days. "The very best place to see a rodeo is in a small Western town," Larry McMurtry writes. "One can be assured of a colorful occasion, and the show will have a summer evening and a long Western sundown setting on it."

Small town, summer evening, a long Western sundown— perfect.

"My god, this is beautiful!" my wife, Luscaine, says as we drive down Gurley Street, Prescott's main drag, toward the courthouse plaza. She is right. Beautiful—if something of an anomaly. In a region where the dominant architectural style is made up of variants on sunbaked adobe, Prescott is a town marked by graceful Victorian gables and cupolas and gingerbread.

The centerpiece is the Yavapai County courthouse plaza, which could have been plucked from the heart of Illinois or Indiana. The handsome courthouse is fringed with soaring elms that on this summer day provide plenty of cool shade for the dozens of people who lollygag on benches or stretch out on the grass. There's even a covered bandstand. How much more all-American can you get? It may be impossible to take in the square without conjuring up 1950s movie musicals, but it is an impressive place, an inviting place.

I park the car, and my wife and I loop the plaza a couple of times on foot. The wind swirls through the elms. People we meet on the sidewalk nod and smile. A guy in a lawn chair panhandles us, never rising to his feet, and it is the friendliest panhandling I've ever encountered. We walk to the main entrance of the courthouse, a white stone building with columns out front and a clock tower up above. It was on these steps that Barry Goldwater announced his quixotic campaign for the GOP's 1964 presidential nomination, and that seems perfectly apt for a candidacy steeped in Western conservatism. Besides, Prescott was sort of a second hometown for the Arizona senator. His uncle Morris Goldwater was a Prescott business and political leader and helped organize the first Prescott rodeo in 1888. When Barry Goldwater made his announcement, he shared the stage on the courthouse lawn with the statue of Buckey O'Neill. It's hard to get away from Buckey's shadow in Prescott.

William Owen O'Neill arrived in town in 1882 at age twenty-two after stays in Tombstone and Phoenix. He evidently was quite a player at the faro table. His nickname came from his skill at being good at "bucking the tiger": Faro cards had tigers on their backsides. Over the next sixteen years, he established himself as one of Prescott's most important citizens. Court reporter, newspaper editor, probate judge, short story author, prosperous mine owner, school superintendent, Yavapai County sheriff, tax assessor, mayor of Prescott—he held all these titles before achieving the one for which he is best known, captain of Troop A of Teddy Roosevelt's Rough Rider regiment. Buckey must have gone to Cuba in part hoping to blot away a measure of notoriety he had achieved during a courthouse lawn hanging in Prescott. Buckey commanded a local militia unit there to serve as an honor guard. When the trapdoor fell, Buckey fainted.

In Cuba, however, he showed no lack of bravery as troopers who had taken cover watched him calmly go about his business with a cigarette in his mouth as bullets whizzed past him. When asked about his lack of concern, Buckey would give his famous line: "The Spanish bullet is not molded that will kill me." But on July 1, 1898, Buckey took a Spanish bullet in the head, and it most certainly did kill him. Almost instantly Buckey became a legend. After a local fund-raising campaign and a legislative appropriation, Prescott officials acquired the services of Solon H. Borglum, "America's first cowboy sculptor," to create the statue of Buckey that would serve as a monument to all Arizona Rough Riders. At the unveiling in 1907, thousands of people crowded onto the courthouse plaza to cheer for old Buckey, the fainting episode of twenty years earlier all but forgotten. It was July 3. Rodeo time.

The Victorian look of the plaza and the surrounding buildings is no accident. In the mid-1860s, Abraham Lincoln designated Prescott (which is pronounced *press-kut*) as the capital of the fledgling Arizona Territory, picking a village that still needed to be laid out over the only existing town of any consequence in the territory, Tucson. Lincoln and the other Republican leaders viewed Tucson as a community dominated by Texans with pro-Democrat, pro-Confederacy leanings, so they didn't trust placing the seat of power there. Prescott popped up along the banks of Granite Creek, with the early leaders determined to make it a tidy Midwestern oasis in the middle of Apache country.

Despite the Midwestern trappings, Prescott became a sure-enough Wild West town as mining boomed, cattle ranches took root, and rail lines opened in the years following the Civil War. The new town became home to the sort of carrying-on that would cause the most open-minded people back in, say, Peoria to blush. Montezuma Street on the west side of the courthouse plaza soon was known as Whiskey Row, with one saloon squeezed next to another. Drinking, brawling, gambling, and whoring—all were mainstays of life in Prescott, with some shooting thrown in from time to time.

The jewel along Whiskey Row was the Palace Saloon, which in one incarnation or another might be as old as the town itself. Records at Prescott's Sharlot Hall Museum indicate it could have been opened by one Isaac Goldberg, on the dirt road that was Prescott in 1864. The Palace went down in flames in 1883 along with the rest of Whiskey Row. The saloon came back to life in a new, allegedly fireproof incarnation that featured a twenty-foot oak bar that became known as the best in the West. At this point, the Palace was the quintessence of Western saloons, with the fabled oak bar, poker and keno tables, dancing girls (including the notorious Little Egypt), gunfighters like Virgil Earp (who once was Prescott's constable), Wyatt Earp, and Doc Holliday, and even three heavy chandeliers, from which, one imagines, feisty cowboys swung when fisticuffs broke out over a poker game or a dance-hall girl, just like in the movies. In spite of the new Palace's alleged fireproof status, it went up in flames along with the rest of the business district in July 1900 after a blaze broke out at the O.K. Lodging House. Aghast at what was happening, Palace patrons and employees freed the oak bar from its moorings and carried it across the street to the safety of the courthouse plaza. Other concerned citizens rescued cases of whiskey. As the walls of the Palace and the other downtown buildings collapsed in flames, there had to be sighs of relief from the plaza lawn. At least the bar and the whiskey had been saved. Thank god. And then someone decided to serve drinks to the people watching the fire. Why not? It was a hell of a show. Less than a year later, the new Palace Saloon opened, this version even grander, with the oak bar in place and the gaming tables liberating miners and cowboys from their hard-earned pay. A half dozen years later, changes in Arizona law curtailed the gambling and the activities of the "hostesses." The Palace began a slow slide into seediness while at the same time becoming one of the best-known rodeo bars in

America. When you showed up in Prescott for the Fourth of July rodeo, you had to have a beer at the Palace.

LUSCAINE AND I get back in the car and drive around the plaza and up Montezuma. There is the Palace and two other famous bars associated with the rodeo, Matt's and the Bird Cage. Nearby is the old St. Michael Hotel, where a lot of Frontier Days fans and cowboys traditionally stayed, a three-story red brick building with arched windows, green and white awnings, and an old-fashioned vertical sign attached to its corner, extending up the top two stories of the structure. The buildings, like most of downtown, are done up in red-white-and-blue bunting for the rodeo.

We go out to look at Thumb Butte, an immense tower of granite that is Prescott's most distinctive landmark. The base of Buckey's statue was hewn from the butte. Then we head back into town to check in at the Vendome Hotel, a small two-story inn a couple of blocks off the plaza, built in 1917. Tom Mix used to rent a room at the Vendome for a year at a time while filming silent Westerns in nearby Slaughterhouse Gulch and the Granite Dells as well as around Prescott itself. In fact, it was while making films in Prescott that Mix moved from stuntman to star. Tom Mix! How much more cowboy can you get? Once in our room, I change out of my shorts and sneakers into my jeans and boots, gearing up for the rodeo. Many rodeos require all members of the press to wear Western attire. Prescott might be among those rodeos that do. Besides, it seems a little unnatural to go to a rodeo not wearing jeans and boots.

AN ODD THING about Prescott: It is perhaps more famous for its rodeo than anything else, yet there is not a single sign downtown to direct traffic toward the rodeo grounds, which turn out to be fairly far from most of the better-beaten paths. A funnel of dust rising into the deep blue sky northwest of downtown signals where it is. It has been about fifteen years since I last went to a rodeo, but one thing I remember: Rodeos in parched small towns in the West always stir up a lot of dust, but not from the arena itself. Rodeo arena dirt is a valued thing, pampered with continual harrowing and watering. If the dirt dries out enough to produce dust clouds, it means someone has fallen down on the job. Instead, the dust rises from the makeshift parking lots and from the open areas where ropers, steer wrestlers, and barrel racers loosen up with their horses. And that's exactly the case here in Prescott. Luscaine and I drive past dozens of horse trailers and fancy pickups jammed into an open field opposite the rodeo arena grandstand. I smile as I park the car, feeling at home.

Prescott's rodeo takes place in a Depression-era arena with adjacent stone buildings constructed by the WPA. In one of the buildings, I meet the general manager, Dennis Rowley, a large affable man who welcomes Luscaine and me to the World's Oldest Rodeo and pledges to do anything he can to help out. Dennis sets the pattern for the summer and fall as I journey to rodeos and bull-riding events across the West. To a person, the rodeo officials I meet are friendly and accommodating. The only time I ever notice Dennis getting the slightest bit testy comes when I am talking to him about the roots of Frontier Days. I say something that suggests to him that I've been in communication with someone from Prescott's chief rival for the claim of "oldest rodeo," Pecos, Texas—which I haven't. Still, he growls, "Ah, those damned people in Pecos."

THERE'S NO BETTER way to get into an argument among hard-core rodeo people than to make assertions about where rodeo started or who has the oldest rodeo. Pecos's claim to the world's first rodeo goes back to 1883 when Henry Slack and several other cowboys from nearby ranches were boasting to each other about who was the best roper. One thing led to another, and soon enough a steer roping was scheduled on July 4 in front of the courthouse. Someone rounded up a small purse while someone else liberated blue ribbons from the trim of a young girl's dress to award as prizes. A cowboy named Trav Windham ultimately won. As for Henry Slack, he lassoed a steer, but the rope snapped, sending him tumbling from the saddle. The fall knocked him out, and Henry wound up with a mouthful of Chihuahuan desert sand as his only reward for his efforts in organizing this "first" rodeo.

Thus began what would become known as the West of the Pecos Rodeo in Pecos. It was an irregular event in the decades to come. In 1979 the rodeo held its fiftieth anniversary celebration, overlooking the contests that had gone on before 1929. But just four years after the golden anniversary blowout, Pecos celebrated the *centennial* of the rodeo, prompting Peter Applebome to note in *Texas Monthly:* "False modesty is not among Pecos's shortcomings."

Five years after the first Pecos rodeo, Prescott held a "cowboy tournament" in conjunction with its Independence Day celebration. The late Danny Freeman argues in *World's Oldest Rodeo* that organizers may well have created (albeit unwittingly) the first modern rodeo with this tournament. The event was created and run by a committee, multiple events took place (steer roping and saddle bronc riding—the two classic rodeo events), spectators paid admission to get in, and an award was given for an all-around cowboy—all of these elements would become mainstays of rodeo everywhere. To the Prescott mindset, these elements are adequate for claiming that its rodeo was the first "real" rodeo. "Oldest" rodeo is a stronger claim for Prescott. Through wars and financial ups and downs, Prescott has held its rodeo every year since 1888. No other rodeo has a longer unbroken streak.

Over the last couple of decades, Pecos and Prescott have sniped at each other over "first" and "oldest" claims. The communities have sought legal claims to their titles: In 1985 Prescott registered the phrase "world's oldest rodeo" with the United States Patent and Trademark Office. Both seem miffed that the Professional Rodeo Cowboys Association won't officially designate "first" and "world's oldest" rodeos. And both have been involved with disputes with organizations ranging from the makers of Trivial Pursuit to the *Encyclopaedia Britannica* over the roles the communities have played in rodeo's roots.

All of which causes a lot of rodeo followers outside the two communities to roll their eyes. Cowboy contests of different sorts certainly took place long before Pecos or Prescott held their first rodeos. There seems to be little doubt that cowboys wagered among themselves about who had the most prowess with bucking stock as far back as when the first outfits started moving cattle up the Texas trails in the 1860s. The binding of these kinds of events to Independence Day predates both Pecos and Prescott. In the last third of the nineteenth century, nationalism ran high in America as the fractured republic mended, and as Manifest Destiny became reality. Nowhere was patriotism celebrated with more zeal than in the West. Marching bands, baseball clubs, and fireworks might be in short supply in remote Western towns, but there were always plenty of horses and steers around. Staging a cowboy contest was a way any frontier community could commemorate the signing of the Declaration of Independence. In 1872 a group of Texas cowboys who arrived in Cheyenne, Wyoming, decided to celebrate Independence Day by staging an impromptu wild steer riding contest. Three years before that, cowboys held a bucking horse contest on July 4 at Deer Trail, Colorado, with an Englishman named Emilne Gardenshire of the Mill Iron Ranch winning the event after staying aboard an outlaw bronc named Montana Blizzard for a full fifteen minutes. For his feat, Gardenshire received a new suit of clothes and the title Champion Bronco Buster of the Plains.

Some Texans say an event organized by Major Jack Hays of the Texas Rangers should be counted as the first rodeo. This affair took place in San Antonio just west of San Pedro Creek in 1844 and involved Rangers, Comanche warriors, and Tejano vaqueros competing in riding and shooting contests, with the winners receiving Spanish blankets, knives, and pistols. A Ranger named John McMullin was the all-around winner, with a Comanche named Long Quiet coming in second. One interesting aspect of this event is that it exemplifies the multicultural fabric of rodeo that stretches from Long Quiet all the way to the Brazilian cowboys who are among the dominant bull riders of the early twenty-first century. Another interesting aspect is that it predates cowboys, who came into being on the cattle trails leading out of Texas and across the Indian Nations following the Civil War. Likewise, the annual branding roundups in Santa Fe, New Mexico Territory, in the 1840s took place in the precowboy days. New Mexicans stake their claim to the birthplace of rodeo on these roundups because they included contests to determine the best ropers and calf throwers. I've heard claims that similar sorts of contests accompanied roundups held by the Five Civilized Tribes in Indian Territory in the years before the Civil War. Thus some Oklahomans argue that rodeo took birth there.

A page on the Oklahoma Historical Society's Web site states: "Although the [Wild West] shows later dissolved, the competitions evolved into rodeos, the *only national spectator sport originating entirely in the United States*" (emphasis mine). This is as amusing as all the claims and counterclaims about who held the first rodeo. The fact is that rodeo took root in Mexico during the years when it was still New Spain.

By 1537 New Spain was so overrun with wild cattle and horses, which had been introduced to the area only twenty years earlier, that Spanish authorities required ranchers to brand and castrate their stock at an annual roundup. This yearly roundup became known as the *rodeo del ganado,* and it afforded ranchers and their vaqueros an opportunity to socialize and celebrate on the tab of the hacienda that sponsored the *rodeo.* Francis Edward Abernathy writes: "They had a barbecue and bands played and people danced, and this celebration became meeting and mating time for the rancher-frontiersmen of Spanish Colonial and Mexican times. Natural exhibitionists as all males are, the vaqueros and the young sons of the *hacienda* showed off their skills and their bravery to win the hearts of the women present and to arouse the envy of their peers." Out of this evolved the tradition of the *charro* (the man on horseback), the national symbol of Mexico. The contests that allowed the charros to exhibit their bravery and finesse became known as *charreadas.* The events (*suertes*) in charreadas are similar to rodeo: roping, team roping, bull riding, "bull tailing" (an event with some similarity to steer wrestling), bucking-mare riding, and so forth. Enough so that modern charreadas held around Texas are often called Mexican rodeos by Anglos.

It's logical to assume that the vaqueros who taught the first cowboys their trade also told them about charreadas. Some of those early cowboys quite possibly saw charreadas themselves and tried to reenact the suertes in their own cowboy contests at roundup time. And out of this, rodeo was born. As Dee Brown writes: "It was no accident that the Spanish word for round up, *rodeo,* came into use early as the name for the most popular sport in the West."

AFTER TALKING TO Dennis Rowley, Luscaine and I walk across the dusty road to Prescott's rodeo arena. Charreada is on my mind as I sit down on a bleacher to watch the afternoon slack.* The champion of the first Prescott rodeo was a Mexican American cowboy named Juan Leivas, from a ranch on Arizona's Date Creek. No doubt Leivas knew about the grand Mexican horseman tradition, the way of life called *charrería*. He was a great roper—"able to throw a long *reata* far and accurately through the brush," as Danny Freeman writes—and a talented bronc rider. And he was a living bridge spanning charrería and "the world's oldest rodeo."

The grandstand at Prescott is covered with a canopy of angle iron and corrugated tin, so we are out of the glare of the sun. A breeze keeps me cool in spite of my boots and jeans. Down on the arena floor, a calf shoots out of a roping chute, pursued by a cowboy atop a galloping quarter horse. The cowboy twirls a lariat as he chases the calf. Suddenly the loop shoots out and snags the calf by the neck. The horse stops as soon as the cowboy throws the loop, the rope between the saddle horn and the calf snaps tight, and the calf is whipped to the dirt. Meanwhile, the cowboy dismounts without any display of effort and runs toward the calf while moving hand over hand down the rope. The horse takes a step or two backward to keep the line tight. When the cowboy reaches the calf, he lifts it and drops it onto its back—a maneuver called flanking. Then he gracefully falls into a crouch and wraps a short length of rope, called a pigging string, twice around three of the calf's legs, and

---

*Usually more ropers and steer wrestlers sign up for timed events than the time allotted for the rodeo performance can accommodate. *Slack* is the term used for elimination rounds that most often take place in the morning, before afternoon rodeos, or in the afternoon, before evening rodeos. Admission to slack is free or costs only a dollar or two. Family and friends of the cowboys make up the sparse number of spectators—along with hard-core roping and bulldogging fans.

cinches it with a half hitch. He springs to his feet, hands held high. The judge on horseback dips a small flag to signal the timer to stop his watch. Now another watch is running, this one to ensure that the calf remains bound for a minimum of six seconds. The roper's horse steps backward again, keeping the rope as taut as a strand of newly strung barbed wire. The knot holds. The judge signals two high school boys, who rush to free the calf from the loop and to untie the pigging string. The calf springs to its feet, looking around as if it is trying to figure out what has just happened. One of the boys slaps its rump to send it in the direction of the exit gate. The announcer calls out the time—no penalties, so the time will hold up, and it is a good one, enough to ensure the roper will compete in an upcoming round of roping. All this takes less than twenty seconds, from the moment the calf bolts out of the chute until it trots through the exit gate.

"I kind of feel sorry for those poor little calves," Luscaine says. She's a Texas girl, with family going back in Austin through at least three generations. Yet she has never seen a rodeo before today. Calf roping probably isn't the best event to introduce her to the sport. "It has to hurt them to be jerked like that. Then picked up and slammed to the ground."

"I was always told as a kid that it doesn't hurt them," I say. "They're a lot tougher than we are."

Luscaine doesn't look convinced.

In the fifteen years or so since I'd been to a rodeo, I've forgotten just how complicated and fast each event is. I try to think back to that last rodeo. It had to be Ponca City, Oklahoma— 1987 or '88. I was a down-on-my-luck newspaper reporter, living in Stillwater, commuting to Ponca City to work on the *News.* I'd gotten back into journalism a few years earlier after a disastrous spin in politics, and it was hard for me to see that my newspaper career was going anywhere. I was broke, living in a trailer house, and foundering in an unraveling marriage. Though I didn't understand the symptoms at the time, I know now I was in a long-running siege of depression; I was only in my early thirties, yet believed I'd already wasted my life. I was drinking too much at times and smoking weed a little too often.

My best work for the *News* was a number of feature stories from neighboring Osage County, known in Oklahoma simply as the Osage because the county followed the boundaries of the Osage Nation. It was vast ranching country, and often as not, my articles dealt with ranchers. Because of this, the *News* decided I was a natural to cover the annual 101 Ranch Rodeo in Ponca City. I had a curious reaction. I got mad. I thumped my chest for the benefit of the managing editor and threatened not to show up. But in the end, he convinced me to go—without actually having to tell me to cover the rodeo or else my ass was fired. I went out to the rodeo grounds and immediately fell under rodeo's spell, just as I always had when I was a kid. I ended up having a great time hanging around the stock contractor and the cowboys.

Late that night, as I drove through Ponca country near White Eagle on my way back to Stillwater, I wondered why I had reacted angrily when first asked to cover the rodeo. I sorted through possible reasons and decided it must have had something to do with Cowboy Don, who was then still a complete mystery. I realized I was going to have to find him, or at least find out what became of him, if I was ever going to have peace in my life.

I DON'T KNOW if Cowboy Don ever saw the rodeo in Prescott, but I am certain he never competed there. My wife and I spent a couple of hours in the Sharlot Hall Museum going over ledgers in which rodeo officials recorded entry fee information for Frontier Days in the '50s. Someone named Gib Stratton won the bull riding a time or two. But no sign of Don Stratton. Not too surprising. A lot of rodeos take place over the Fourth of July, so many that Independence Day has become known as the Cowboy Christmas because cowboys have the opportunity to zip from rodeo to rodeo to pick up as much day money as possible. He definitely was present at another Independence Day rodeo, the Black Hills Roundup in Belle Fourche, South Dakota, for several years during the 1950s and early 1960s. I've made a stab at locating day sheets (the daily roster of who's performing at a rodeo) for the Belle Fourche rodeo during those years, without luck. So I can't say if he entered bull riding or any other events there, although I suspect that he did at one time or another. I also suspect that he never came away with any day money.

I've called Cowboy Don a rodeo cowboy, but some people would take offense at that. To be sure, he held a membership card in the Rodeo Cowboys Association for several years in the '50s and '60s, which ostensibly meant he was qualified to enter sanctioned rodeos, and which set him apart from the thousands of amateur cowboys who never made it to the RCA/PRCA ranks. "But anyone can get a card, if he wants to bad enough," one of Cowboy Don's acquaintances from that time told me. "That doesn't really mean anything." Cowboy Don had a hard time learning how to ride bulls. One problem was his body type. The best rough-stock riders are usually built along the lines of Freckles Brown: short and thin and lithe.* Cowboy Don was built like me. He was lean enough in his younger days, but he stood over six feet tall with long legs and a stiff awkward-

*Bull riders like Justin McBride and Terry Don West have classic rough-stock rider builds: both are five feet eight and weigh 140 pounds. Adriano Moraes (five feet ten, 185 pounds) and Owen Washburn (six feet two, 175 pounds) are top bull riders whose builds defy the classic mold.

ness. Some riders can overcome their body type, but Cowboy Don wasn't able to do it. He never was much of a competitor. And that's why some people would challenge my calling him a rodeo cowboy. "What he was," said an old friend of his, "was a rodeo bum."

A rodeo bum. There's no precise definition for it. It can be a good-natured term for anyone associated with rodeo. But it can also describe a character whose soul is infected by rodeo addiction. He can't make any kind of living from it, yet he can't turn loose from it, either. He batters his body, has no future, and has *left a long string of friends, some sheets in the wind, and some satisfied women behind.** He has few possessions besides what he's wearing on his back. He knows the finer points of hitchhiking and sleeping out in the rain. He shows up at a rodeo, looking for whatever work he can find, maybe persuading the stock contractor to give him a job bucking hay or wrangling the cattle and horses in the pens behind the arena. If he draws enough pay for this, he'll blow it on entry fees. And he'll lose his events. Then he's off for the next show.

Or at least that is how it was for Cowboy Don.

Not that he didn't have his appeal. In fact, under the right circumstances, he had appeal by the bushel. "He was a charming guy, in his way," my mother once told me. Other women who knew him in his rodeo days concur. "I remember him," a woman in Tulsa recalled. "I met him at a dance once, a tall guy in a white-on-white Western shirt and a black hat. He was something else." The way she said *something else* carried a lot of weight with it: attractive, yet perilous. Mom placed him squarely in the category of rodeo cowboys who were wild and crazy, which seemed to be the dominant category in the 1950s,

---

*from Billy Joe Shaver's "Ride Me Down Easy"

and that was what made him desirable. Beyond the charm, however, was a near toxic combination of bullshit and cunning. His guile was endless. "Helllllooo darlin'!" he'd begin a beer-fueled phone call to one of his half sisters. The call would last an hour, two hours, maybe more, and would always conclude in the same way: He'd ask for money. He'd be rebuffed, of course. And his half sister wouldn't hear from him again for months or years. Mom was very young when she met him, barely out of her teens, yet she figured him out a lot quicker than other women in his life did. She came to realize that life with a rodeo bum was no kind of life for her: Wild and crazy all too quickly turned into irresponsible and self-destructive. "He couldn't keep a commitment," she told me. "I do know that." She talked to him by telephone one last time in the spring after I was born. He was in Austin for the rodeo held in conjunction with the Travis County Livestock Show. Before he rang off, he promised to call back. He never did.

Sometimes you can't snag the ribbon tied to the calf's tail, no matter how hard you try. Sometimes you can just watch it run. Then you get up, dust yourself off, and put that calf out of your mind. That's what Mom did with Cowboy Don.

WE LEAVE THE SLACK and drive to the plaza to get a late lunch. Parking is hard to come by, and I end up sticking the rental car in a slot near the alley running parallel to Montezuma. We walk up the alley to enter the Palace Saloon through the back door.

"Look," Luscaine says, pointing to a four-wheel drive pickup parked in the alley. It has a bumper sticker reading IF IT'S TOURIST SEASON, WHY CAN'T WE SHOOT 'EM? I picture the guy who owns the truck. A guy pissed off by the taming, the softening of the West. A guy who lusts for the freedom enjoyed by the cowboys, miners, and railroaders of old, never mind the hazards they faced. But maybe I'm wrong. Maybe the truck's owner is just some real estate agent trying to affect some sort of macho pose or be funny. Sadly, I decide it's probably the latter.

But Prescott does seem to be a community in dispute with itself about its Western heritage in general and the rodeo in particular. One day, I asked one of the rodeo directors, Ray Lesniak, about this, and he concurred. "You are absolutely right," he said. "There are people here who want everything to be like it was in the 1880s. Then you have people who want nothing at all to do with the Old West. A lot of people blame the changes in attitude on the influx of people from California." Those Californians get blamed for a lot. Hearing someone curse Californians for the ruin of Austin is almost a daily occurrence for me. Ray said, "We now have gated communities in Prescott. We don't need them here."

If you look at documents on Frontier Days in the archives at the Sharlot Hall Museum, you learn that in the 1930s, Prescott billed itself as "the Cowboy Capital of the World." Nowadays, as you enter Prescott you pass a billboard encouraging you to visit downtown to experience "Real Charm," whatever that is supposed to be. But you don't see anything about cowboys. I sense a lot of people would prefer to transform Prescott into something resembling Sedona, seventy miles to the northeast. Sedona is set against imposing bluffs of red granite. Surrounding the town are breathtaking rock formations that tower above the desert. The landscape exudes a kind of mystical spookiness, and Sedona has become a favorite of the New Agers as well as of upscale tourists. You find spas and crystal shops on the main drags along with sophisticated restaurants, boutiques, and jewelry shops. The sidewalks are crowded with people who seem ready to drop a dollar at every turn. Sucking some of those dollars into Prescott would delight many in Yavapai County.

And so you have Prescott in transition. The railroad tracks are gone, replaced by a shopping center. The depot has been made over into an office building. Bed-and-breakfasts are big business; in fact, in its current incarnation, the old Vendome Hotel has a B&B feel to it. Next door to the Vendome is a shop selling organic candy. You can find massage therapists without much looking. There's a brewpub on the plaza. And Whiskey Row is hardly Whiskey Row at all. Sure, Matt's and the Bird Cage are still in operation. But most of the old-time saloons have given way to businesses like Buckey's Bean Bag; "with over seventy-five coffee blends, fifty tea varieties, and many Southwest gourmet foods, Buckey's is a comfortable and friendly place to ponder your next taste adventure!" Van Gogh's Ear is an art gallery where you might find a trio playing soft jazz, but never a honky-tonk singer. The café in the St. Michael sells lattes. And then there is the Palace.

Luscaine and I tromp into the Palace to find it has been renovated and transformed. No longer an out-at-the-elbows cowboy bar, it has been cleaned up, revarnished, and made ready for tourists. The Palace even hosts dinner theater these days. Sure, the great oak bar is still there, but there are no cowboys, miners, or railroad men bellied up to it. Cheap beer is no longer the draw. Now the menu is the thing. Fried artichoke hearts. Grilled prawns prosciutto. Dishes named after famous Palace patrons—Doc's (as in Holliday) T-Bone, Tom's (as in Mix) mixed grill. Luscaine and I order from the lunch menu, and I get a roasted turkey sandwich with sun-dried tomatoes, carmelized onions, and dill Havarti. The food is good, but I have a sinking feeling as I eat. I'd wager that in their entire lifetimes neither Juan Leivas nor Virgil Earp ever consumed dill Havarti.

On a wall adjacent to our table is a mural based on the film *Junior Bonner*, which Sam Peckinpah shot in Prescott in the early 1970s. I wonder what Junior would have thought about prawns prosciutto.

I SURVIVED growing up in Guthrie in large measure because of the Melba Theater, the town's only indoor picture show, located along a block of Harrison Avenue that was also home to the Vencedora snooker parlor and a beer joint. Once a vaudeville venue, the Melba was a wonderfully shabby movie house with a floor sticky from generations of discarded gum and spilled colas. The air smelled musty. The upholstery on the seats and the stage curtains seemed ready to disintegrate from age at any moment. You could see as many as three different movies a week there. In the late 1960s through the mid-1970s, something of a renaissance took place in American cinema, and I savored many of its fruits from my stuffy seat in the Melba. I came to love films directed by the controversial Sam Peckinpah.

One evening in 1972 I tagged along with my mother to the theater to see *Junior Bonner*, Peckinpah's new rodeo movie. The promise of seeing Steve McQueen portray a rodeo cowboy was enough for her to see the movie at the Melba, which many adults in Guthrie found too run-down. I was sixteen years old, and I'm sure I had qualms about going to the show with my mother—god only knows what my friends would say. But I'm glad I did.

In the extremely narrow genre of rodeo movies, *Junior Bonner* ranks with Nicholas Ray's *The Lusty Men* as the best. One of the few McQueen movies that failed to rock the box office, it nonetheless gave the star the opportunity to turn in one of the best performances of his career. McQueen was notoriously touchy about being short. Legend has it that he refused to work with leading ladies taller than he—and there were many of them. While filming, legend also has it, he stood on platforms designed to elevate him to the height of his fellow male stars. But in *Junior Bonner,* McQueen's stature and build worked to his advantage. He looked like a rough-stock rider (well, maybe his hair was a little foppish for most rodeo cowboys of the time). He carried his body the way rough-stock riders who've seen a few too many rodeos carry theirs. He obviously studied rodeo cowboys while preparing for the role. The rest of the cast was terrific as well. Ida Lupino and Robert Preston as Junior's mom and dad. Ben Johnson as the stock contractor. Dub Taylor as the proprietor of the Palace. The underappreciated character actor Bill McKinney as Junior's younger rival. Joe Don Baker as Junior's obnoxious sellout of a little brother.

Peckinpah shot *Junior Bonner* as cinema verité during the 1971 Frontier Days, so Prescott itself can be considered a character in the film. Peckinpah collaborated with cinematographer Lucien Ballard, and the team beautifully filmed the rich hues of the landscape and the unique look of the town. Peckinpah had a good script from which to work, one well rooted in Prescott's traditions. Jeb Rosebrook was a New York City native who ended up spending much of his boyhood in Prescott. After an absence of fifteen years, he returned for the 1970 Frontier Days and immediately noticed that change was impinging on the community he'd known so well. "That Fourth of July," he wrote in *Arizona Highways* many years later, "I sat in Matt's Saloon listening to a country band and thought of the rodeo that was a Prescott tradition, and the change in the Yavapai County landscape of ranch country I had known since boyhood. The genesis of an idea and a character was born. His name was to be Bonner. He would change my life." Rosebrook was a published novelist at the time. *Junior Bonner* made him a successful screenwriter.

At its essence, *Junior Bonner* is the Freckles Brown story: Aging rodeo cowboy proves himself one last time by riding an unridable bull. In Junior's case, the bull is Sunshine, which threw him just a week earlier. And the rodeo at which he rides the unridable bull just happens to occur in his hometown of Prescott. Said Rosebrook: "It also tells the story of a family trapped in a changing West." Junior arrives in Yavapai County just as bulldozer operators are leveling the old family ranch house to make way for expansion of his brother Curley's trailer-house development. Driving his convertible and pulling a horse trailer while searching for his father in the dusty, noisy turmoil, Junior jousts with a front-end loader operated by a man who looks more like a filthy robot than a human being. It's a classic confrontation: the solitary Western hero standing up against tradition-destroying machines bent on progress. In the end, Junior has to back down, reversing his convertible just before the front-end loader's operator can drop the machine's load of rock and dirt on Junior's car. While Junior loses the confrontation with the machine, he proves himself at the rodeo by riding the unridable bull, a triumph for the solitary Western hero. It is the fundamental appeal of rodeo, and Peckinpah captures it beautifully.

At sixteen, sitting in the Melba with my mom, I was captivated by Junior's need to ride in order to prove himself. I'm still captivated by it. Sure, *Junior Bonner* has its flaws. Knowledgeable rodeo fans can pick it apart—especially one bronc montage in which, if you look carefully, saddle bronc riders appear to be competing against bareback riders. And, yes, some of that "man out of his time" stuff is a little romanticized. But I love that movie. As much as anything, it brought me to Prescott.

AND NOW IT IS evening. The dusk sky is clear. I park next to a pickup with a message stuck on its back window: HEY SIERRA CLUB, SAVE THIS BIRD . . . There is an image of a hand, middle finger extended in a classic gesture. I go into a stone building where rodeo officials and a scattering of cowboys are scoffing hot dogs and chili pies before the rodeo gets rolling in a few minutes. I walk to a small room in the back of the building that is functioning as a makeshift pressroom, where Ray Lesniak is dealing with the broadcasters and reporters covering the rodeo.

I get a day sheet from Ray and ask about the turn-out. The term *turn-out* in rodeo has nothing to do with the fan attendance at the performance. Instead, it is the list of cowboys who will not make it to the rodeo, even though their names are listed on the day sheet. When the absent cowboy's turn to ride arrives, the stock handlers will "turn out" into the arena the animal he's drawn, unridden, unwrestled, unroped. The animal is in essence the winner by forfeit.

The most famous turn-out in rodeo history occurred in 1995 at the National Finals Rodeo in Las Vegas. The notorious bull Bodacious had smashed the face of champion bull rider Tuff Hedeman just two months earlier. Tuff got his nickname for good reason. The injury was bad enough to drive most bull riders into retirement, but Tuff was back to compete at the NFR after eight weeks of painful recovery—never mind that he'd lost twenty pounds and a lot of strength while mending. Then he drew Bodacious. Trouper that he was, Tuff faced one of the most difficult decisions of his life, one he said made him sick to his stomach. Tuff opted to turn out Bodacious rather than risk further injury or quite possibly death. Bodacious charged through the open gate and into the arena while Tuff watched with one of the saddest expressions ever captured on video.

Turn-out is a problem at rodeos taking place during Cowboy Christmas week. Cowboys scatter-shoot entry fees to different rodeos. If a rider does well at one rodeo, he might forgo the other rodeos he's entered. That makes perfect sense to the cowboy, who is trying to win as much money as he can. But the prospect of no-shows leaves rodeo promoters itchy as all get-out. Prescott is one of the top twenty-five rodeos in the nation, and the ticket buyers expect to see championship-quality riders. Too many turn-outs can dash that expectation. Worse, too many turn-outs can mean that not enough cowboys showed up to have a meaningful event, never mind the quality of the riders.

"I've been involved in rodeos," Ray is telling me, "where the stock contractor has to take money out of his pocket to pay some of the hands working the pens to ride so that the fans will have a full show. You know, maybe you don't have enough bronc riders show up. So you pay some of those guys fifty bucks to go out and ride. They're not any good, but the fans get to see bronc riding."

I suspect that in his day Cowboy Don got money on occasion for doing that.

The prospect of turn-outs is causing me some concern now. "What about Jesse Bail?" I say. "Heard anything from him?"

"Don't know about Jesse," he says. "He's not on the day sheet for tonight."

"So no way to tell if he'll be here or not?"

He shrugs. "Not really. Depends on how he's doing somewhere else. I haven't heard anything."

Twenty-three-year-old Jesse Bail from tiny Camp Crook, South Dakota, is another reason I've come to Prescott. He is a rising star in the PRCA ranks. He's one of rodeo's top saddle bronc riders, continuing the tradition of terrific South Dakota bronc riders that stretches back to Casey Tibbs and beyond. He's also one of the PRCA's best bull riders. Although he qualified for the National Finals Rodeo for the first time when he was just twenty years old and has gone back to Las Vegas every year since, a lot of people in rodeo think that even greater accomplishments lie ahead of him. Some even think he has the makings to be the next Larry Mahan or Ty Murray, a multi-event rough-stock rider who can capture multiple all-around cowboy titles.

Jesse was coming off a successful 2002 season. During the winter half of the season he was the point leader in both saddle bronc and bull riding—the first time a cowboy ever led two events. During the summer season, he topped the bull-riding competition. He claimed all-around titles at the big-money San Antonio Livestock Exposition; the Puyallup (Washington) Fair and Rodeo; the Navajo Nation Fourth of July Rodeo in Window Rock, Arizona; the San Angelo (Texas) Stock Show and Rodeo; the Jaycee Bootheel Rodeo in Sikeston, Missouri; and the Deadwood Days of '47 Rodeo in his home state. He won saddle bronc riding titles at the U.S. Smokeless Tobacco Cup Finale at Las Vegas, the West of the Pecos Rodeo, and at Deadwood. He won bull-riding titles at Puyallup, Washington; Clovis, California; Guymon, Oklahoma; Caldwell, Idaho; Molalla, Oregon; and Dodge City, Kansas. And he finished the year with more than two hundred thousand dollars in purse money. Coming into 2003, he had a chance to hit a million dollars in career earnings. While a million dollars might be chump change these days to many professional basketball players, it remains a landmark achievement for cowboys competing in the PRCA. Compared to his fellow South Dakotan, and occasional traveling buddy, Tom Reeves—an outstanding cowboy who won the 2001 world championship for saddle bronc rider—Jesse is approaching the million-dollar mark in a hurry. It took Reeves more than a decade to do it. In fact, after twenty-one years on the PRCA circuit, Reeves's career earnings stand at $1.5 million. The way he's going, Jesse should top that number in another three or four years.

"He's a good hand"; that's how top Professional Bull Riders (PBR) star Justin McBride described Jesse to me in standard cowboy understatement. A good hand—and also a throwback in an age of specialization among rough-stock riders. Jesse is also a sure-enough ranch kid who has spent his whole life around cattle and horses and loves nothing better.

I took an immediate liking to Jesse the first time I spoke to him on the phone. When he told me he'd entered the Prescott Frontier Days, I knew I'd want to see him ride there. I doubt if we'll have a chance to talk, though. It is Cowboy Christmas week, after all. Last year during Cowboy Christmas, he logged an astonishing 17,479 miles while competing in six states and two countries. He won $33,456 for his efforts. Cowboy Christmas this year promises to be nearly as hectic. He told me he plans to drive to Prescott the day he is set to ride, rosin his "riggins," take his shots at his bronc and his bull, then immediately get back behind the wheel and drive three hundred miles to Window Rock, hoping to repeat as all-around champ at the Navajo Nation's Fourth of July Rodeo. But at least I'll get to see him ride. If he doesn't "turn out."

Suddenly the lights go out. Ray sighs. The power has been on the fritz all afternoon, and someone from the county is poking around breaker boxes trying to figure out what's wrong. Ray and I leave the small pressroom and walk outside, where he retrieves a cigar he's stuck in a chink in the mortar of the rock wall. I tell him I'm going to head to the arena to meet up with my wife. "Have a good time," he says, lighting his cigar.

THE ARENA IS packed, as it will be for every rodeo performance for the 2003 Prescott Frontier Days. The venue is not nearly as large as, say, the rodeo grounds at Cheyenne or Pendleton. But thousands of people will file in and out of the grandstands during the Prescott Frontier Days' run. Most of the crowd is made up of rodeo regulars from northern Arizona, but there are a fair number of out-of-staters who come year after year, including a contingent of officers from the Los Angeles Police Department, who drive the four hundred miles between LA and Prescott annually.

"There's nothing I hate worse," Luscaine says as we work our way through the crowd, "than drugstore cowboys. But some of these ranchers here are pretty attractive. You know? You can tell they spend most of their lives outdoors in the sun. You can see it in their faces. The white shirts and the straw hats—there's something really appealing about them. They're real."

Exactly. Where we live, there are no small number of guys who "cowboy up" every day for their jobs writing insurance forms or drilling out cavities in teeth in the bright glare of fluorescent lights. They drive big-assed four-wheel drive pickups that will never leave the pavement, even though they've paid extra money for massive brush-guard grillwork on the front, and will never carry a load more substantial than a couple of sets of golf clubs. They might spend their weekend evenings two-stepping and line dancing (dance steps they learned at a class) at some sort of nightmarish urban or suburban rendition of Mickey Gilley's nightclub as it appeared in the movie *Urban Cowboy* twenty years ago. There they'll hop around to the tortured, soulless pop tunes that masquerade as country-and-western music these days. These drugstore cowboys might have spent some time when they were kids on pony rides at a petting zoo, but otherwise they are unacquainted with the back of a horse. Yes, I know precisely what she means. And I know why she hates them. Who loves a phony? We don't see many men here tonight fitting that bill. Thank god.

I've always associated rodeos with pretty women in the stands, and there are plenty of them here tonight. To many women, there is something immensely erotic about rodeo cowboys. Sara Davidson writes in *Cowboy: A Love Story:*

> I've always loved cowboys. The way they look has a great deal to do with it. The sight of the Marlboro Man on a billboard can give me a jolt of longing as I drive through traffic on my way to work. I imagine that the way some men respond to the sight of a woman in seamed stockings and a garter belt is the way I feel when I see a man in chaps. The rough leather directs the eye up the legs to the place where the leather stops, just below the groin. The tight-fitting jeans, the boots with spurs, even the hat with its rakish, playful shape contributes to an image that I find deeply appealing.

Appealing. Even if, as she later writes, they can be "men who cheated, lied, did not listen, and could not be counted on."

Cowboy Don.

When my mom and her friends went to rodeos in the 1950s, they dressed a lot like the cowboys themselves: hats, boots, jeans, long-sleeved shirts with pearl-snap pockets, Western belts. They wore their hair bobbed, and too much makeup or gaudy jewelry was frowned on. All things considered, they were a pretty prim lot of young women. That had started changing by the time I was going to rodeos as a kid in the 1960s. Tonight I see women who, yes, might be wearing a hat and boots, but with halter tops cropped just below their breasts and impossibly tight jeans that begin maybe four or five inches below their bare, pierced navels.

But a lot of the crowd is dressed like summer crowds everywhere dress these days: shorts and T-shirts and sneakers or sandals. Generic America. The good news is that there are plenty of exceptions to the generic look here tonight. The guy who sits next to us, after we've found a couple of vacant grandstand seats, is beefy and sun blistered. Suspenders hitch up his Levi's below his big belly. His hands are large and swollen, with scraped knuckles and thick calluses. His head is big, too, shaped like a fishbowl. His face is wrinkled. A gray bushwhacker's mustache droops over his mouth, completely camouflaging his lips except when he speaks. His black hat is big, the crown an uncrimped mound of felt, the brim flat. A sidekick's hat. Think Hoss from *Bonanza*. The hat's the same, only black instead of white. My guess is that this man has never lapped the foam off a latte or sampled sushi in his entire life.

THAT THIS MAN is wearing Levi's interests me. Looking around at the brands of jeans, I see a lot more Levi's than I thought I would. This is reassuring, for I am wearing 501s myself.

Growing up in Guthrie, I developed a sort of blue jeans snobbery, favoring Levi Strauss & Co.—one that I think most boys and men of that time and place shared. As a kid, I started out wearing brands like Lee or Wrangler because they were less expensive than Levi's. Of course, I wanted Levi's 501s all along, but Mom would tell me I was growing too fast. She couldn't justify the investment Levi's demanded when there was a chance that I'd outgrow them before they were even broken in. So I wore my Lee jeans and Wrangler jeans with a sense of shame. There I was, stuck in kids' jeans when the cowboys, oil-field roughnecks, snooker hall regulars, and motorcycle riders I admired all wore 501s.

I was thirteen before I got my first pair of Levi's. The denim was drenched in indigo dye, so much so that your hands turned blue if you handled the jeans too much before washing them the first time, and they were as stiff as a Baptist preacher's sense of humor. And what a process washing was. Then, as now, I laundered mine five times (sometimes more) in scalding water, with a little bleach thrown in, to begin the fading process before wearing them the first time. I never will forget yanking my first pair out of the dryer and pulling them on. I felt like a cowboy.

Of course, the *real* cowboys, the ones who drove cattle up the trail out of Texas, never wore jeans. One of them, Teddy Blue (E. C. Abbott), recalled in his classic memoir, *We Pointed Them North:* "[W]e had a high-crowned white Stetson hat, fancy shirts with pockets, and striped or checkered California pants made in Oregon City, the best pants ever made to ride in." No mention of denim at all. And if you look at Wild West show and rodeo photographs taken through the turn of the twentieth century, you don't see cowboys in jeans. Although by World War II, Levi's certainly were standard rodeo attire.

Levi's were all I remembered rodeo cowboys wearing when I was young, although pictures I've seen recently show that some were indeed wearing Wranglers back then. The very few photos I've seen of Cowboy Don from the late 1950s and early 1960s all show him in Levi's, tucked into his cowboy boots. But that's all changed now. Today, Wranglers are de rigueur at rodeos, so much so that a recent *El Paso Times* article notes that while Wrangler or Cinch jeans for men are appropriate at a rodeo dance, "No real cowboy would mix Levi's and boots."

Cinch jeans?

Wrangler conquered rodeo with a marketing siege that can trace its source to 1947, when the company signed on as a sponsor of the Rodeo Cowboys Association. By the 1980s the company's persistence and shrewd promotions paid off, and Wrangler was the undisputed king of rodeo, leaving Levi Strauss & Co. and any other contenders capsized in its wake. Texas country singer George Strait, who has had close ties to rodeo throughout his career, set the standard for how rodeo goers should look: white hat, crisp Western shirt, starched and ironed Wranglers, a Western belt with a trophy buckle, roper boots. Variations on the style developed over the next twenty years—singers like Garth Brooks brought black hats back into fashion, ropers transmogrified into variations of lace-up boots. But Wranglers held solid as the jean of choice.

At least as far as men were concerned. True, many women in rodeo also wore Wranglers, but Rocky Mountain jeans also claimed a substantial share of the female market. Rockies were more expensive than Wranglers. They were more of a fashion brand—or at least what was perceived as fashion in the small cities and towns and wide-open spaces from which rodeo drew its primary fan base. Tight-fitting Rockies turned eyes and in-spired country songwriters. And teenage girls growing up in this culture yearned for their first pair of Rockies in the same way I yearned for my first 501s.

The male market for Wranglers seemed impenetrable for years. Then in 1994 some sales reps for the Rocky Mountain Clothing Company began noticing that a growing number of rodeo cowboys were forsaking Wranglers for some of the looser-fitting jeans being marketed by The Gap and, yes, Levi Strauss & Co. By this point, my beloved Levi's were considered contemptuously as "mall jeans" in the cowboy world, and most Western-wear stores no longer carried 501s. Seeing a possible crack in the Wrangler stranglehold, Rocky Mountain found that many Wrangler customers wanted "relaxed fit" jeans and that Wrangler wasn't providing them that option. In 1995 Rocky Mountain unveiled the prototype of its new jeans at the U.S. Team Roping Championship finals at the Lazy E Arena—a large indoor rodeo arena located just outside my hometown of Guthrie—with a "trade in your Wranglers" promotion. Rocky Mountain was successful. Hundreds of pairs of Wranglers were exchanged for these new jeans. And the Cinch brand was born. By 1996 Cinch had an aggressive marketing and merchandising campaign rolling. In some ways, the campaign followed the Wrangler lead: signing up top cowboys to endorse the product while sponsoring rodeo events. Soon, world champions like Tuff Hedeman, Fred Whitfield, Cody Ohl, and Marvin Garrett were sanctioning the Cinch label, as were top PBR cowboys like Chris Shivers, Owen Washburn, Luke Snyder, and Mike White. And Cinch sponsored PBR events and other competitions on the periphery of mainstream rodeo.

So that explains some of the green and red labeled jeans here tonight. But make no mistake about it: Wrangler is still the champion, at least in the PRCA venues. "How many of you are wearing your Wranglers?" rodeo announcer Randy Corley calls to the crowd from his booth opposite the grandstand. A bellow of pro-Wrangler sentiment is his response.

I feel content in my Levi's, though—even if they are mall jeans that, sadly, aren't American made anymore. I guess cowboys are supposed to be independent, aren't they?

THE NEXT AFTERNOON, July 4, I'm back at the arena. Every rodeo I've ever attended exuded patriotism at every turn, and Frontier Days in Prescott isn't any exception. *This Is My Country* is its theme. Before things get rolling, we're led through singing and pledging and praying. The prayer includes a request of the Almighty to look after the welfare of the animals in tonight's performance. Corley reads a long poem extolling patriotic virtues. Then the grand entry begins.

Virtually all rodeos begin with a grand entry. It serves as an opportunity for the announcer to set the stage for the events to come. Grand entries are always showy, always crowded, always patriotic. At some point during the grand entry, the announcer will introduce the VIPs to the crowd—the rodeo's manager and other officials, the stock contractor, the rodeo queen and her court, any local or state politicians who might be present.

This afternoon, riders by the dozen enter the arena in the traditional serpentine formation, all carrying banners representing corporate sponsors. Rodeo has become nothing if not an opportunity to market products at every turn. I scribble down brand names into my notebook: Dr Pepper, Outback Steakhouse, Resistol, Wells Fargo, Justin boots, Coca-Cola, Coors, U.S. Smokeless Tobacco. Not to mention the ubiquitous Wrangler. I'm writing as fast as I can, but it's hard to keep up. The riders' chaps are emblazoned with DODGE—and not for Marshal Dillon's town in western Kansas but for the manufacturer of Ram pickups. The bucking chutes no longer have numbers but instead bear the names of businesses. "Comin' out of the Outback Steakhouse gate is Stormy Sagers of Rush Valley, Utah— any folks from Utah here tonight? He'll be ridin' a bronc named Headlight. And just a reminder, folks, tonight's saddle bronc riding is brought to you by the good people at MacMillan Construction." The grand entry itself has a corporate sponsor, Whiskey Row Partners. Even the comedy performances by barrel clown Martin Kiff have a benefactor—Bank One. Recognition of the rodeo's all-around cowboy is funded by the casino at the small Yavapai tribal reservation on the edge of Prescott. Across the arena from the grandstand, you can see giant inflated replicas of a silver Coors Light can and a black Jack Daniel's bottle. The cowboys themselves are so plastered with advertising slogans that they look like NASCAR cars.

Next the rodeo queen and her court make their entrance, sponsored by Western Warehouse. Back in the mid-1970s, rodeo royalty began to adopt Farrah Fawcett's *Charlie's Angels* hairstyle. While those flowing locks long ago faded from style for the rest of America, they never really left the world of rodeo queens, sweethearts, and attendants. You understand why they've kept the long hair when you see these young women astride their horses. Their hair emphasizes the symmetry of their rides. There's a graceful flow that begins with the horse's mane and arches upward through the rider and the long hair falling down onto her shoulders from underneath her hat. Then the flow dips downward and rolls through the feathering of the horse's tail. These women are always good riders, and their agility on horseback is immensely appealing. The image they present is at once wholesome and just a little sexy. "Next to the cowboy heroics of bronc and bull riding, rodeo queens are asked to play out a cowgirl fantasy," writes Joan Burbick in *Rodeo Queens and the American Dream*. I suppose that's true. My own fantasy of cowgirls is that they are strong, resourceful, comfortable outdoors, good with animals, athletic. And pretty, in a well-scrubbed sort of way.

Now galloping into the arena is the ringmaster of the show, the stock contractor, Harry Vold. In his late seventies, Vold has white hair and a belly that suggests he hasn't missed many meals. Yet he rides with extraordinary grace, waving his white hat at the crowd. He's a well-known figure at Frontier Days, as he is at many rodeos—a celebrity among stock contractors, a man who has come a long way since he took in his first rodeos as a horse trader's son in Canada. By the time he was sixteen, he was riding broncs. Shortly thereafter, he signed up with a Wild West show and also took up auctioneering. When he was twenty, he hauled a load of horses to a rodeo in Montana, and that hooked him on the stock contracting business. "People from the neighboring town saw that show, and they wanted those horses," Vold once said. "I made them a deal. That's when it all started, and I haven't been smart enough to stop yet." Vold's career began at a time when a successful contractor relied on horse sense and some good luck, and it has continued into an age of scientific breeding of bucking stock. He told a reporter that gathering a good pen of bucking stock was a lot like creating a football team. "You put together the very best guys,

and they go through a tryout period to determine who the best
of the best are. You search all over the country for them. Finding good stock doesn't just happen. You have to look for them."
His stock has appeared at the National Finals Rodeo ever since
the event began. Vold also has received about every award possible, including being named honorary chief of Canada's
Sarcee (Tsuu T'ina) tribe—Chief Many Horses.

Kirsten Vold, Harry's daughter, has managed the Harry
Vold Rodeo Company since 1998. She's established herself as
an astute businessperson throughout the world of rodeo. But in
the arena, it's clear that Chief Many Horses is the person to
reckon with this afternoon, as he was last night and as he will
be at each Frontier Days performance. To start things off, his
company has trucked in some completely wild "outlaws"—
horses unable to be broken for riding—for an event I've never
seen before, called team bronc riding. The idea is for a team of
three men to grab hold of one of the wild horses and saddle it.
Then one of the men climbs on and tries to guide the horse
across a finish line to win what purports to be a race. This is by
no means a standard rodeo event, and what happens down on
the floor of the arena is chaos manifested in dirt, hooves, horse
flesh, bruised human beings, and damaged human pride. The
horses rear and kick and at times fall to the ground and roll
around in their attempt to keep from being saddled and ridden.
Some teams never even manage to get their horses saddled. If
a horse is saddled, chances are the rider will be hurled skyward
before any progress is made toward the finish line. More riders
get banged up in the team wild-horse riding than in any other
event I'll watch tonight. Eventually Corley announces a winner, though I can't for the life of me figure out how the winner
is determined. "You have to be crazy to do that," Ray Lesniak
said one evening as he was talking about the team bronc riding.
As I watch the members of the riding teams limp toward the

gate, some of them only able to move with the help of shoulders to lean on, I understand why he thinks so.

As soon as the wild horses are herded from the arena, steer wrestling (which I still tend to call by its old-fashioned name, bulldogging) gets rolling. It's the fastest event in rodeo. The world record time is a mere 2.4 seconds. In most arenas, a run of five seconds or less is considered a good one. The steer bursts through a chute, encouraged to run sometimes by a shock from a hotshot or sometimes by a firm twist of the tail. Once the steer crosses a line to start the event, two cowboys on horseback take up pursuit, sandwiching the steer between them. The rider on the right side of the steer is a helper in the event, a hazer, whose purpose is to keep the steer from veering away from the cowboy on its left, the contestant, the bulldogger. When the opportunity is just right, the bulldogger slides from the right side of his saddle as his horse is in full gallop. For a moment, he is airborne, his face scarce inches away from the steer's left horn. In a split-second series of moves, the bulldogger hooks his right arm under the steer's right horn and grasps its left horn with his left hand. At virtually the same time, he slams his feet into the ground—he is wearing boots with "doggin' heels" to give him traction in the dirt—and plants them to bring the steer to a halt. Then he hammerlocks the steer to the ground. The impact of the rider leaving the saddle cannot cause the steer to tumble. It has to be wrestled down from a standstill. If the steer does stumble from the contact of the cowboy leaving his horse, the bulldogger has to allow the steer to regain its feet, then wrestle it to the ground, thus costing the cowboy precious seconds in an event that allows no seconds to spare. The competition is complete when the steer is lying on its side with all four feet facing the same direction. A mounted judge then snaps down a flag he's been holding upright, signaling the timer to stop the watch.

To be able to pull all this off, a bulldogger has to be a strong man. It helps if he is a big man because leverage is the key to making all these moves work. Even though a bulldogger might weigh two hundred pounds or more, his adversary will weigh at least twice as much. And the dogger's hazer has to be talented, able to read the steer's run just right. Mom always told me that good hazers are among the most talented people you'll see in a rodeo. They are so important that a cowboy who wins money in the event will usually give a fourth of his prize to his hazer.

Though bull riding is the event that most often causes deaths in the arena, I've heard a lot of cowboys say that bulldogging is the most dangerous. It is a breathtaking thing to watch a man that size fly off his horse at a speed of thirty-five miles per hour, then set his feet and wrestle the steer that quickly. But the wear and tear on the bulldogger's body during a successful run is staggering. Things go wrong. Fairly often. Sometimes man and animal both end up rolling head over heels in what's called a hoolihan—a physically painful experience for the cowboy. To top it off, a hoolihan is a foul, so the bulldogger will get no score for the event. Good-bye entry fee, hello ruptured pride and bruised ass. At other times a cowboy ends up doing the equivalent of a belly flop on the dirt as he misses the steer altogether. And worse things can happen.

Louise L. Serpa captured things going awry for a bulldogger in a great photograph called "Miscalculation," shot at a rodeo in Tucson in 1983. The cowboy, Clay West, has his right arm in the correct position, but he missed the steer's left horn with his left hand. At the moment Serpa snapped the shutter, West's left hand had veered like—well—an unhazed steer to the right side of the steer's snoot. West's mouth is open beneath his handlebar mustache, and the look on his face is pained. I like to think he's saying, "Oh shit" at that instant. The left side of his body is jammed against the steer's left horn, which has to hurt, and he knows he's going to tumble to the ground just ahead of the steer, meaning he'll probably get popped by a hoof or two as the steer thunders over him.

The worst possible thing that can happen to a bulldogger is getting "hung up." His foot goes through the stirrup instead of sliding out of it when he dismounts. The horse yanks him off the steer and drags him until his boot comes off. In the text accompanying a collection of her photos, Serpa writes:

> I watched a man get killed that way, right in front of me, in Yuma. It's horrifying to see the horse dragging the rider, right there, and not be able to do anything about it. He was dead before he got to the end of the arena because he went right under the horse, and the horse just pummeled him to death in a panic. I saw the same thing happen recently in Sonoita, but fortunately, the rider's boot came off. The boot went right through the stirrup, but the boot came off his foot—so he was banged up, but he was alive. The horse was so panicked by this whole thing happening underneath him that he tried to jump the end of the arena. The horse was all right, but it could have finished the rider.

Even successful bulldogging takes its toll on the cowboy. Serpa notes: "This is the worst thing in the world for knees on a human being . . . because you're down there stopping the steer with your legs out . . . You can drive a horn into your body very easily if you miscalculate . . . And the steer weighs five or six hundred pounds."

Today the cowboys—including a couple of brothers from La Junta, Colorado, named Jace and Keo Honey, who fail to score in spite of their sweet names—walk away from steer wrestling relatively unscathed. No one racks up a particularly outstanding score. Ben Bates Jr. of Mexican Springs, New Mexico, and

Calvery Hogue of Phoenix split the day money, each scoring times of 5.7 seconds.

The action moves from the timed event chutes to the bucking chutes for bareback riding. If some cowboys believe bulldogging is the most dangerous event, others think that bareback is the one that ensures that all the contestants are beaten up by the time the ride is complete. The horse—and old-time rodeoers contend that the term *bronc* is reserved for saddle broncs exclusively, that there is no such thing as a "bareback bronc"—is outfitted with what's known as a bareback rigging, or "riggin." It is essentially a flap of leather with two large metal D rings on each end and something approximating a suitcase handle attached with stainless steel bolts at the middle. The rigging is draped over the horse just behind the withers and cinched tight using the D rings, leaving the handle directly above the horse's back. The rider mounts, grasps the handle with his riding hand, and leans far back with his feet up high on the horse's shoulder, almost like he's relaxing in a recliner. The chute opens and the cowboy tries to keep his back as close to parallel to the horse's back as possible while "raking" the horse using spurs that have dull five-edged rowels, which look sort of like miniature gingerbread men. Because the spurs are not sharp, the raking doesn't hurt the horse. But it looks good to the judges and helps with the scoring. Each time the thousand-pound horse bucks, it smashes the back of the rider with its own body, a sensation something akin to being pounded by a boulder. Meanwhile, the handle is yanked with terrific force with each buck, and you wonder how a cowboy can come out of a career as a bareback rider without having his riding arm stretched out to be six inches longer than his other arm. Moreover, the cowboy is expected to keep his nonriding arm raised—it's a disqualifying foul for him to touch the horse with his free hand—and to somehow control the ride.

This afternoon Phil Smith of Springhill, Louisiana, does the best job of surviving the beating and controlling the horse and making it all look good. He receives a score of 79 for his ride on the horse called Hanger.*

Martin Kiff, the barrel clown, or barrel man, is a thirty-nine-year-old Californian. He now takes the spotlight in the center of the arena for a standard feature that is practically as old as rodeo itself: the clown's comedy shtick. Kiff is dressed in his regular outfit: silver hat; yellow, red, white, and blue shirt; Wranglers; and yellow socks. Below the hat is a yellow wig, and his face is smeared with yellow greasepaint, with his eyes and mouth outlined in white. The clown's persona in these acts is as a sort of Peck's bad boy, with the announcer playing the role of the long-suffering straight man. So Corley begins with, "What in the world are you doin'?" as Kiff wheels a set of golf clubs onto the dirt. What unfolds is a series of gags and puns built around making a golf shot, with *shot* being the operative word,

---

*A perfect score in bareback, saddle bronc, or bull riding is 100 points, though no one ever achieves a perfect score. Judges evaluate the cowboy's riding technique on a scale of 1–50. They score the animal's difficulty to ride on the same scale. The totals are tallied to give the cowboy his score for the ride. In order for a cowboy to win a rough-stock event, he has to ride well and his horse or bull has to throw a lot of challenges his way. For some reason, bull riding is always scored higher than bareback or saddle bronc riding. These days, a good score for a bull ride is in the 80s, while a good score for a bareback or saddle bronc ride is in the 70s. Some longtime rodeo fans believe that modern scores are being inflated in order to appease a new generation of fans. Just twenty years ago, a saddle bronc score in the 60s was considered a good one. Defenders of modern scores say they occur because today's cowboys are better trained and today's rough-stock animals are better bred and more difficult to ride. The naysayers believe that TV producers think higher scores play better to younger viewers and to the advertisers wanting to pitch products to them.

as Kiff yuks it up about a shot from a gun and a shot from a whiskey bottle. Pure vaudeville, corny—so bad that it's funny. And the crowd loves it. When I was a kid and watched these routines, I missed out on most of the banter from the clown, but now, armed with a portable microphone, Kiff is easy to hear around the arena. Kiff performs the role of the buffoon so well that you'd never guess he holds an English degree from Cal Poly and spends much of his free time reading, writing, and designing Internet Web sites.

When Kiff completes his routine, tie-down roping (the official term for calf roping these days) begins. The calves seem to have the upper hand on the cowboys tonight. Four ropers fail to score at all. One breaks the barrier too soon and has ten seconds added to his time, ensuring he'll finish out of the money. In the end, Dustin Koyle of Albuquerque takes the go-round with 9.9 seconds.

After watching team wild-horse riding, steer wrestling, and bareback riding, the audience seems to be rendered a little lethargic by the relative tedium of calf roping. The traditional rodeo brass band music that has been playing throughout the earlier events gives way now to George Thorogood and the Destroyers' "Bad to the Bone." In comes a souped-up Dodge rig with loud exhaust pipes. A long stock trailer attached to it has ONE-ARMED BANDIT emblazoned on the side. The crowd roars its approval for the music and the truck. Something about this seems familiar to me. Then I realize it's John Payne, a whip-snapping trick rider from Shidler, Oklahoma, a small town in the Osage. I remember writing about him for the *Ponca City News* years ago.

Payne has a great story. As a kid and a young man, he was eaten up with cowboying. But as he got a little older, he decided he needed to take a more practical approach to life than spending all his time messing around with horses, so he learned how to be an electrician. One day while he was on a job, he struck a live wire. He was severely shocked, losing one of his arms as a result. As he recovered, he decided he was going to do what he loved, practicality and disability be damned. He started working with horses again. Soon he developed a rodeo specialty act that extended beyond horses to include longhorns and cow dogs. As a rider, he proved to be awe-inspiring, standing on his saddle at full gallop, twirling a rope or snapping a bullwhip while doing so. He never shied away, just because he had only one arm, from stunts other trick riders did. In fact, he chose "One-Armed Bandit" as the name of his act, putting his disability up front for all to see. He became a hit at rodeos in Oklahoma and Kansas, and his reputation spread, so much so that he was named specialty act of the year for eight consecutive years by the PRCA. No small accomplishment for a guy featuring trained animals in his act at a time when other specialty performers are using motorcycles, pyrotechnics, and other whizbang elements in their acts.

This afternoon Payne is riding a disabled horse—he has just one eye—named Rusty. "Other people," Corley intones over the PA system, "might have had this horse put down because it just has one eye. But John saw the possibilities in this horse and made him into a top performer." And Corley's right. Payne and Rusty leap onto the bed of the truck, then climb onto the top of the stock trailer, coming to a dime stop right at the trailer's edge. Payne is standing on the saddle, snapping his whip. Then Rusty dances in a circle on the trailer's narrow top, and I notice for the first time that the horse is wearing a pirate's patch over his missing eye.

Payne and Rusty dismount from the trailer. A hatch in the trailer opens and several buffalo charge out into the arena. I sense that the crowd catches its breath collectively at the sight of the buffalo. But maybe that's just me. I'm a sucker for buffalo, sentimental about buffalo, a romantic when it comes to buffalo. I would have loved to have witnessed firsthand one of the buffalo herds on the southern plains before the great slaughter of the late 1800s—tens of thousands of bison darkening the grassland for as far as the eye could see. Just viewing these few buffalo running onto the dirt at Prescott is enough to make me feel weak in the knees. I like to think the audience is reacting the same way.

Buffalo have a reputation for being all but impossible to train. Yet Payne has them scampering around his truck, striding much more gracefully than cattle can, fur oscillating with the breeze, their large heads noble in the arena lights. Now Payne herds them onto the bed of his truck, then up on the top of the trailer. So much for buffalo being untrainable.

With the buffalo back in the trailer, one of Payne's helpers drives the rig out of the arena as Payne gallops on Rusty, dipping off one side of the saddle, then crossing over to the other side of the saddle for another dip.

Payne leaves the audience jazzed for the next competition: the classic rodeo event, saddle bronc riding. Space for snobbery is scarce in the world of rodeo, but where it does exist, it's usually associated with bronc riding. At most rodeos, saddle bronc is the only event the audience sees that grew out of real-life cowboys' daily routines during the heyday of the great ranches. "Rodeo is show biz—its relationship to ranch work is oblique at best," Larry McMurtry writes. No cowboy needed to wrestle steers as part of his job. He seldom, if ever, needed to rope a calf, although he roped steers regularly. Team roping was not found on the ranch, either. And cowboys sure as hell never rode bulls as a requirement for drawing their wages from the foreman.

But breaking horses was something in which all cowboys took part. Horses buck ferociously the first time they are saddled and a rider climbs on board. Ideally the cowboy would have been able to stay on the horse until the horse tired of bucking and began to resign itself to a life serving as transportation. Not many cowboys could ride bucking horses consistently. Those who were able to stay on were valued by the ranchers who employed them, so saddle bronc riding was a skill cowboys tried to achieve. Boasts and subsequent wagers over whether a particular rider would be able to ride a particular outlaw horse were the centerpiece of the old cowboy contests in ranching country, just as bucking-mare riding was a centerpiece of the ancient *charreadas*. Other events can be eliminated, but rodeo would not be rodeo without saddle bronc riding.

Saddle bronc riding is about style and grace and precision. It has its dangers, but the chances of getting killed are far less than in bull riding, and injuries among saddle bronc riders are fewer than among bareback riders or bulldoggers. Yet it is the most difficult rodeo event to master. Judges keep a fine eye on the horse and the rider. Every move the cowboy makes must be synchronized with that of the bronc in order to create eight seconds of fluidity. The cowboy's form should be perfect, poised. He should be upright in the saddle, with his nonriding arm lifted above his head.

As in bareback riding, the cowboy must "mark out" his horse at the first jump from the chute—his heels must be touching the animal's shoulders. If the rider fails to mark out, the judges disqualify him. If he successfully marks out, the judges score the ride primarily on the cowboy's ability to control the horse and his spurring action. Using spurs that are subtly different from a bareback rider's, the saddle bronc rider ideally will rake from the horse's shoulders to the back of the saddle, his toes turned outward. To control the horse, the cowboy has only a single thick rein attached to the bronc's halter. It's remarkable that the cowboy is able to manage the bronc at all.

A good bucking horse—and for decades Harry Vold has had the reputation of providing the best bucking horses in the world—kicks more than once per second during the ride. Sometimes all four hooves are off the ground. At other times the horse rears back so far on its hind legs that it is almost perpendicular to the ground. It wriggles its body while forcefully snapping its head from side to side, in a maneuver called sunfishing. It ranges over a good deal of the arena while doing all this—in what Larry McMurtry has called "the dance of gravity." *Dance* is an apt description. For all the bucking and rearing and running and wriggling the horse goes through, it must help the cowboy out by doing these things in a rhythmic way. An ideal ride seems to be choreographed. But in reality it is pure improvisation on the part of the horse and the cowboy. It is a thing of beauty.

Today's lineup of riders is heavy with Canadian cowboys from Alberta. Like South Dakota, Alberta has a long tradition of producing outstanding saddle bronc riders. But tonight it is John Donnelly of Unionville, Nevada, who proves to be the most beautiful in the arena, scoring a 74 aboard Storm Barn Snuff.

The rodeo has been running for close to two hours, and I sense the slightest bit of impatience from the people in the grandstand. They're ready for the big event—bull riding. But there's still team roping and barrel racing to come, plus another comedy routine by Martin Kiff.

Team roping involves two ropers, a header and a heeler, whose goal is to snatch a running steer by its horns or neck and by its hind legs. These steers are large, weighing maybe two or three hundred pounds more than a wrestling steer. As with calf ropers and steer wrestlers, team ropers begin with their horses in a three-sided box area adjacent to the chute. They have to wait for the animal to get a running start before they can begin their pursuit, with the header taking a slight lead. Then the header, riding to the left of the steer, tries to lasso both horns, one horn and the head, or the neck. Roping any other part of the steer is a foul. If he makes his catch, he veers the steer to the left to expose its rear legs to the heeler. The heeler then attempts to rope both hind legs—if he catches only one, a five-second penalty is assessed.

Team ropers do not have their ropes secured to the saddle before attempting their catches. Once a roper's loop has found its mark, he wraps the loose end of the rope around his saddle horn before the rope goes tight. This maneuver is called "dallying," and it occurs so quickly that the casual fan in the grandstand might never even notice it. And it's a tricky move. When I was hanging out with cowboys in Osage, I kept running into ropers missing fingers because of mistakes they made with their dallies.

Sometimes even this most sedate of rodeo events can turn deadly. Ronald Reagan's commerce secretary, Malcolm Baldrige, was a team roping heeler. In 1987, while practicing at a ranch in California in preparation for an upcoming rodeo, Baldrige's horse reared and toppled backward onto him. The horse got up unharmed, but the commerce secretary was crushed. Those who rushed to his aid found his belt buckle lodged against his spine. Baldrige died a short time later at a nearby hospital.

Still, cowboys well into their forties and fifties, and older, can compete successfully in team roping. Indeed, Prescott's Chuck Sheppard, who was a world champion team roper in the mid-1940s, continued to participate in team roping into his eighties. That's one of rodeo's most attractive features. The contestants range from teenagers to retirees. Another attractive feature of rodeo is that for years women have taken part in the competition.

In the flow of a rodeo performance, women's barrel racing typically occurs just before bull riding. It seems to whet the crowd's appetite for what is to come. It is fast and simple. The rider zips into the arena, guides her horse around a cloverleaf course of three barrels, then zips back out. It is the one rodeo event that involves no judges—just a timekeeper. The only way a rider can foul is if she knocks over a barrel. Not to diminish the horsemanship of the riders, but the real athlete here is the horse. A horse that shows the instinct for becoming a terrific barrel racer can cost the rider as much as fifty thousand dollars. Then the rider can invest untold hours training the horse, all aimed toward successfully competing in an event that's over in seconds. So the accolades a winning rider receives are more in recognition of the weeks she spent working her horse in a practice pen than of a performance that lasted a quarter of a minute.

Good times in barrel racing vary from rodeo to rodeo, based on the size of the arena and the configuration of the barrels. But in the end, only hundredths of seconds separate money winners from those who go home with nothing. Tonight, good scores are in the 17-second range. Rising barrel racing star Sheri Sinor-Estrada of Alamogordo, New Mexico, posts a 17.4, tonight's best time. Four other riders also score in the 17s. This kind of close competition always stirs up a crowd. As the rider loops her barrels, she reins her horse as close to each barrel as possible, leaving the barrel rocking. *Will it tip over? Will it stand?* You move to the edge of your seat and hold your breath. *Yes! She made it!* Or, *Ah, that's too bad.* . . . For a crowd that's been guzzling beer and wolfing down nachos and hot dogs for more than two hours, barrel racing is a cold slap in the face. An ideal way to wake up for bull riding.

Bull riding is finally here. As if to emphasize that this is "the Event," a crew scurries onto the field to set up a temporary fence in front of the bucking chutes, as a pickup hauls away the

CHASING THE RODEO · 69

racing barrels. Bruce Springsteen's "Born in the U.S.A." blasts from the sound system. Everything is ready.

Bull riding is a bit of a paradox. It is a relatively new event in its present form, not having turned up as a standard competition in rodeos until after the turn of the twentieth century—twenty or third years after those early rodeos in Pecos and Prescott. And yet it harkens back to something ancient. Some of the oldest historical records reflect human beings' obsession with competing against bulls. More than any other creature, bulls epitomize power and virility—they did to the ancients and they do today to the crowds in rodeo arenas.

Games honoring the sea god, Poseidon, were held in Thessaly, on the Greek peninsula, and featured acrobats grasping the horns of charging bulls, then performing handstands and other feats. In Knossos, the Minoans included bulls in their worship services. As part of the rituals, both male and female athletes took part in bull vaulting. In one maneuver, a bull vaulter grasped the horns of a galloping bull, flipped over its head, landed on its back, then somersaulted over the rear of the bull to land on the ground. In another, an athlete leaped from an elevated platform, over the bull's head and onto its back. Sometimes a bull vaulter grabbed the bull's horns in order to be flung into the air, at which point he or she performed flips and twists before lighting on the ground. At other times, one athlete distracted the bull by challenging it from the front while another athlete rushed the bull from the flank and performed a handstand on its back. After the vaulting performance was finished, the bull was typically killed as a religious sacrifice.

In centuries to come, battles with bulls were a standard event at the Colosseum in Rome. Still later, bullfighting became an obsession of the Moors living in North Africa. When they conquered Andalusia, they took bullfighting with them, and by

1040 the Spaniards had adopted the event, which they called
tauromaquia. In Portugal, bullfighting on horseback took root,
with the emphasis on good horsemanship rather than on the rit-
ualistic killing of the bull (although bulls are typically slaughtered outside the arena shortly after a Portuguese bullfighting
event). Bull baiting and bull running became popular in other
parts of Europe, especially in England. Bull baiting involved
trained mastiffs attacking a tethered bull, but bull running involved people assaulting the animal. An account of one such
event details how the bull was prepared by having its horns,
ears, and tail cut off; its nose stuffed with pepper; and its
fur slathered with soap. The bull was set loose and towns-
people pursued the beast, pelting it with stones and sticks, until
it dropped to the ground from exhaustion. Then a butcher
slaughtered it. Animal-rights activists may have no love for the
bull-riding event practiced at rodeos today, but it's a damned
sight more humane than what our forebears did to bulls in the
name of sport.

At a rodeo, once in the bucking chute, a bull is outfitted with
a flat, braided rope, which is wrapped around its massive chest
just behind its front legs and over its withers. One end of the
bull rope, called the tail, is fitted through a loop on the other
end, and is tightened above the bull's backbone. Leather is
braided into the rope (which otherwise is made of strands of
polypropylene or more traditional fibers) to form a grip for the
cowboy. Wearing a thick yet soft riding glove that's taped onto
his hand, the cowboy grasps the rope at the leather section and
runs the tail through his pinkie or index finger. Brazilian bull
riders introduced the practice of winding the tail around their
hand in what's become known as the suicide wrap—a rider can
have difficulty freeing himself from the rope once he's dismounted. Also attached to the rope is a cowbell, which dangles
from the bull's chest. The rattling of the cowbell might do

something to encourage the bull to buck once it's out of the chute, but the purpose of the cowbell is to act as a weight to pull the rope free from the bull once the cowboy has released his grasp. While parading under the simple name of *bull rope,* this is a fairly complicated device, one costing as much as $250—or more if hand-braided. Even a custom-made rope undergoes all sorts of further treatments to get it just right for the rider. It is stretched before a ride and treated with rosin to make it sticky, which is where the phrase "rosined his riggins" comes from. Some cowboys are picky about the leather handgrip. I over-heard a conversation in which one rider asked another how he stiffened up his grip. The other rider advised dousing the leather with tincture of benzoin, then letting it sit on the dash-board of a pickup to allow the sun to bake it.

Like all bucking stock, bulls also are fitted with another rope, this one called a bucking strap, or a flank strap. The flank strap is among the most controversial accoutrements in all of rodeo. Animal-rights activists allege that the strap, which goes around the bull toward the rear of his midsection, is purpose-fully affixed over the animal's genitals and cinched tight to cause it excruciating pain. On the other hand, the Professional Bull Riders organization maintains that the strap's purpose

is to enhance the natural bucking motion of a bull and to en-courage the animal to extend its hind legs when trying to get his rider on the ground. The rope is fleece-lined and does not hurt the bull. A common misperception is that this strap somehow irritates or is tied to the bull's testicles. This is simply not true. That would cause the animal pain and dis-courage him from bucking or even moving—exactly the op-posite of the desired behavior. The flank strap never covers or goes around a bull's genitals, and no sharp or foreign ob-jects are ever placed inside the flank strap to agitate the ani-mal. Furthermore, a flank strap cannot be too tight around

the bull's flank or the bull will be too uncomfortable to perform. Pulling the flank strap too tight would restrict a bull's
motion, resulting in an inferior performance by the bull and
quite possibly a reride for the bull rider. The flank strap is
designed for quick release and is removed immediately after
the bull exits the arena.

The truth probably lies somewhere between the two positions. As one old rodeo hand told me, "It don't hurt 'em none,
not really. Just makes 'em a little itchy." If so, bulls don't like
feeling itchy. As soon as the flank strap is on, the bull starts
doing its best to get out of the chute, kicking and slamming the
wooden sideboards, sometimes nearly climbing out over the top
of the gate. It's a hell of a chore to get the bull rope and the
rider in place with all this commotion from an animal weighing
between seventeen hundred and twenty-two hundred pounds.
Some of the hands around the gate use two-by-fours to leverage the bull's body into a position that allows the rider to climb
down the sideboard to mount his draw. Once the cowboy has
his hand in place and the rope secured—with a final slug of his
free hand to the gripping hand—he gets his body situated as
best he can on the back of the bull, gives the gate hands a nod,
and rides what must feel like a hurricane out into the arena.

A bull has strength enough to "easily jump over a five-foot
fence or lift the back end of a car off the ground with his
horns," note Wayne S. Wooden and Gavin Ehringer in their
Rodeo in America. I've never witnessed a bull picking up the
back end of a car, but I have seen one fly out of the chute with
all four hooves higher than the top of the gate. As soon as it
lands on its feet, the bull starts spinning and bucking and doing
everything possible to rid himself of the cowboy. In most of
the rides I've seen, the cowboy is simply rag dolled off the side
of the bull within two or three seconds after the gate opens.

The force is just too much for a rider who typically weighs around 150 pounds.

This is nothing at all like ballet, at least not to the spectator. There's none of the beauty here of saddle bronc riding, none of the grace. And a cowboy simply can't control the ride like a competitor can in saddle bronc or bareback, although he will win points from the judges if he appears to have some control. There's no marking the bull out or anything similar to that. The point is to survive. Donnie Gay, the greatest bull rider of all time, has many times likened it to a sort of dance, one in which the bull has absolute power—but one that's not nearly as graceful as the ballet of saddle bronc riding. "It's sort of like a waltz, but you gotta let the bull lead," Gay says. Sometimes a rider has the opportunity to rake a little for the judges' benefit, but for the most part, he uses his legs and heels to hang on until this violently awkward dance is done.

Out comes the first bull, Charlie Brown, who drills Avelino Baca of Bosque, New Mexico, soon after he breaks through the gate. The other bulls on tap for tonight—Freightrain, Scruffy, Plum, Spiderman, Brindle Bob, and the rest—all prove better than the riders. After the last horn sounds, it's the bulls 8, the cowboys 0.

THAT NIGHT I make a quick trip to a supermarket adjacent to the location of the old Prescott depot. In the parking lot a large tent has been erected to house the rodeo dance. In the shadows, a cluster of *compañeros* share a gallon jug of Gallo wine from the grocery store while listening to the music coming from the tent. I step under the canvas to check out the scene. A band saws away while couples sway to the music.

I think about rodeo dances. They could be pretty intense affairs. Usually they followed an afternoon rodeo, and the revelers were wired from the action they witnessed just a few hours earlier and from no telling how many beers they'd consumed over the course of the day and evening. They were boisterous, with crowd noises always threatening to drown out the offering from the band, which was usually mediocre at best though no one seemed to care much. Above all else, they were events gooey with sexual tension and the promise of violence. Rodeo contestants showed up, looking for women. Sometimes the women they set their eyes on were in the company of dates, but that seldom slowed them down. Of course there was always a contingency of what are sometimes called "buckle bunnies" or "shiny brights" as well—young unattached women smitten by cowboys, rodeo groupies ready to find love in the front seat of a pickup truck parked outside. But even with buckle bunnies there for the taking, there were always cowboys who went for the women with dates. Inevitably, these dates were the sort of men who would love nothing more than to acquire bragging rights for having stomped the shit out of a rodeo cowboy. One thing leading to another, as it always does, a fight or two or a half dozen would break out before the band played "Faded Love" for the final time. Peckinpah satirized all this in a *Junior Bonner* brawl scene set in the Palace. Extravagantly choreographed and lasting for several minutes, the scene features drunken battlers throwing punches and elbows as well as smashing chairs and beer mugs and tables and mirrors and banisters and about anything else that might have been found in the Palace, circa 1970. The fracas comes to an end when the band plays a warbly, only slightly off-key rendition of "The Star-Spangled Banner."

Tonight's dance seems sedate, so I don't hang around for very long. I stroll up to the old Santa Fe depot that has been refurbished into an office building and look up at the A. G. Edwards sign. Financial services. But not a sign of tracks anywhere. I sit down on the sidewalk and think about the best scene in *Junior*

Bonner. Junior and his dad, Ace, end up at this very depot, seated on a bench facing the tracks. Junior confesses that he's broke and can't help Ace out with his latest scheme. Using only facial expression and body English but not a single word, McQueen conveys all there is to be said about a son coming up short in his father's eyes. For a moment he seems to be ready to bolt. But finally he and Ace have a kind of reconciliation, punctuated by Ace's retrieving Junior's Western hat from across the track—earlier Ace thumped it from Junior's head to show his displeasure in him.

I lean back on my elbows and stare up at the sky. I wonder what it's like for such things to occur between fathers and sons. I've never experienced it.

THE NEXT MORNING, Luscaine and I are up early, taking a walk in the cool, evergreen-fragranced air. At the First Congregational Church, a pancake breakfast is under way—a traditional part of the celebration surrounding rodeos in small towns in the West. Local and state politicians are there to glad-hand and flip flapjacks—another part of rodeo tradition. This year, Arizona Governor Janet Napolitano is here to take her turn with the spatula. It must be a good respite for the governor to get up here in the high country. In her first year as governor, she's had to deal with a terrible wildfire season as well as the worst fuel-shortage crisis to ever hit the state. By comparison, pancake batter sticking to a grill must seem like the most minor of concerns.

Luscaine and I make our way back to the Vendome, where we claim a couple of chairs on the gallery and settle back to watch that other mainstay of the small-town rodeo fiesta, the parade. A family of locals set up lawn chairs in front of us and I overhear a woman with a raspy voice say, "Seeing that man from the funeral home reminds me. We used to have a priest here whose last name was Body. *B-o-d-y. Body.* You used to read obituaries in the paper that ended with 'Father Body will officiate.' Used to crack me up to read that. You know, funeral, body, Father Body."

She laughs. A young woman with her says, "That is *so* Prescott. I had a teacher in middle school whose name was Mrs. Stoner."

"Well, honey, I went to a dentist named Dr. Hurt."

More laughter. "That is so Prescott," the young woman says again.

The family becomes quiet when a color guard of slightly bent, silver-haired men from the American Legion Post march past with the colors, bringing all of us to our feet. They are followed by Miss Rodeo Arizona. Then the grand marshal, Governor Napolitano, rolls by in a surrey with—you guessed it— fringe on top. She has the political gene, no doubt about it. She waves vigorously from one side of the surrey to the other. And her face registers absolute delight with the applause she receives.

Rodeo royalty move past the Vendome, as does a contingency of the Arizona department of the U.S. Marshals Posse. Where do they find all these damned horses? The kids who clean up the horseshit mounds along the parade route must wonder the same thing. I close my eyes and the parade scenes from *Junior Bonner* run through my mind. Peckinpah shot the actual Prescott parade and, as with so many things he dealt with in his films, he got it just right. Riders dressed like mountain men. Clowns. An endless stream of Shriners. Hometown floats with varying degrees of hokeyness. Spectators on rooftops. That's just how it must have been in Prescott back in the '60s and '70s. And that's how it was in my hometown back then as well.

My mind drifts back to when I was a student at Guthrie Junior High School. Two-thirds of the parade has already gone ahead of us, and we know there's no way we're going to make it through to the end of the parade without stepping in horse-shit. It's the third week of April, but this Saturday is more like a June day, with the temperature approaching ninety. I'm wearing jeans and a T-shirt beneath my band uniform, and I can feel sweat trickling down my legs and back. The heat is cranking up the odors of the horse manure to eye-watering intensity. The good news is that this torture is soon to end. The band has made a left turn off Oklahoma Avenue onto Second Street. A block down Second, then a left turn onto Harrison Avenue. A couple of blocks up Harrison, and the parade is finished. At the corner of Harrison and Second, we come to a standstill for some reason. A good bandsman would keep his eyes straight forward like a soldier at attention, but what the hell, we're almost done, so I'm looking around. I glance over at Edna's Lounge, a beer joint that in an earlier incarnation was known as the Blue Belle Saloon. Suddenly a guy in a Paladin hat and vest emerges from Edna's open door—on horseback. I guess he catches me looking at him, for he raises a can of Coors in a salute in my direction. All I can do is smile.

I think back on Paladin's salute, open my eyes, and peer out at the array of floats passing the Vendome. Something is missing and now I realize what it is. No marching bands. Of course. It's Independence Day week. Schools are closed. Today I'm wishing I could be out there on a float rolling down Prescott's streets. Maybe on a horse. Decked out in boots and a Western hat. Maybe I could run into Ace and Junior Bonner. Better yet, maybe someone dressed like Paladin could raise a beer in my direction as I ride by.

THE SUN IS HIGH overhead with only puffs of clouds in the distance. Everything in the Frontier Days arena is glaring.

Behind the bucking chutes, the rough-stock riders gather. Prescott, like most outdoor rodeos, offers nothing more than a fence or two and a stretch of grass to serve as a locker room for the cowboys. The cowboys pick their place on the fence and mark it with their riggins. Then they open their travel bags and pull out their riding duds. No athletes get filthier in the course of their sport than rodeo cowboys. Their boots are so battered that Goodwill would reject them. Their jeans are smeared with dirt, bullshit, mud from maybe twenty different states, along with a little bit of blood and possibly a splash or two of beer. Their hats have been trampled and reshaped dozens of times. Their shirts are usually the most reputable looking item of clothing they'll slip on, especially if it bears the names of corporate sponsors.

"Cowboys are the most superstitious athletes," former bull rider Louis "Bubba" Murphy told me. "One superstition I had was that I never washed my riding clothes. Things got pretty rank as the year went on." Judging by what you see along the fence at Prescott, Bubba wasn't the only cowboy with this particular superstition.

Rough-stock riders as a whole aren't particularly modest. They drop their jeans in plain sight of anyone who might be strolling past, to begin wrapping themselves with Ace bandages and slathering on analgesic cream. In fact, analgesic cream is in such strong supply that its odor threatens to overwhelm that of manure from the pens and chutes. Once they're taped and into their riding clothes, the cowboys rosin their bull ropes, take dry rides on bronc saddles mounted on the dirt, and fiddle with their bareback rigs. They put on their spurs and chaps. Some do stretches and other warm-up routines that would make any aerobics instructor proud. More than a few of them dip snuff and find some buddies to bullshit with. Others don't want to talk to anyone at all. You'll always find at least one rider sitting by himself, his face buried in his hat.

Jesse Bail arrives, nods to acquaintances, shakes a few hands, then heads to a fairly remote place along the fence to get ready for his bronc and his bull. He already has several thousand miles under his belt for this Cowboy Christmas week. As soon as he picks himself up after his bull ride this afternoon, he'll pack his rope and his bronc saddle back in his bag and hightail it for Window Rock, 299 miles northeast of here, hard against the Arizona–New Mexico border, for the evening performance of the Navajo Nation Fourth of July Rodeo.

I AM WATCHING from the crowded grandstand. Ray Lesniak told me that he has seen so many rodeos over the years that he never feels particularly compelled to watch one now. The age-old saying goes, "You've seen one rodeo, you've seen 'em all." It has to be something "extra special" to bring Ray to an arena, something like watching the great Ty Murray ride—"pure poetry in motion." I'll see five rodeo performances while I'm in Prescott and they will be largely alike—the same patriotic poem, the same grand entry, the same music, the same specialty act, the same comedy bits by the clown. But each timed and riding event is a unique little drama unto itself, and that fascinates me.

Take the team bronc riding this afternoon. The horses do a particularly good job of stomping the would-be riders. I watch one horse leap over a fallen cowboy, clipping him in the back of the head with a hoof. The blow is strong enough to send the rider sliding on his belly for what seems like three or four feet. He does not get up without help.

I'm wondering how Jesse will do in today's go-round of saddle bronc riding. He faces tremendous competition. The great Dan Mortensen, a five-time world champion saddle bronc rider, is one of his competitors. A lot of eyes are on Mortensen this year, for if he wins another world title, he will tie Casey Tibbs for the most-ever saddle bronc championships, a record many rodeo fans thought no other rider would ever achieve. Also competing is Cody "Hot Sauce" DeMoss, a Louisiana cowboy who claimed the saddle bronc championship at the Houston rodeo earlier in the year (Houston titles carry a lot of prestige and also come with a big paycheck). A cadre of other top riders are on tap: Scott Johnston, originally from Australia but now calling Gustine, Texas, home; Justin Arnold of Atascadero, California; Scott Miller of Waco, Texas; Rance Bray of Dumas, Texas; Jeffery Willert of Belvidere, South Dakota; and Bradley Harter of Aledo, Texas.

Jesse rides a Harry Vold bronc named Springboard and notches a 74, a decent score, but the judges give Bray a 76 and Johnston a 79. So Jesse takes home day money for third place.

When the bull riding comes around, Jesse is first out of the chute on a bull called X1. But he bucks off before eight seconds are up. Jesse is packing his bag while Jaron Nunnemaker of Willits, California, scores an 82 on Plum, which will hold up as the best ride of the afternoon.

As the crowd disperses, I come across a young guy holding an ice bag on the back of his head, dried blood in his hair. I recognize him as the team bronc rider sent sprawling in the dirt after taking a horse hoof to the noggin. He's talking to a young woman who is concerned about how hurt he is. But the cowboy isn't interested in discussing what happened to him. He's wonky from the blow to the head and is jabbering about all sorts of things. At one point he tells the young woman, "I met Jesse Bail back there. He talked to me for a while. He's a nice guy." He shifts the ice bag.

"Really? You met him?" the woman says without too much enthusiasm.

"Yeah. Great guy." He smiles, then starts jabbering about something else.

I wonder how many miles of highway Jesse already has behind him, as I leave the arena.

⇥ 3. RANGING OUT ⇤

The Daddy of 'Em All
Cheyenne, Wyoming—July 2003

DENVER INTERNATIONAL Airport seems to be closer to Omaha than to the Mile High City itself. It sits out on the prairie, surrounded by snow fences, with the downtown skyline far away. The airport's distinguishing feature is the terminal roof, a long stretch of translucent nipples that reminds me of nothing so much as a nursing mother dog lying on her back. I've flown to Denver where I'll rent a car and drive to Wyoming to attend Cheyenne's version of Frontier Days, the most famous rodeo in the world, "the Daddy of 'Em All."

My plan is to skirt Denver, and I take a loop that leads me past a Conoco refinery and other industrial sites. But when I hit the intersection with Interstate 25, which leads to Cheyenne, I turn back toward Denver after making a split-second decision that I'm not quite ready to leave. I find a restaurant and stop for a cup of coffee. I stretch my legs and plant my heels on the seat opposite me in the booth, my knees aching. I watch the traffic on the access road and think about Cowboy Don.

COWBOY DON was not your typical rodeo bum. At least not in terms of his family background. He was no ranch kid. He was a city dude.

In 1909 his father, Don Carlos Stratton Sr., arrived in Denver. Even though Denver got its start as a rough-and-ready cow town, my grandfather was not a cowboy at all. Instead, he was a dapper man, a self-educated accountant who knew much more about corporate boardrooms than he did about corrals. He had black hair and piercing eyes so dark that they were almost black—"Stratton eyes," a family member told me. Despite his features and his name, he most likely had no Hispanic heritage. All evidence suggests he was named after Don Carlos Buell, a Civil War general from the Midwest.

My grandfather was born in 1871 in the small town of Austin just up the road from Louisville on the Indiana side of the Ohio River. Stratton is a fairly uncommon surname in the United States, and that region where Indiana and Kentucky meet along the Ohio is the breeding ground to which many of us can trace our antecedents. By the time my grandfather was grown, he lived in what was then a Stratton stronghold, Pewee Valley, Kentucky, about fifty miles from Austin. While there, he married a woman ten years older than he who had children from a previous marriage, thus engaging in a pattern of complicated family relationships that would be visited on his children.

In June 1898 my grandfather traveled to Lexington to join the First Kentucky Infantry as it prepared to enter Buckey O'Neill's war against Spain. But my grandfather saw nothing of the Rough Riders or Cuba. Instead, he served in Puerto Rico, where he contracted malaria, which would afflict him for the rest of his life. Because of this, he drew a pension as a disabled soldier. Not long after the end of the Spanish-American War, he followed the lead of his distant kinsman Winfield Scott Stratton and departed the Ohio River Valley for Colorado's Rocky

Mountains. W. S. Stratton achieved wealth beyond the imagination of the most fanciful of Indiana dreamers. He hit the mother lode at Cripple Creek, won the moniker of "Midas of the Rockies," and is honored by a statue in Colorado Springs. Don Carlos Stratton never accomplished anything worthy of a statue, but he became a successful Denver businessman, working with companies that dealt with oil and gas exploration, mining, and real estate development.

For several years, he kept the books for one of the more exotic Denver businesses, the Savery Savory Mushrooms Company, located at 107th and Federal Boulevard, in what was then farmland north of the heart of the city. C. W. Savery began producing his Savory Mushrooms in the 1920s—a risky undertaking, for mushrooms were a relatively unusual food for the American palate and had been cultivated in the United States only since the turn of the twentieth century. By the time my grandfather went to work for him, Savery's enterprise included thirty-two buildings for growing mushrooms and another thirty mud huts to accommodate the Mexican American women who did most of the labor for him.

My grandfather worked for Savery for five years, and while there, he did the same thing he did at the oil exploration, real estate, mining, and other companies at which he was employed in Denver: He cooked the books so he could take home extra cash in his pocket.

DRIVING ON Interstate 25, heading due north out of Denver, I pass the area off to the west where Savery's mushroom empire once flourished. Nothing remains there now except a few building foundations and the stone footing for the water tower that had been designed to look like a Savery Savory Mushrooms can. It's a hundred miles straight up the highway from Denver to Cheyenne. Denver hugs the foothills of the Rockies, but the

foothills disappear as you move northward, giving way to un-
dulating grassland studded with occasional stone outcroppings.
The sky seems impossibly big here. Clouds roll by, casting
shadows on the rolling hills, creating a sort of kaleidoscopic effect. Color and light dance across the endless wide-open spaces.
Room enough to dream and scheme. At the Wyoming state line,
a metal sculpture of a buffalo stares down at the interstate from
a hilltop to the east. I pass a cluster of discount fireworks stores
on the Wyoming side of the line.

In a few minutes I'm entering the outskirts of Cheyenne. I
pull into a truck stop, gray puffs of diesel exhaust floating past
my rental car in the parking lot. I go inside and get a tasteless
buffet lunch. Surrounding me are burly truck drivers, most with
tattooed arms, fussing over mileage logs while picking at their
food. It is Cowboy Don's kind of place.

MY GRANDFATHER embezzled for the reason most embezzlers
ply their trade. He wanted to live better than his salary would
allow. He never went for the single big score. As an accountant,
he knew better. Instead, he took a little here and a little there
and kept it up for years. The endless columns of handwritten
ledger entries revealed to C. W. Savery and the others who employed him nothing about which to be suspicious. "Know your
stuff," Savery used to say when asked about his secret for success. "If more people would study their failures and delve
deeper into necessary information regarding whatever enterprise in which they happened to be engaged, there would be
fewer business flops." Savery apparently never delved very
deep into his own books, however, because he never caught on
to my grandfather's creative bookkeeping. By the mid-1930s,
Savery Savory Mushrooms had flopped, a victim of disease that
wiped out the company's crops. The loss of the money my

grandfather stole from Savery in the late 1920s couldn't have helped matters.

My grandfather walked a narrow line in Denver. He knew many of the rich and powerful men of his time while simultaneously keeping a fairly low profile. Another trick of the successful embezzler: Never call too much attention to yourself. Records about him are hard to find, especially for his first ten years in the city. But by the 1920s, he was living comfortably in eastern Denver.

But his family was in turmoil. His wife, Mary (called Monie by the family), died at age sixty-three in 1924. My grandfather, then fifty-three years old, didn't grieve the loss of his first wife for long. He enjoyed a drink, another Stratton-family trait, and he especially enjoyed sharing a drink in the company of the ladies. Soon he encountered a free-spirited New Yorker named Anna who was some twenty-five years younger than he. It's safe to say he'd never before met a woman quite like her. She was a pistol.

CHEYENNE IS one of the most famous place-names in the West. A number of my friends have come here just because of the name, conjuring up images of mountains and relics of ranching empires as they made the long trek. To a person, they all have been disappointed by what they found at Cheyenne. Or, more accurately, what they failed to find at Cheyenne. "Ain't no place to go but Cheyenne," a character in *On the Road* says, "and ain't nothing in Cheyenne." The community does not pretend to be anything more than what it is, a small state capital and a military town. And, above all else, a transportation hub. The only time things get fanciful around here is that ten-day period in July when Frontier Days flips everything upside down and knocks loose the cobwebs. Otherwise Cheyenne is pretty much your standard blue-collar Western town, not much different from, say, Temple, Texas. A place where the opening of a regional-distribution-center Lowe's Home Improvement Warehouse is celebrated news because of the four hundred jobs it promises. A place where a poll of local diners revealed that the Applebee's across the street from the mall is the best restaurant in town. Things get pretty scruffy along the outlying stretches where Interstates 25 and 80 intersect and main rail lines for the Union Pacific and the Burlington Northern cross paths. Truck stops, fast-food restaurants, convenience stores, and a lot of motels. A lot of eighteen-wheelers on the highways. A seemingly endless procession of trains on both rail lines. None of which must have any appeal to tourists looking for the authentic West.

Now I get to experience what many fans endure when they show up for a big rodeo in a small town—a harrowing search for lodging. I turn onto a street called Lincolnway (U.S. 30), which skirts the south side of Cheyenne, and find the motel where I'd made a reservation. The old inn must have been "beat" already by the time Jack Kerouac drifted through Cheyenne at rodeo time in the late 1940s. The ensuing years have not made things any better. It hugs the Union Pacific tracks, and just as I step out of the car, an Amtrak train thunders past, causing the building and parking lot to tremble. *Great*, I'm thinking. *I should get a lot of rest here.* I step inside the office and discover I'm not going to have to worry about whether I'll be able to sleep here. The codger at the desk tells me my reservation has been lost. And, sorry, they're full up. I go back to the rental car feeling a mixture of relief and despair. Glad I won't have to listen to trains all night. But where the hell am I going to stay? Some four hundred thousand people swarm into Cheyenne, a town with a population of around sixty thousand, for the Daddy of 'Em All. Motel rooms become as rare as purple mountain majesties in

Cheyenne during Frontier Days. And there are no nearby communities. I might have to drive to the closest purple mountain to find a place to rest my weary head.

The young woman at the Holiday Inn on Interstate 80 laughs to herself when I ask if there might be a vacancy—I'm hoping for a cancellation. No, she says, not likely there will be any cancellations. She gives me a phone number for the chamber of commerce and says they monitor the availability of rooms during Frontier Days. "Good luck," she says as I turn to leave. I hear her giggle again as I walk away. I should have known better than to even stop at the Holiday Inn. In many small Western towns that host big rodeos, fans make reservations as much as a year in advance for motel rooms, especially at places like Holiday Inn.

Back in the car, I call the chamber and a woman there tells me I'm in luck. Days Inn has a single room. She gives me the motel's number and I immediately call. Yes, there is a room still open. I'm warned it is a smoking room but I take it. The clerk says okay, but she also warns me about the rates. Tonight will be relatively inexpensive, since this is not considered to be a "rodeo night." But tomorrow is a rodeo night, as are the remaining nights I'll be in Cheyenne. So the rate will be double what it is for tonight, she says. Since I have no other choices, I agree, even though I'm thinking I probably could get a decent room in midtown Manhattan for what I'll be paying to sleep at the Days Inn in Cheyenne, Wyoming. I give her my credit card number, then rush to the motel to claim my room.

Days Inn is on Lincolnway, not too far down the street from the run-down motel where I thought I had a reservation. The room does smell like an ashtray (I leave the window open the whole time I'm there) and the carpet appears to have been ground with the grime of ten thousand pairs of trucker boots. But the bathroom's clean and the bedding is unsoiled. It will work. I plop down on the bed. As these things go, the search wasn't nearly as bad as the time I tried to find a room one night in Jackson Hole, Wyoming, when the rodeo was in town. I hadn't slept much for two days and was desperate for a place to crash, and the Datsun B210 I drove wasn't exactly cut out for sleeping. After being laughed at every place I stopped, I finally nabbed what probably was the last available bed in Jackson Hole at a pleasant little place called the Woods Motel. I've never had a room I enjoyed more.

Through the open window I hear rain begin to fall outside on the highways and railroad tracks of Cheyenne. Almost immediately I'm asleep.

ANNA LOCKWOOD Newell could trace her roots to some of the first English families to settle in America. In 1630 her Lockwood kin were among seven hundred Puritans who traveled to the Massachusetts Bay Commonwealth in eleven ships that came to be known as the Winthrop Fleet. Descending from a Winthrop Fleet family carries cachet in some circles, but it didn't mean anything to Anna. By the time Cowboy Don was born in 1930, Anna had cut connections with her family in the East. Eventually she had become a mystery name to Lockwood family researchers. No one knew what ever became of Anna.

The Lockwoods eventually made their way south to New York, where they developed into furniture merchants of some prominence in Brooklyn. In 1881 the *Brooklyn Daily Eagle* reported: "Brooklyn has a reputation for artistic work in this line, and among the concerns which stood first for excellence of workmanship, elegance of design, and beauty of finish is the house of Jacob W. Lockwood of Fulton Street. Artistic furniture that is worth the title is one of his specialties and the selections which may be made would please the most fastidious tastes." Lockwood was "catering to a demand on the part of the public for beauty in the common surroundings of everyday life." Jacob Lockwood was Anna's grandfather.

My grandmother was born in Brooklyn to Mary Lockwood and William Newell in February 1895. Just six months later William died. He was only twenty-eight years old. Mary remarried and had other children, but her life was to be cut short as well—she developed a stomach blockage that killed her when Anna was seven years old. Not surprisingly, Anna was shunted from relative to relative among her Lockwood kin. No evidence exists showing that she had anything to do with her father's family after his death. Later in life, Anna used different identities. Usually her first name was Anna, but sometimes it was Ann or Anne, sometimes Joanne or Joanna, sometimes Joan. Most of the time she gave Newell as her maiden name, but almost as often she listed Lockwood, sometimes even Westlake. Being orphaned that young, she must have been confused about just who she was. After she reached puberty, she discovered sex was a way for her to gain acceptance. When she was in her teens, she stirred up a family scandal by attempting to seduce one of her male relatives. Not too long after that, she disappeared from her maternal family's records. Maybe she left on her own, maybe she was invited to leave. No one knows.

She married a man who practiced law in midtown Manhattan and soon had four children: three daughters, and a son who perished at a very young age in the great influenza epidemic of 1918. New York at that time had plenty to offer a young, free-spirited woman as ready to flaunt convention as Anna was.

And so she had lovers.

One of her affairs was with a businessman from Denver, one of her husband's clients, whom she met while he was in New York on business. I don't know how long the tryst lasted, but Anna wound up pregnant and she was certain the Denver man was the father. So she packed up her young daughters and headed to Colorado, abandoning the East Coast and memories of an unhappy childhood forever. The evidence suggests she didn't trouble herself with getting a divorce.

In Denver, she learned some hard lessons. Not surprisingly, her husband's soon-to-be former client already had a wife and family, and when Anna turned up in Denver, he delivered the news that he would not be abandoning them for her. She had no money or prospects for getting money. Whatever unhappiness she may have experienced as a child, she had always lived in comfortable surroundings. For the first time in her life, she experienced abject poverty. She took a tiny, dingy, often frigid apartment off an alley in downtown Denver. The family often scavenged to get by. One of her daughters remembered a day when she and her sisters were hungry and locked inside the apartment. Looking out the window, she spotted an apple that had been discarded in the alley. She and her sisters formed a sort of human ladder out the window in order to retrieve the half-rotten apple, which they then ravenously ate. Given these circumstances, it probably was a blessing that Anna miscarried.

While it's possible that Anna worked during this time, she also became a Rocky Mountain Blanche DuBois, depending on the kindness of strangers. Her daughter told me that a substantial number of men visited the apartment after Anna recovered from the miscarriage. Seventy-five years later, her daughter vividly recalled nights when she stayed out of sight, beneath a table next to the bed, while her mother and one of her male callers rocked the mattress just inches away from her. Her daughter speculated that many of these were business transactions in which the stranger's "kindness" was delivered up front. She wound up pregnant again and gave birth to a daughter named Peggy, although she, like her mother, would come to use different names—later in life, she called herself Emily Snyder and only close friends knew her as Peg. Not long after Peggy was born, my grandfather met Anna. And fell in love with the woman a quarter of a century his junior.

CHEYENNE CAME into existence by happenstance. Or at least that's the southern Wyoming lore. Shortly after the Civil War, General Grenville M. Dodge led a survey crew into the area to map the route of the Union Pacific Railroad. The crew had worked hard for days on end and Dodge knew he needed to set up a camp so that his workers could rest. At sunset one evening, miles from the last site designated as a station and knowing that the Rockies loomed not too far ahead, Dodge glanced around and announced, "Good as any." And Cheyenne was born. But it turns out reality was more complicated than the legend—as is always the case in the West. True, the site for Cheyenne did not sit on a major river or other readily apparent geographical attraction. But beneath the grass, the spot had a lot to recommend it as a prospective major railroad terminal. Dodge needed to find the right combination of granite topped by sedimentary rock to support the tracks as they approached the Laramie mountain range ahead. At the Cheyenne site, his engineers discovered they stood on a narrow ramp of uneroded sedimentary rock that led to the granite summit of the Laramies. This discovery resolved many concerns Dodge held about how and where the rail line should cross the mountains. He may have thrown down his hat and announced "Good as any," but he did so with some good science backing him.

Cheyenne sprung up in anticipation of the railroad that was creeping westward, and in its early days it was a sure-enough feral place. It had a graveyard before it had its first structure— a raiding Native American war party slew two members of Dodge's survey crew before they finished plotting the town. At one point, more than half the buildings in town were saloons. Still in a sort of no-man's-land as far as governmental authority was concerned, Cheyenne's first citizens turned to vigilantes to provide law enforcement. When a body drilled with bullet holes turned up on the dirt streets, it was hard to tell if it was a murder or merely a "legal" execution carried out by the vigilantes. When the first Union Pacific locomotive finally came snorting into town, about four thousand of the West's most disreputable riffraff were on hand to greet it—and figure out ways to make money off it. Games of chance were the big draw, and by 1868, a year after the first train's arrival, one of its disgusted founders bemoaned the town as "the gambling center of the world." The West's most notorious shootist and best-known card player, Wild Bill Hickok, drifted into Cheyenne to partake of the gambling possibilities and ended up acquiring a wife there. He left Cheyenne to go to Deadwood in the Dakotas to find a fortune in gold but, of course, found a grave instead.

Which, from the point of view of the town's emerging leadership, was probably just as well. These men had big plans for Cheyenne. They dreamed of an elegant city that would be lorded over by cattle barons of refinement and good breeding, some of them with English pedigrees, a city with no place for a ruffian like Wild Bill strutting around with twin Colt revolvers planted in the red sash wrapped around his waist. By 1880 they'd achieved much of their goal.

During the early 1880s Cheyenne was a cattleman's paradise, maybe the greatest cow town the West has ever known. The town's population stood at fourteen thousand people, a number of them sophisticated businessmen from the East who'd come to Wyoming to profit from the cattle boom. With managers living on their ranches to take care of business, many of the ranch owners opted to live in town, enjoying the creature comforts they were used to back east. By the mid-1880s the cattlemen living in Cheyenne had made so much money that the town was dubbed the wealthiest city per capita in the world.

The street now called Carey Avenue was a jeweled row of large houses with immaculate lawns and low iron fences, reflecting architectural styles as diverse as Old English country houses and French villas. But the epicenter of style and grace for the cattle barons was the club they established.

The Cheyenne Club allowed the men who had been made millionaires by cattle prices to sip wine and otherwise behave in the way that proper gentlemen in London would. David Dary writes in *Cowboy Culture:*

> The facilities included a dining room, reading room, and billiard room on the first floor, six sleeping rooms upstairs, and a kitchen and wine room in the basement. Trained servants were brought from the East to wait on the members. The best liquors money could buy were shipped by train to Cheyenne, along with all sorts of delicacies to please the tastes of the wealthy cattlemen. The racks in the reading room contained the latest copies of *Harper's Weekly* and major eastern newspapers, including the New York *Tribune* and the Boston *Sunday Herald-Traveler*. Here and there were, naturally enough, copies of livestock journals, including the *Breeder's Gazette* published in Chicago.

Paintings by well-known artists like Albert Bierstadt and Paul Potter adorned the walls. Members who dined there usually wore tuxedos and abided by rules that would have made Wild Bill cringe: No smoking in the public rooms. No alcoholic beverages in the reading rooms. No games played for a "money stake." And no games played at all on the Sabbath—in the new sophisticated Cheyenne, churches were beginning to compete in number with the saloons.

But the paradise of cattle empires in Wyoming came to a dreadful end during the years 1886 and '87. Things actually started going awry a couple of years earlier when the bottom

fell out of cattle prices because of overstocking by Texas cattlemen looking to get richer and richer. Prices never fully recovered until after 1890. At the same time, free range disappeared
steadily as barbed wire demarcated private ownership of land
that cattlemen had thought they would be free to use forever for
grazing. Then drought set in across the West in the spring and
summer of 1886. Michael Wallis writes: "It left throats parched,
grasslands withered, and streams and water holes dried up.
Nearly all of cow country was seared brown as tobacco, drier
than the heart of a haystack." As far north as North Dakota,
ranchers reported summer temperatures rising as high as 120
degrees in the shade. Bad as the summer was, the upcoming
winter of 1886–87 would be much worse. Blizzards roared
across the plains that season, from Canada all the way down to
South Texas, killing cattle by the tens of thousands. The mother
cows that didn't die in the horrendous cold miscarried their
calves as they tried to survive, so ranchers lost the better part of
two generations of cattle. A lot of fortunes perished with those
frozen carcasses and fetuses out on the range. A year after the
terrible winter, Theodore Roosevelt, who'd owned two ranches
himself on the northern plains, wrote:

> The best days of ranching are over... The great free
> ranches, with their barbarous, picturesque, and curiously fas-
> cinating surroundings, mark a primitive stage of existence as
> surely as do the great tracts of primeval forests, and like the
> latter must pass away before the onward march of our people;
> and we who have felt the charm of the life, and have exulted
> in its abounding vigor and its bold, restless freedom, will not
> only regret its passing for our own sakes only, but must also
> feel real sorrow that those who come after us are not to see,
> as we have seen, what is perhaps the pleasantest, healthiest,
> and most exciting phase of American existence.

Cheyenne beat out other communities to become the seat of government when Wyoming became a state in 1890, but it was obvious the town would never again hit the sort of cultural highs it enjoyed when the cattle barons ruled. It would be a successful community, drawing on revenues from the railroads, government, and the army post (eventually to become an air force base). But merely being a successful small city would not etch a place for Cheyenne in America's imagination. And the people of Cheyenne wanted their city to be known for more than just being a place where rail lines crossed each other. To achieve this, Cheyenne came to look back fondly at the likes of Wild Bill Hickok—or at least at the spirit that the untamed souls of the West possessed—and that "most exciting phase of American existence."

Of course Cheyenne had never been entirely rid of the wild ones. They may not have had rule of the town as they did before the cattle barons took control, but they remained a presence. Someone had to work the cattle, after all, while the barons dined in their tuxedos. If you wanted to find someone who knew about breaking broncs and roping steers, all you had to do was stop by the Old Red Barn at the intersection of 20th and O'Neil. Officially dubbed the Great Western Corral, the Old Red Barn was one of the oldest buildings in town—a drawing of it appears in a business directory for Cheyenne published in 1868, the year after the town was founded. Serving as a station for stage and freight companies, it became a gathering place for Cheyenne's less gentrified inhabitants. Shirley E. Flynn writes of the Old Red Barn: "It was a man's world frequented by sporting types wanting a wager, gentlemen in need of carriage horses, cattlemen signing on a crew, and those engaged in the selling of horse flesh of all varieties. It was a good place to get the pulse of the community."

Buffalo Bill Cody owned a ranch in North Platte, Nebraska, around two hundred miles up the Union Pacific line from Cheyenne. Cody was a frequent visitor to the Old Red Barn, leaning on a fence and observing the young men who were breaking the "broom-tails" for market. Some of these men he hired to perform in the extravaganza he called "Wild West." At the time, being a member of Cody's "Wild West" troupe was the pinnacle of fame in the United States. That some of the hands hanging around the Old Red Barn made it to the big time in show business only encouraged others to try to hone their skills. Maybe Cody would give one of them the nod the next time he was in Cheyenne. They held contests among themselves to prove who was the best on the back of a "waspy" bucking bronc. A few of the young cowboys even tried their hand at pulling off the most famous and most dangerous of all the events in a performance of Buffalo Bill's "Wild West": the reenactment of the Deadwood Mail Coach robbery. And they were pretty good at it.

So Cheyenne had a coterie of would-be showmen just waiting for an opportunity to let their talents shine. The opportunity arrived in 1897, courtesy of the Union Pacific. And, in a roundabout way, courtesy of Buffalo Bill.

For all practical purposes, rodeo as a profitable American spectator sport can be traced back to the Independence Day celebration in 1882 in North Platte. Cody had already made himself famous as a showman, performing in theaters beginning in the 1870s. So he was a natural choice to chair the Fourth of July committee in 1882 when his hometown wanted to stage a bigger-than-life patriotic celebration. Cody's Old Glory Blowout left no one in North Platte disappointed. As part of the Blowout, he persuaded North Platte businesses to donate prizes for roping, shooting, riding, and bronc-busting events, which Cody would eventually call feats of "Cowboy Fun." Elizabeth Atwood Lawrence writes in her excellent anthropological study of rodeo: "He expected to attract about a hundred cowboy contestants, and actually got a thousand. This unprecedented and unexpected success gave him the impetus for his future enterprise [Buffalo Bill's "Wild West"]. Thus 1882 marks the beginnings of both the Wild West show and one part of . . . its successor—rodeo." Lawrence notes that Cody's dramatization of the American West transformed the entire region into a place of romance and glamour. Before "Wild West," Americans regarded cowboys as among the lowest of the low in the social pecking order. Cody's shows, along with the plethora of dime novels that celebrated Buffalo Bill's adventures, both real and imagined, suddenly transformed the cowboy into an American hero—arguably *the* American hero. This occurred just as the United States Census Bureau declared that America's period of frontier settlement was officially over. Americans wanted heroics and they already were nostalgic for the end of the frontier era. Buffalo Bill's "Wild West" performances packed 'em in, and the Old Glory Blowout inspired towns like Pecos and Prescott to stage their own competitions in celebration of the West, although it would be a stretch to say Cody's extravaganza was a rodeo. At North Platte, Cowboy Fun was just a part of a much larger spectacle. At Pecos and Prescott, it *was* the spectacle.

Meanwhile, things in Cheyenne were "practically dead" by the late 1890s, in the view of the Union Pacific's general agent. The railroad's traveling passenger agent, Frederick Angier, was charged with creating events in communities along the line that would encourage out-of-towners to buy tickets for excursion trains. The railroad would profit from ticket sales; the businesses in the towns hosting the events would profit from money spent by the tourists. He'd already arranged successful Corn Day and Potato Day events in some towns along the north–south line in Colorado. So what could he do in Cheyenne?

While stranded at a rail siding at a ranch outside of town, he watched some cowboys struggling to load a wild horse into a stock car. The idea struck Angier of staging some sort of cowboy contest in Cheyenne, to "revive the thrilling incidents and pictures of life that may be reproduced in form by those who were once actors in that period." It made perfect sense. No town held a closer association with the Old West. And there were those cowboys hanging around the Old Red Barn, aching to perform. Cheyenne businessmen readily signed on with Angier to stage the first Daddy of 'Em All in September 1897.

Frontier Days was a success from the start. Shirley E. Flynn writes: "All the night before [the first Frontier Days performance], trains piled into Cheyenne, disgorging hundreds of fun seekers, pioneers, settlers, and cowboys. And they came chugging in the morning of the celebration, too, from the south and east. The chartered Union Pacific excursion train from Denver arrived at noon, carrying, besides a band, more visitors than all the rest put together." It was standing room only at the fairgrounds. The next year's event was even more successful, sanctified by an appearance of none other than Cody himself and a "Wild West" performance. A few years later, the event was big enough to attract Theodore Roosevelt, who rode in a Studebaker touring car in the Frontier Days parade.

The Daddy of 'Em All quickly established itself as America's biggest, most prestigious rodeo. It owed much of its success to Denver. Thousands of Denver residents traveled north to take in the rodeo every year, the most affluent of them taking the by-invitation-only *Denver Post* Special.

BY THE TIME of the 1930 census, Don Carlos Stratton had married Anna, and the family lived in a comfortable house in east Denver. The census lists Peggy as his stepdaughter. But Anna's three daughters from her first marriage are nowhere to be found. About the time she began her relationship with my grandfather, Anna placed those girls on a train for Los Angeles, where they were met by an uncle. He soon had parceled them out to foster homes and orphanages, and the trauma of their childhoods got no better. They never again lived with their mother. Many years later, one of them attempted a reconciliation, only to be rebuffed by her mother. Anna told her she'd just as soon not have anything to do with her first three daughters.

Anna considered her family to be her new husband, her daughter Peggy, and the child she was carrying. Don Carlos Stratton Jr. was born in May 1930. Cowboy Don—though he certainly was not raised a cowboy. For his first four years, he knew shady streets and pleasant parks and a spacious home with plenty of room for a kid to get into mischief. He was ignorant of ranch animals and bunkhouses and wide-open spaces. He came to learn about rodeo early on, however, through the stories my grandfather told him about Cheyenne.

My grandfather loved to rub shoulders with the rich and powerful. In Denver, there was no better chance to do so than to ride the *Denver Post* Special up to Cheyenne for Frontier Days. He finagled his way into a ticket every year he had a chance to do so. The rules on the train were pretty tight, including no women allowed as passengers, except for the salaried "hostesses" on board who were there to serve as dance partners. "Wives thought we were running a rolling cathouse," said *Denver Post* official Alexis McKinney, quickly adding that the allegation was not true. Shoptalk was prohibited among the businessmen. The trip was to be dedicated to fun and to fun only: drinking, dancing, maybe shooting some dice on the floor of one of the passenger cars. Once they arrived in Cheyenne, my grandfather and the other passengers carried the party to the Plains Hotel, then to the rodeo arena. Inevitably some of the revelers would become so caught up in the fun at Cheyenne that they would miss the train's return trip to Denver. My grandfather came back from Cheyenne with tales of cowboy heroics to share with his young son as he sat on his father's knee.

The Strattons also braved the chills of January to attend the newly established indoor rodeo at the National Western Stock Show. Though the rodeo made its debut at the National Western in 1931, it became one of the country's top rodeos just a couple of years later, thanks to the participation of some of the best cowboys in the world and appearances by the famous bucking bronc Midnight.* What later became Cowboy Don's obsession with rodeo can be traced back to those National Western shows he saw when he was barely able to walk.

But it probably would not have become an obsession at all if Cowboy Don's world had not been tipped upside down in 1934.

On the Saturday after Thanksgiving that year, a Denver deputy sheriff named Lindquist stopped my grandfather at Union Station, the elegant railroad hub in Lower Downtown. Lindquist pulled the frail man aside from the crowd and asked him where he was going.

"I'm heading back to Home Lake," he said to the officer. The malaria he carried ever since the Spanish-American War had flared up, and he'd been convalescing at the Soldiers and Sailors Home in Home Lake, about two hundred fifty miles south of Denver, even as he knew he was being investigated for

---

*Today the National Western is the first major rodeo to occur in the PRCA's yearlong rodeo season (a much less significant rodeo in Odessa, Texas, gets rolling a few days before the National Western so it can lay claim to being the actual first rodeo of the year). The purse at the National Western ranks among the very best in rodeo, so it is an important first stop for cowboys attempting to qualify for the National Finals.

embezzling. "I just came to Denver to visit my family for the holiday."

Lindquist looked the elderly man over. My grandfather was sixty-three, but he seemed older than that—his health had gone down in a hurry over the past year or so. His face was pale. The dark eyes had gone dull. He was bent, seemed feeble.

My grandfather read the deputy's face for a moment, then said, "Marcus Bogue?"

The deputy didn't answer. He sighed, then said, "Pops, you've got to come with me."

My grandfather glanced at the train, sighed himself, and nodded. "I can't walk all that way—"

"There's an automobile waiting for us."

For four years my grandfather had a good racket going at the offices of Conway-Bogue Realty Investment Company in the U.S. National Building. He was an officer of the corporation, holding the titles of secretary and treasurer. But Marcus Bogue and his partner, John Conway, were tough businessmen. They kept a close eye on their money, and they weren't about to stand still once they discovered their bookkeeper had been absconding with funds. On May 1, 1934, Conway-Bogue fired my grandfather, although he claimed he was let go because of a lack of business. After spending the summer and early fall straightening out the books, Marcus Bogue was ready to make his move. He could document that my grandfather had taken $2,556.50 out of the company coffers for his own use. Denver's district attorney Earl Wettengel agreed to prosecute a single felony count of embezzlement. The charge was filed in Denver's Second Judicial Court on November 24, the same Saturday that my grandfather was arrested.

Sick and tired and at his wits' end, my grandfather accepted the allegation. When he went before Judge Charles C. Sackmann two days later, he pleaded guilty. Sackmann set a further hearing for December 1 and fixed bail at twenty-five hundred dollars. Anna could not come up with that much money, so my grandfather was remanded to the city jail. He immediately began an application for probation. Besides listing the standard information about family, prior convictions (none), health (poor—"enlarged glands"), and so forth, he entered a glittery roster of personal references: Denver's legendary mayor, Ben Stapleton; Colonel William Danks; Schuyler Peck; George P. Williams; George D. Kimball; and Dr. Fred Beasley—men he'd rubbed shoulders with at his Shriners lodge and in various business dealings. He entered a defendant's statement in which he fessed up to more than the charge against him:

I got in debt and tried to live over my means. I tried to have a nice home for my wife and children, so started embezzling this money over a period of four years [from Conway-Bogue]. The amount was about sixteen thousand dollars. I was using this money to buy a home . . . and supporting my wife and two small children. I also embezzled two hundred dollars from the Ware Bros. when I worked there after working at Conway-Bogue. I expect to pay back all of the money as soon as I get on my feet. I want to go to California where my son is and get work in the line of accounting. I expect to walk a straight line if I get out of this because it doesn't pay to [do] otherwise. I am in need of medical attention now in order that I might be prepared to get employment.

It was a substantial amount of money to embezzle, roughly equal to $220,000 in today's economy. There seemed to be no way this frail old man could ever pay back all the money as he promised. Still, probation officer Edmund Young recommended restitution and no jail time, based on my grandfather's personal references, his poor health, and his clean criminal records. After hearings on December 1 and 4, Judge Sackmann had other opinions. On January 5, 1935, the judge executed an instrument to deny probation. Two days later, he sentenced my grandfather to three to five years of hard labor at the state penitentiary in Canon City. My grandfather would never again ride the *Denver Post* Special to Cheyenne for Frontier Days. And Cowboy Don would never again have a father.

I DRIVE NORTHEAST on Lincolnway, which soon becomes Sixteenth Street. Even though Frontier Days is still a day away, downtown is already decked out for the celebration. The sidewalks are crowded, with at least three-quarters of the men and a lot of the women wearing Western hats. Sixteenth itself is jammed by tandem rear-wheel pickups pulling horse trailers. I creep forward. I ease past the Wrangler, a Cheyenne landmark. It is an enormous bright redbrick Western-wear store, three stories high with white trim. Its name is spelled out in huge letters, each more than a story tall, mounted on the roof. I watch whole families in tourist T-shirts and shorts and sandals invading the Wrangler to pick up something, *anything* somewhat Western to wear to tomorrow's rodeo.

Now Cheyenne's best-known building comes into view. The Union Pacific Depot occupies an entire block, a fortress of stone and brick that's three stories high with a mammoth clock tower shooting up into cloudy sky. Since its construction in 1886, it has had the reputation for being the most majestic depot in the West. The depot no longer functions as a train station, but it is undergoing restoration and renovation. A temporary sign hanging on its side announces that a brewpub will be opening in it soon, joining a museum and offices.

I turn off Sixteenth and work my way through downtown, heading in the direction of the golden-domed Wyoming capitol. The closer you move to the heart of Cheyenne, the more pleasant the city becomes, echoing the glory days of the cattleman's

paradise. Treelined neighborhoods of tidy houses are dominant. I notice that several mailboxes along the street feature
Wyoming's trademark image: a cowboy riding the first superstar among rodeo animals, the bucking bronc known as Smokey.
Enough meandering, I decide. *I'm here for a rodeo.*

I swing over to fabled Carey Avenue, Cheyenne's most
prestigious residential street in the 1880s, and drive northwest,
crossing through Lion's Park until I reach one of the gates leading to Frontier Park, home of the rodeo grounds. I tell an at-
tendant at the gate that I'm here to pick up media credentials,
and he directs me to a gravel parking lot near the Old West Museum & Store. I lock up the rental car and stroll over to a small
building, shaped like a house, that serves as the media office. Inside I get the once-over—I'm in shorts and a T-shirt. The guy
who hands me my press badge says, "You know you can't wear
that when you go to the rodeo."

I know. I was able to scrape by in Prescott with Levi's and
boots, with a short-sleeved golf shirt, as my usual rodeo attire.
But Cheyenne is strict about enforcing the PRCA's rules for
media attire. Western hat, long pants, boots, and a long-sleeved
Western shirt.

"I have my stuff back at the motel," I say.

"That's good, because we wouldn't let you in with that pass
if you weren't dressed right."

I smile. He tells me what time I can pick up the day sheet
and the turn-out list for tomorrow. I step outside and look over
at the arena. Tractors and trucks zip around the livestock pens.
People scurry about, stepping out of the way of the tractors and
trucks at just the last second. Everybody seems in a hurry to get
somewhere, to get something done. Everybody seems to have
too much to do and too little time. And no one seems to be in
the mood to talk to a nosy writer from Texas. So I head back to
the motel.

In the room, I open my suitcase to check on my hat. It's a terrific hat, a classic. Resistol "'Self-Conforming' Western, Made in Texas, U.S.A. Stockman's Long Oval." I bought it almost twenty years ago from a Western-wear store in the Osage in Oklahoma. I'd worn it to the annual spring tribal dances held by the Osages in Hominy, and to the annual spring shinny games held by the Poncas along the banks of the Arkansas River, near White Eagle. I'd worn it to the Ben Johnson Father's Day Steer Roping in Pawhuska. All of this in Oklahoma. I'd brought the hat with me to Texas and worn it to a rodeo in Burnet County and to the Futurity cutting horse event in Fort Worth (held at the Will Rogers Coliseum). I take the hat out of the suitcase. My attempt to safely cushion it by packing it with socks and underwear has not been successful. The brim is bent in a couple of places, the crown caved in. I manipulate the hat for a moment or two and it comes back to form, more or less. Not that it matters much. The hat is showing some wear. It had some sweat stains and a couple of dirt smudges on the underside of the brim before I packed it. I place the hat on my head and peer into the mirror. Damn, a Western hat looks right on me, even though it doesn't exactly complement the T-shirt featuring masked Mexican wrestlers, and the Bermuda shorts that I'm wearing. I take the hat off and think about the last time I wore it. Maybe twelve, thirteen years ago?

I remember. I was in a cutting-horse practice ring near Belton, Texas, mounted on the back of a white mare. She decided I wasn't half the horseman I thought I was—she was right—and took off on me. She zipped me around the pen for what seemed like forever, bucking and dipping her head, before whipping me from the saddle by running me under a low-hanging live oak branch. I hit the ground flat on my back and blacked out.

When I came to, a guy named Odell had stuck his fingers

beneath the waistband of my jeans. He pulled my pelvis up off the ground and shouted, "Breathe!"

I breathed. He did it again. I breathed again.

"You're all right," he said.

I stood up, brushed the dirt from my jeans, retrieved my Resistol, and climbed back on the horse in true cowboy fashion. I finished out the afternoon at the pen, then went home and soaked in Epsom salts and swallowed some aspirin. I was stiff and sore for two weeks, but I eventually got over it. More than a decade later, X-rays and an MRI revealed that I had actually broken my back in two places with that spill. But hell, a man's gotta carry on, right? At least that's the kind of bullshit I used to say to myself.

I spend the next half hour or so ironing my shirts. I had not owned a Western shirt for years until the previous week, when I bought four Panhandle Slims. In the old days, Panhandle Slim was the standard in cowboy shirts. But I had to dig around for a while at the store to find the brand. Resistol, Wrangler, and other brands seemed more dominant, most of them emblazoned with brand names on their collars, breast pockets, and, in some cases, backs. Some of the shirts had giant splotches of bright colors forming various geometric patterns. Informally these are called Brooks & Dunn shirts, I learned, named after the well-known country duo that popularized the look. I'd feel uneasy in that kind of shirt, remembering too well the days when wearing something like that to a rodeo was a pretty good invitation to get a mudhole stomped in your ass, as they used to say, by cowboys outraged by your audacity. About as flashy as anyone ever got when I was a kid was Casey Tibbs in his purple chaps. And he only got away with that because he was *Casey Tibbs*, the greatest bronc rider of all time. My idea of appropriate is your basic Western shirt: pearl-snap buttons, two breast pockets with flaps, cut from cloth with a simple pattern—or better still, plain white. I finally found some Panhandle Slims that fit the bill, stuck on a rack in a corner of the store.

I picked out the four shirts I liked best, then headed toward the cash register. But I made the mistake of passing by the boot section. A pair of black calfskin boots with simple yet elegantly stitched uppers caught my eye. I'd planned on wearing a pair of black Nocona bull hides I'd owned for years (reheeled twice, resoled god knows how many times) at Cheyenne, so I wasn't shopping for footwear. But these looked great. I placed my shirts on a fitting stool and picked up one of the boots. I looked at the price tag and swallowed hard. Then I glanced inside and understood the reason for the price. These were Luccheses, the Cadillac of Western boots ever since Sam Lucchese (pro-nounced *lou casey*) immigrated to the United States in 1880 and set up shop in San Antonio—the best boot you can buy short of having a pair custom-made for you. Like a fool, I sat down and put one on. It was the most comfortable boot I'd ever put on my foot. I sighed. A few minutes later I left the store with the shirts in a bag and the Luccheses in a box under my arm. And the debt on my Visa card considerably elevated.

I slip on one of the Panhandle Slims, then step into a pair of Levi's. I dig the Lucchese's out of my suitcase and put those on, then add the Tony Lama belt I bought in Prescott. Finally I slide my old Resistol hat onto my head and look in the mirror. *Good enough, cowboy. Let's rodeo.*

ANNA AND HER children lost everything when my grandfather went to prison. Suddenly she faced the same poverty she'd known when she first came to Denver. She and her two children left the family home at 1925 Holly Street and began an odyssey of moving from apartment house to rooming house that would go on for a decade. Denver school records show that Cowboy Don lived at five different addresses during his kindergarten and first-grade years alone. Then things got worse. During the second grade, Anna moved the family to six different places, and Cowboy Don attended four different schools. She finally took him out of school altogether for a while. In spite of all this, he appears to have been a good student. After he finished the first semester of the second grade, he skipped ahead to the second semester of the third grade. Once he'd completed that, school officials allowed him to jump fourth grade entirely, as well as the first semester of the fifth grade.

He attended several grade schools in Denver, but the one where he turned up the most often was Ebert Elementary. It was there that he encountered Neal Cassady. Cassady was four years older than Cowboy Don, and nothing suggests that Cassady had the slightest idea who he was. But Cowboy Don knew all about Cassady. He had to. Everybody at Ebert did. Among the kids in the neighborhood, Cassady was a legend for his sports accomplishments on the Ebert playground. Later, his antics and his free-flowing style of conversation would inspire Beat Generation writers like Jack Kerouac, Allen Ginsberg, and John Clellon Holmes. In the 1960s, he became a founding father of the hippie movement as the man behind the wheel of Ken Kesey's celebrated psychedelic bus.

Cowboy Don's and Cassady's paths crossed repeatedly in Denver in the 1930s and '40s. Cassady and his friends hung out at a combination bar/pool hall/hotel on Glenarm and Fifteenth—a place where you could buy beer as soon as you were tall enough to lay money on the bar—and at Pederson's Pool Hall a half block away. A half block in the other direction was the apartment building where Anna and her children eventually resided. She pulled Cowboy Don out of school once he finished the sixth grade, and he got a job cleaning up after Cassady and his friends at the pool hall. Later, he worked as a pin monkey at a nearby bowling alley.

Cassady was a singular person, as students of the mythology of Kerouac and Kesey know. But he and Cowboy Don were similar in many ways. Just as Cassady became a petty criminal, so did Cowboy Don, amassing a sizable file (according to one of his half sisters) at the Denver Police Department. Both had absent fathers: Cassady's lost to booze, Cowboy Don's to prison. Cassady's mother died when he was young. Anna was a selfish woman who, while physically present, was emotionally absent. Neither boy knew what a stable home was. Both became womanizers and had multiple wives. Both had itchy feet. Neither ever fully recovered from their Denver experiences.

Never mind recovering from the Grateful Dead's lyrics. Cowboy Neal at The Wheel of the Bus to Never-Never Land was no cowboy. Cassady was a hipster, never plugged in to Denver's cowboy culture. He was all about Charlie Parker and Miles Davis, not Hank Williams and Lefty Frizzell. Cowboy Don, on the other hand, listened to Hank and Lefty and heard the poetry of his life. Rodeo offered him direction in an otherwise adrift life. He took jobs working the pens behind the chutes during the Denver rodeo as a teenager, and when summer came around, he hitchhiked to Cheyenne to do the same at Frontier Days. When he had the chance, he asked the experienced riders to show him a thing or two about how to stay on the back of a bull. No collegiate rodeo training or rodeo schools for him. He learned what he could the old-fashioned way: by getting his ass tossed into the mud.

My grandfather served three years of his sentence at Canon City, then was paroled to California to live with his first son, Carlos. Of course he never made good on his pledge to pay back all the money he embezzled. After that much time in prison, his already precarious health was shot to hell and he wasn't able to work much. He died within ten years of being paroled, confined to a veterans hospital in LA, where he suffered from dementia brought on by arteriosclerosis. Cowboy Don was sixteen when the old man died, and he didn't learn about his father's death until it was too late for him to attend the funeral. If it upset him, he took it out by ranging out to rodeos around Colorado and surrounding states.

In fact, Cowboy Don was at the point in his life where he would do a lot of ranging out. Anna left Denver about the time my grandfather died. It seems possible she might have inherited something upon his death. Although she struggled in poverty during those years while he was in prison, she had the means to acquire a small piece of property in Albuquerque, where she eventually opened a trailer court. She also hit the road with her other business venture. She owned and operated midway games at carnivals through the West. Cowboy Don traveled with her, learning how to work as a carnival roustabout and how to sucker marks out of their money once the midway was open. Usually they worked carnivals set up in conjunction with a rodeo, so Cowboy Don could pick up some extra money wrangling live-stock behind the chutes and he could try his skill on the back of a bull from time to time. The open road was his home now, not downtown Denver. And he loved it.

THE BRINDLE BULL looks at me, or maybe he looks through me. Up the way, a group of wranglers are trying to move bulls from one pen to another. Three bulls give them no problems. But a fourth has decided to stop in the alleyway. He's not fighting them. He's just stopped. A man on horseback tries giving the bull a couple of swats with his lariat. The bull is content standing where he is. "Why, you cantankerous son of a bitch," the man on horseback says. The men clatter the fence and try to manipulate the stubborn bull. If any of this affects the brindle bull I'm looking at now, he doesn't show it. He chews his cud in the soft sunlight. His tail swats at an invisible something on his flank. Occasionally one of his ears flickers. But nothing seems threatening about him. He is as peaceful as an old yard cat taking in the sun. This is exactly how you want a bull to behave on the day it is going to come out of the chute. Rodeo movies like to portray bulls in the pens as snorting, angry, dirt-pawing, vicious sons of bitches, frantically trying to hook anything they can see, in or out of a pen—which is exactly the way you want a bull not to behave. Bulls have a relatively small energy reserve. If they spend the morning agitated, they will wear themselves out before they ever enter the chute. The explosion out of the gate won't be an explosion at all. The bucks will be halfhearted, and the spins will be slow, like a washing machine set on the gentle cycle. The cowboys will be pissed off because their bulls won't be holding up their end of the deal; the scores will be low in spite of the cowboys' best effort. Most of the stock back here behind the chutes is placid, just like the brindle bull. Except for the one stubborn bull stuck in the alleyway and the commotion surrounding him, it's a pretty peaceful place.

I tarry too long here with the brindle bull and have to trot to catch up with a group of tourists being given a tour behind the chutes. The tour is made up mostly of kids, each of whom gets a plastic Old West peace officer's badge as a souvenir—okay, I get one, too. The tour is led by a woman on a plodding old horse, and her horse seems to be getting far more attention from the kids than any of the rodeo stock are getting. She takes us through the pen area while another woman points out the horses, steers, calves, and bulls. Then we're taken to the arena itself, allowed up-close looks at the chutes and the cowboys' ready area. And then we head back to the museum on the rodeo grounds, where our tour began.

The two women involved with this tour are among the throng of volunteers who make Frontier Days possible each year. It takes dozens of unpaid assistants to make Prescott's

Frontier Days a success, but in Cheyenne, the volunteer army numbers more than twenty-five hundred. There are only a handful of full-time employees who work for Frontier Days. Then there are the workers employed by the stock contractors, and some other hands temporarily employed by the rodeo. But the overwhelming majority of people here are kicking in gratis work, answering to a calling of civic pride. At least *some* of them do it for civic pride. Others do it—well, it's a rodeo after all, and people want to be part of the excitement. I met volunteers who came from all over Wyoming as well as from Fort Collins and Greeley, Colorado. If I'd looked hard enough, I suppose I could have found volunteers from as far away as Denver.

Everything about Frontier Days is as big as the Wyoming sky. Its promoters now boast that it is the world's largest rodeo. The most contestants. The biggest arena. The biggest rodeo grounds (one of the volunteers whispered to me that Frontier Days organizers had recently acquired some extra acreage just so the Daddy of 'Em All could have a larger rodeo grounds than the Calgary Stampede's). The million-dollar purse is the largest of any regular season rodeo, topped only by the National Finals Rodeo. And the nine rodeo performances will draw about four hundred thousand spectators, the biggest audience in rodeo. Even the press pass bouncing against my belt as I walk is huge, by far the largest one I've ever worn.

Maybe the most staggering thing about Cheyenne is the number of cowboys and cowgirls who compete here. This year's Frontier Days features around eighteen hundred contestants, including world champions as well as rodeo part-timers. If you have a PRCA card and the money to pay the entry fee, you can compete against the best in the business, and hundreds come here to do just that.

Take Ryan Rodewald of Colorado Springs. The son of two-time NFR saddle bronc qualifier Roy Rodewald, Ryan was brought up with rodeo in his blood. As an adult, he became an airline pilot, working for a United subcontractor. For a time, he tried to balance both—keeping his flight schedules and competing in saddle bronc. He did pretty well competing in rodeos, but eventually he was forced to make a decision between the friendly skies and the often not-so-friendly arenas. His dad told him that, yes, he'd had a pretty good run, but "goofing around on weekends wasn't going to do much good." Focus on your career, not the rodeo, was his father's advice. Ryan took it and dropped out of the circuit for two years. But now at age thirty-one he's back at Cheyenne, determined to juggle career and rodeo again.

Or take calf roper Terrell Phillips of Edmond, Oklahoma. He's an anesthesiologist by profession, but ropes and horses are his passion. "I got hurt last year and took about a year off, but now I hit about forty to forty-five rodeos a year," he tells a newspaper reporter. "I'm in a group of anesthesiologists so they can cover for me when I'm gone." And so he picks and chooses rodeos on the circuit, competing only at those he likes.

Another roper at Frontier Days is Ty McClary, a Texas native now working as an actor in Southern California. McClary played the hockey player with a roping jones in *The Mighty Ducks*. At Cheyenne, he will be one of the pickup men working the rough-stock events.

Better yet, take Kappy Allen. Born in Austin, she grew up in El Campo, Texas, a town southwest of Houston of about ten thousand people. She was the daughter of Grady Allen, who qualified to compete as a calf roper in the very first National Finals Rodeo. Not surprisingly, she grew up with rodeo and started barrel racing when she was still a child. But Allen turned her focus away from rodeo when she entered college. Her determination combined with her intelligence paid off: She graduated from the University of Texas in 1981 with high honors.

Three years later, she took her Juris Doctor from UT's fa-
mously difficult law school, picking up numerous honors along
the way. That same year she passed the bar exam. In 1986 she
became an adjunct professor at the law school. Known in legal
circles by her more formal name, Kathryn E. Allen, she joined
Graves Dougherty Hearon & Moody, one of Texas's most
powerful law firms, in 1985. Graves Dougherty is a button-
down, charcoal-gray sort of practice housed in an office building on Congress Avenue in downtown Austin. Members of the
firm include two former assistant U.S. attorneys general; a former member of the Office of the Solicitor General, U.S. Department of Justice; a former general counsel to the governor
of Texas; and three former special assistant attorneys general
for the state of Texas. As a civil litigator and shareholder at
Graves Dougherty and as the mother of two sons (she's married to attorney Bob Roller), she seemed to have more than
enough to occupy her time.

But she still aspired to follow in her father's footsteps. "I
had a lifelong dream that I would make the National Finals
someday," she said.

So in spite of the heavy demands on her time, she started
barrel racing in earnest in 1997, when she joined the Women's
Professional Rodeo Association, the organization that represents rodeo's top barrel racers. Barrel racing is often regarded
as a team event, so barrel racers sometimes refer to their horses
as their partners. If the teaming of just the right rider with just
the right horse isn't there, a barrel racer won't be successful. It
took Allen awhile, but she eventually found the right steed, a
quarter horse gelding named Risky Chris. She paid a lot of
money for Risky Chris, but the investment paid off. By 1999 she
was one of the fifteen best barrel racers in the world and she
competed at the National Finals, fulfilling that lifelong dream.

In 2000 she took that dream a step further. Fellow Texan

Charmayne James had a lock on barrel racing world championships through the 1990s. By 2000 the thirty-year-old James had claimed ten titles and didn't seem ready to give up her winning ways anytime soon. Allen, nearly a dozen years James's senior and twice as old as some of the other competitors, seemed an unlikely threat to the champion's throne. But when the NFR concluded, Allen had ridden Risky Chris to the title. Back in Austin, the button-down lawyers at Graves Dougherty were elated. A number of them had organized television watch parties for all ten days of the NFR—no small showing of support, since ESPN tape-delayed most of the performances, with some of them not airing until 3 A.M. The forty-something mom with the demanding legal career was welcomed home with a banner at Graves Dougherty: CONGRATULATIONS! 2000 WORLD CHAMPION BARREL RACER. That must have perplexed some of the stodgy corporate clients who walked through Graves Dougherty's doors that day.

So cowboys and cowgirls from all walks of life clog the highways in southern Wyoming during the days before Frontier Days gets rolling. It takes more than two thousand head of livestock to accommodate so many contestants. The vicinity north and east of the arena doesn't look like the typical rodeo-pen area. Rather, it looks like a small-town stockyard sprung up overnight. And smells like one, too.

I'M ASTONISHED by how much the rodeo park has changed since yesterday. In twenty-four hours, the frantic workers I saw yesterday have completed their jobs. Now everything is ready for the tourists. I walk down Wild Horse Gulch, a sort of hokey, permanent rendition of an Old West town created to allow craftspeople to sell their wares. You can buy a corset here, you can buy a bullwhip here. The local country station has set up its mobile unit across the walkway from Wild Horse Gulch and is broadcasting its music over loudspeakers. I talk to the disc jockey for a while, and he seems excited to meet someone from Austin, regaling me with stories about wild times and wicked nights he once spent there. I'm always amazed by the number of people I meet who tell me about how they misbehaved at some point in their lives in Austin—even someone way up here in Cheyenne.

Beyond Wild Horse Gulch, the Budweiser Clydesdales are being bathed, and this has drawn a substantial crowd. The flawlessly groomed horses are mesmerizing, for whatever reason—a paradoxical combination of brawn and beauty? I find myself joining the tourists to watch, as the keepers tend to the horses with brushes and hoses. The horses seemed to enjoy the bath. They may not enjoy the people massed around the area, but they act as if they are accustomed to it. A bent old man in a white straw hat leans over to me and says, "They could charge a buck a head and people would pay it just to watch these big sons of bitches get squirted with soap and water. You know it?"

"I'd probably pay it," I say.

He jabs me in the ribs with a bony knuckle and says, "I would, too." Then cackles at himself.

I leave the Clydesdales and head in the direction of the Indian village that is a standard part of each year's Frontier Days celebration. The tepees are sequestered inside a wooden stockade. I find myself walking with a couple from Minnesota, and soon we're gabbing like old friends. They are in their late fifties. She is tall and heavy with short dyed red hair capping her head. She wears a sleeveless top and capri pants with sneakers. Her skin is freckled and pale, although the Wyoming late morning sun seems to already be turning it pink. Her husband wears sandals with black socks and baggy shorts and a loose-fitting open-collar shirt. His hair is cut in a silver flattop and I cannot see his eyes behind his sunglasses.

"Aren't you just dying in that shirt and those jeans?" she asks me. "I'm about to burn up."

The radio station up the way announced that the temperature was in the mid-eighties, and for a guy from central Texas, that's almost chilly for July. But I'll give her that the sun is particularly bright right now. "No," I say. "I'm pretty comfortable."

"Marvin," she says, "I think you should get a hat like his. They had some for sale up there." She points in the direction of Wild Horse Gulch.

Her husband grunts something. It's plain to me he won't be buying a hat anytime soon.

I ask, "You come to Frontier Days very often?"

"Heavens, no," she says. "This is the first time we've ever been to a rodeo. I've always wanted to see one. I went up on the Internet to find out about a good rodeo, and from all I could gather, Cheyenne is the place to go. So we started planning this trip a year ago. You have to start early."

"You have any trouble getting a room?" I ask.

Marvin grunts again.

She says, "Oh, no. See, we're retired, and we spend the summers traveling. We have an RV. But we had to get our reservation in at the RV park last summer. And I think we were pretty lucky to get it. Have you been to other rodeos?"

"Yeah," I say. "A few."

"Are they all like this? I mean, I never expected anything so—*humongous.*"

"No, they're not all like this. Cheyenne is special."

"Marvin, look there. It's the Budweiser Clydesdales!" Marvin twists his head, grunts, and they're off to see the big horses.

I go inside the Indian village, but nothing much seems to be happening. I stop at a concession stand advertising fry bread only to learn that the electricity is out—rolling power outages in California, problems with the breaker boxes in Prescott, and now the electricity is out at the Indian village in Cheyenne. Seems to be a theme of the summer.

"I've got some hot dogs that we warmed up before the power went out," the man in the concession stand tells me. "But I can't do any fry bread." He shrugs in the direction of the dead deep-fat fryers.

"That's okay," I say. "All I really want is some lemonade."

"Lemonade? That I can do for you."

I gulp the lemonade from the plastic cup and head toward the carnival midway on the west side of the arena. Well, the terms *carnival* and *midway* really don't do justice to what you find at Frontier Days. It is more like an amusement park with every sort of ride you could fathom available to churn your stomach and torture your inner ear. The midway itself seems at least as large as the one at the state fair of Texas, which, of course, being in Texas, is supposed to be the world's largest. Sizzling fajitas, barbecued turkey legs, sausage on a stick, hot dogs, hamburgers, french fries and fried onion blossoms, corn dogs, funnel cakes, cotton candy—the scents of all these and more swirl together, a heady bouquet. I walk up the rows of carnival games, listening to the barkers.

I know very little about my grandmother's carnival business, and I'm sorry for that. I do know that she traveled in style, by carny standards. She preferred Cadillac convertibles, and she managed to buy one just about every year—as I said, she was a pistol. I don't know where Anna took her games. I indulge a fantasy that she set up shop here in Cheyenne, though.

I WIND MY WAY around the massive arena to the museum. Just inside the main entrance are the trophy saddles, ten of them: calf roping, steer roping, team roping (one each for the champion header and champion heeler), steer wrestling, barrel racing, bareback riding, saddle bronc riding, bull riding, all-around.

Ever since the Union Pacific started sponsoring the Frontier Days' trophy saddle for saddle bronc riding in 1902 (which it continues to do), a saddle from Cheyenne has been one of the most prized awards in all of rodeo. To the mind of many cowboys, only an NFR championship means more.

A blue-haired volunteer for the museum steps up to me. "Can you tell the difference between the saddles, honey?" she asks.

"Well, that one's a doggin' saddle," I begin, pointing to the one with the slick surface that allows a steer wrestler to slide off quickly.

"You know about rodeo saddles then," she determines. And I smile. There is a rich smell of leather coming from the saddles. I'd like to reach over and touch one, but I suspect that would violate museum rules. So I keep my hands to myself. The saddles have been crafted by Court's Saddlery Company located in Bryan, Texas. And each one is a beauty. My guess is that it would cost upward of two thousand dollars to buy a similar saddle from Court's. Maybe more. Some of the cowboys and cowgirls who will win these saddles will proudly display them as trophies in their homes. But most of the ropers, bulldoggers, and barrel racers will make full use of them in rodeos to come. Cowboys who ride into an arena aboard a trophy saddle from Cheyenne are accorded a lot of respect.

The museum is modern, well lit, with professional displays. To walk through it is to be impressed by the important place, the essential place, that Frontier Days has played in rodeo history. When Ike Rude, the biggest rodeo champion of the time, won a calf-roping title here in the 1920s, Douglas Fairbanks Sr., the biggest movie star of the time, was on hand to personally present Rude with his championship check. Rude thought so much of Frontier Days that he once uttered, "Hell, yes, I'd go to Cheyenne just to hear the band play." Rude was, as they say, a piece of work. Born four years before the Spanish-American War, he started rodeoing in his home state of Oklahoma, in 1910 at age sixteen. He finished his career in 1970 as the Vietnam War raged on—he was seventy-six that year and competed in the steer roping at Cheyenne. In that sixty-year span, he won eight championships at Cheyenne—the last a steer-roping title when he was sixty-two years old.

Casey Tibbs, Freckles Brown, Bob Crosby, Dick Truitt, Andy Jauregui, Larry Mahan, Roy Cooper, Donnie Gay, Jim Shoulders—the roll call of great cowboys who have competed and won at Cheyenne is staggering. Shoulders is arguably the best of them all. The grand Oklahoma cowboy won a remarkable four all-around titles here in Cheyenne, and there is plenty here to honor him. But I am at the museum mostly to find some photos of Ikua Purdy.

Purdy was born in 1873 in Waimea on the Hawaiian island of Kauai, the descendant of Irish and native-Hawaiian ancestors, one of whom was the famous King Kamehameha. It is a surprise to many mainlanders that Hawaii is home to large cattle ranches, particularly on the Big Island. In fact, cattle raising in Hawaii goes back to the late 1700s. Vaqueros were invited to the islands by the king of Hawaii in the 1830s to help run these ranches, thus establishing the *paniolo** tradition. Purdy was arguably the best paniolo ever.

He began working rangeland as a teenager and soon established himself as one of the best working paniolo in the territory, especially adept at using the rawhide lariat known as a *kaula ili*. Hawaiian singer and storyteller Clyde Kindy Sproat says:

---

*Paniolo is the Hawaiian word for cowboy. It is a corruption of the word *Espanola*.

Our paniolo had to catch wild cattle. They would set up ropers at the edge of a *kipuka* (a densely overgrown piece of
land entirely surrounded by newer lava). The cattle would
run by on the fly and the cowboys had to be ready with
horses in good condition. They'd only get one swing of the
lasso to catch a longhorn or it would get away. Therefore,
when Hawaiians first encountered rodeo-style roping of
fast-running cattle, it was what they did everyday.

Purdy drew on his experiences at the edge of kipukas to be-
come a champion in roping contests that took place on the Big
Island, Oahu, and Maui. Eben Low, a rancher and sugar planter,
became more and more impressed by the rodeo skills that
Purdy and other paniolos exhibited, and wondered how they
would measure up against the best talent on the mainland.
Eventually he sought out an invitation for Purdy and Archie
Ka'au'a to compete at Frontier Days in 1908. By that time,
Cheyenne had become the biggest and best-known rodeo on
the planet, and victors at Cheyenne were usually accorded the
title of world champion for their event. So Purdy and Ka'au'a
were to compete against the world's finest cowboys. The Frontier Days committee responded by welcoming the Hawaiian
cowboys—"Bring your saddle and lariat; horses will be provided at the rodeo."

Purdy, Ka'au'a, and Low traveled to Cheyenne, where the
paniolos immediately became a sight to be seen by the curious.
While cowboy fashions on the mainland had changed since the
years of the South Texas wild-cow hunters, the paniolos still
looked a lot like vaqueros, with brightly colored island accoutrements. Their saddles also looked foreign, again reflecting va-
quero tradition more than cowboy tradition. Moreover, Purdy
and Ka'au'a did not speak English, and the Westerners who

gathered around them on street corners had heard nothing like the Samoan-based language the paniolo spoke.

The rodeo promoters were glad to have the paniolos there because Frontier Days already was as much a spectacle as it was a rodeo. Why not throw in some strange-talking oddities like Hawaiian cowboys wearing colors so bright they'd shame a peacock? It would make the show even better. But no one expected the paniolos to do well in the competition. Shock hung over Cheyenne after Purdy and Ka'au'a dominated the first day of steer roping.

The *Cheyenne Daily Leader* reported on its front page: "Two brown Kanakas from Hawaii provided the big sensation at Frontier Park yesterday. Iku Purdy and Archie Tiini, lithe youngsters from the far Pacific, invaded the heart of the American cow country and taught the white ropers a lesson in how to handle steers." The paper thus managed to misspell both names and call the thirty-five-year-old Purdy a youngster. The report continued: "Here was something new—the idea of a Hawaiian cowboy defeating a real cowboy at the cowboy's own particular game—and the crowd made the most of the novelty. Their performance took the breath from the American cowboys, and they are demanding that the whites who are to rope today let slip no opportunity to beat the time of the Honolulu experts."

The "Honolulu experts" showed up the "American cowboys" again the next day as Purdy bested Hugh Clark—who had won the 1905 saddle bronc championship—to claim the steer roping title. Ka'au'a finished third. Eden Low, who also took part in the roping, finished sixth. The *Daily Leader* ran a headline bemoaning Wyoming's loss of both the steer roping and saddle bronc titles (Oregon's Dick Stanley won the riding championship). At least the reporter spelled the names correctly in the accompanying story.

Purdy, Ka'au'a, and Low returned to Hawaii as heroes and were celebrated with great aloha in hulas and songs like "Hawaiian Rough Riders," "Pu'u Huluhulu," and "Waiomina"—*Famous are Ikua and Ka'au'a / Both mischievous with the lariat.* Purdy never again competed at Cheyenne. He continued to work as a cowboy for the next thirty years, mostly as the foreman of the Ulupalakua Ranch in the uplands of Maui. While esteemed in Hawaii, he died—on Independence Day, 1945—without ever getting the recognition he deserved on the mainland. He was not inducted into the Cowboy Hall of Fame until more than fifty years after his death. But I'm happy to see his picture is up in the museum at Cheyenne.

"OH MY GOD!" the girl shrieks. "I've died and gone to heaven!"

She is maybe fifteen years old and her dad has just brought her to the cowboy ready room on the east side of the arena. The ready room at Cheyenne is considerably more sophisticated than the one at Prescott—or rather the lack of one. Justin Sports Medicine's trailer has been backed up adjacent to the area, so cowboys can get taped up and smeared with analgesic cream inside with a modicum of privacy. But the ready room itself is simply a space under the arena grandstand separated from the spectators only by chain-link fencing. And now about a half dozen other teenage girls climb onto the metal steps that hug the fence, hook their fingers through the chain links, and coo over the hard-bodied young men who are stretching their bull ropes and working on their saddles and bareback riggings.

"I can't believe it," one girl sighs.

Another squeals.

Most of the cowboys are unfazed by the attention. They're already concentrating on the horses and bulls they've drawn and can't afford to be distracted by a gaggle of silly teenage girls. Although I do see one bareback rider glance at another rider, then roll his eyes in the direction of the girls. The other rider shakes his head—jailbait. They both grin, then continue getting ready for the rodeo.

The first girl's dad says, "All right, girls, we need to go find our seats."

"I want to stay here forever," groans his daughter.

"Now, c'mon," says the dad. "The rodeo is going to start before too much longer." The girls reluctantly release their claw holds on the fence, with a lot of sighing, and tromp up the metal steps.

The steps lead up to a metal platform bridging the main alleyway that runs from the pens to the bucking chutes. A handful of rough-stock cowboys are standing on the platform, gazing out toward the pens at the horses or bulls they've drawn.

"You ever drawed him before?"

"Yeah, twice. He's not so bad, but you gotta watch what you're doing."

"That right?"

"He'll come out and drive hard to the right. Now that's what you got to look out for. Then he'll crack you back to the left and start into a spin. But he'll come out of it pretty good after the buzzer. He'll work with the clowns."

"Good to know."

"But you gotta watch him coming out of the gate."

This is serious business for these guys up on this platform. Their tense expressions will crack into brief smiles if fans recognize them. There might be a handshake and a quick exchange of pleasantries. But then the stern visage is right back. They flee the platform as soon as they are able to have a good look at their draws—back down to the shelter beneath the grandstand.

Other cowboys are not nearly so cranked up. A rider from inside the chain link calls out to a blond in her late thirties, eyes hidden behind big sunglasses, who is trying to get up the stairs as fast as she can. He calls to her twice before she turns to look at him.

"Oh, hi," she says, trying her best to sound enthusiastic.

"I had a great time last night," the cowboy says.

"Oh, yeah," she says. "It was—fun."

"I'll look for you."

"Yes, please do."

Then she zips up the stairs.

Outside the ready room, a group of four young riders gathers in a circle. One of them digs a footbag out of his pocket, tosses it, and a game of Hacky Sack is under way. But it's like no other Hacky Sack I've ever seen before. They bounce the bag off the spurred heels of their boots, so there's a jingle with each move. And they use the brims and crowns of their hats to fling the bag. They appear to have a lot of experience playing this cowboy version of Hacky Sack. I'm guessing no one saw anything quite like it at any Grateful Dead concert during the '80s.

"Aren't these kids something?" asks a volunteer who sidles up to me.

"Yeah," I agree. They are something.

I head into the arena.

NOWHERE IS the bigness of Frontier Days more manifest than in the arena itself. I perch myself above the bucking chutes and peer out at the vast stretch of tilled dirt. Maybe three of Prescott's arenas could fit into this one. Circling the arena is a racetrack just a shade over a half mile in length. And as rodeo events unfold in the arena, horses and chariots and trick riders race around the oval, lending an air of the Roman circus to Frontier Days.

The grand entry begins with the mellifluous voice of Justin McKee, the best rodeo announcer I will hear throughout my travels, reverberating through the air. He is thirty-five years old, was born in the Flint Hills of Kansas but currently lives in Lenapah, Oklahoma. McKee is a rancher with a slim, athletic build—he's also a steer roper and team roper. On his ranch, he maintains a large herd of cows used for breeding bucking bulls. He's a regular on the Professional Bull Riders' television broadcasts. "In the West they say we're slow to change," he says in his Oklahoma drawl. "And that is true, my friends. We're proud of that. We're still proud to say, 'God bless America!'" A quartet sings "The Star-Spangled Banner." Then the theme from *Bonanza* roars over the public address system, and the 107th Frontier Days is off and running.

Chief Many Horses, Harry Vold, is one of three contractors providing stock for Frontier Days. The rough-stock riders will face his horses and bulls. McKee announces that Vold is back in Cheyenne for the umpteenth time. After acknowledging the applause from the crowd, Vold takes his position on horseback, near the gates. McKee calls Vold "the Duke of the Chutes."

Cheyenne is so big that it features three bull-riding events in a single rodeo performance, and one of those begins the competition. There's no time to cordon off a space in front of the bucking chutes for the bulls. Instead, a platoon of pickup men in matched shirts—lassos circling the air—envelop the area, ready to take control of the bulls and lead them to the exit gate once the ride is complete. From just below me, Ray Thurston, from Tabernash, Colorado, rips out of the chute on a bull that spins and deposits him on the dirt long before the buzzer sounds. The next rider fares no better. Then Seth Redding rockets out on his bull, only to get catapulted maybe eight feet straight up in the air, off the bull's back. The crowd groans as he falls to earth. And so it goes with this first round of bull riding. The bulls end the round with a decided advantage over the cowboys.

As steer roping begins, I slide down into a chair. The bull riding seemed particularly intense. A good way to start the show. But also a little frightening. Cowboys die competing in rodeo on a fairly regular basis, particularly bull riders. There's an old saying in rodeo, often attributed to Jim Shoulders, that goes something like, "No one wants to see a wreck where somebody's killed. But no one wants to miss it if it happens." Cheyenne has many proud claims about its place in rodeo history. And there's at least one claim that it's not proud of: It was the site of the most famous fatality in rodeo history. That event proved the old saying to be untrue. Thousands of people witnessed that particular wreck. And probably every one of them would have preferred to have missed it.

LANE FROST* was twenty-five years old in 1989, a true star of rodeo, right up there with Ty Murray and Tuff Hedeman. But the first half of 1989 wasn't turning out to be stellar for him. He hadn't ridden as well as in the past, and he'd messed up his teeth in an accident in Texas just a month earlier. For the first time in a long time, he was not ranked among the top fifteen PRCA bull riders. When he came to Cheyenne, his teeth were still wired from the Texas accident. It seemed his fortunes might be turning around here, however. He qualified for the short-go (the rodeo's finals round) on Wednesday, and he believed he was riding well enough to put himself in a good position to claim the championship on Sunday afternoon—July 30.

Rain had settled in over Cheyenne for the two days prior to the short-go, and the arena floor was a lake of mud. The clowns and the barrel man were struggling in ankle-deep slop, while

---

*The Frost family's account of the death of Lane Frost appears at http://www.lanefrost.com, a Web site maintained by Sharon Mahrley.

the chute hands wore yellow slickers to keep dry. Maybe the muck helped Marty Staneart, a California cowboy who became the first person to ride the famed bull Mr. T that afternoon, much to the soggy crowd's delight. Staneart's feat was accomplishment enough to become part of Cheyenne lore. But it was quickly overshadowed by what happened next.

Frost had drawn a bull called Takin' Care of Business—although the cowboys sometimes called him Bad to the Bone. Frost knew the bull. It had bucked him off at a rodeo in San Angelo, Texas, earlier in the year. So Frost considered his draw a bad one. As it turned out, Takin' Care of Business gave Frost the sort of tough ride that bull riders love, one that allows them to score high marks with the judges. After the buzzer sounded, the bullfighting clowns, Bobby Romer and Rick Chatman, got Takin' Care of Business out of his spin and headed in a straight line, the textbook procedure to allow a cowboy to slide off the bull in the direction of his riding hand—in Frost's case, his left hand.

Frost hit the mud and was trying to rise up to his hands and feet when the bull abruptly pivoted and attacked him. Frost tried to move, but his boots only slid in the mud. The bull smacked him in the back of the legs, knocking Frost flat. Frost did the smartest thing he could do in that situation: He curled into a fetal position while the bullfighters tried to rescue him. But in that next horrible moment, Takin' Care of Business dropped his head and rammed his right horn into Frost's left side. The tips of rodeo bulls' horns are sawed off to prevent the animals from damaging each other while being transported, so Takin' Care of Business did not gore Frost. It was more like a crushing blow. The bull bore down and shoved Frost forward through the mud, then, still bucking, leaped over the fallen rider. Only then were the frantic bullfighters able to lead him away from Frost.

As the judges were tabulating his score—a high one, 85—
Frost managed to rise to his feet, his left arm stiff at his side,
and began trotting toward the gate, waving for assistance with
his right arm. Romer rushed to aid him, but Frost collapsed to
the ground. Frost's traveling partner, Hedeman, was among the
first to reach the injured rider. He and the others who had run
out into the mud to provide aid turned Frost over. There was
no blood or other outward signs of serious injury, yet Hedeman
could tell his friend was not breathing. As the last bull rider of
the 1989 Cheyenne Frontier Days left the chute, paramedics
struggled to revive Frost. It seemed apparent to them that
Takin' Care of Business had shattered Frost's ribs when he
rammed his horn into the rider's side, creating scalpel-sharp
bone shards that had sliced open an artery, causing massive internal bleeding. The paramedics loaded Frost into an ambulance and Hedeman climbed in behind them. Fans in the
grandstand noticed that the ambulance left slowly, without a
siren. At Cheyenne's Memorial Hospital, physicians tried to revive Frost, but they had no more luck than the paramedics. At
3:59 P.M., twenty-nine minutes after Frost left the chute on
Takin' Care of Business, doctors pronounced him dead.

Hedeman left the emergency room to call Frost's folks in
Oklahoma with the devastating news. And he called Frost's
wife, Kellie, who, for the first time since their marriage, had not
traveled with her husband to Cheyenne. Then he went back to
his friend and cleaned the mud from Frost's chaps and boots.

The next morning, Hedeman and Frost's friend Cody Lambert boarded a private jet supplied by the Frontier Days committee to fly Frost's body to Oklahoma. More than three
thousand people turned out for the funeral at the First Baptist
Church in Atoka, where Clem McSpadden delivered the eulogy. "Lane had one great quality that separates him from much
of this generation today," McSpadden said. "He knew no greed.

To the people he baled hay with in Choctaw County, and the people he worked cattle with, he was just what he was." Then Frost was buried in the cemetery down the road at Hugo, just a few steps from the grave of his hero and mentor, Freckles Brown, who'd died a couple of years earlier of cancer.

The death of Lane Frost affected the rodeo world as no other loss had. He was the biggest star ever to be killed by a bull in the arena, and he died at the world's most famous rodeo. He had made a name for himself as a world champion rider and was on the cusp of achieving even greater fame. He was a handsome young man with a winning smile and his looks could have carried him into a career in film—something he'd wanted to explore ever since he saw the miniseries starring Robert Duvall and Tommy Lee Jones and based on Larry McMurtry's *Lonesome Dove*. In fact, he'd signed up to do some film stunt riding, hoping that would lead to more movie work—he'd planned to show up on the movie set shortly after he left Cheyenne. And, within a few years, the formation of the PBR and the emergence of sports agents in the world of rodeo would have opened doors for the young rider to make more money than he ever dreamed of.

The magnitude of the loss forced rodeo to examine its long-held positions on rider safety. Before Frost died, the sport's bravado mandated that rough-stock riders wear no protection beyond their boots, jeans, and Panhandle Slim shirts. In the years after Frost's death, flak jacket–type vests became de rigueur for virtually all bull riders. The most common bull-riding injuries are muscle strains and tears that occur simply as the result of a rider's being jerked around at such tremendous force by such a powerful beast. Most of the serious injuries are caused by the bull's stepping on the rider once he's on the ground. Broken arms. Broken legs. Crushed faces. Relatively few injuries are caused by the horns. A flak jacket offers no protection against muscle damage during the ride and little protection from being stepped on by a two-thousand-pound animal. But should a bull attack with its horns, a flak jacket can shield a rider's ribs, maybe keep them from shattering and from shredding his blood vessels and internal organs. Once flak jackets won acceptance, it became common to see riders who were recovering from head or face injuries wearing protective helmets resembling football headgear. In fact, some riders now wear a helmet as a precaution against injury—twenty years ago, that would have been considered as much a threat to a rider's macho image as wearing ballet slippers. You can even find a PBR contestant or two who eschews boots for Nike sneakers in order to get a better footing in the dirt after dismounting a bull.

Of course this trend has a few detractors among old-line fans. One night in downtown Cheyenne, I stopped in at a tavern for a beer. The guy sitting next to me looked up from his ashtray, studied my Resistol, and said, "You must be here for the rodeo."

"Yes," I said, taking a long draw on a bottle of Coors.

"Been around this rodeo shit all my life," the guy said.

"Yeah?"

"I wouldn't pay a dime to see what they call rodeo now."

"That right?"

"In my day cowboys were tough. Next thing you know, they'll be wrapping these candy asses in a mattress before they let 'em climb on a horse or a bull."

"I don't know. Some of these cowboys seem pretty tough to me."

He snorted. "They ain't worth a kiss of my sorry ass." Then he left the bar and staggered through the crowd toward the door.

STEER ROPING is something of a novelty for most rodeo goers, even if it is one of the two original rodeo events—the other, of course, is saddle bronc riding. Steer roping is similar to calf roping. The idea is to stop a running animal, bring it to the ground, and bind its feet. In the old days when cattle grazed practically as wild creatures on open ranges, steer roping was an almost everyday part of a cowboy's working life. Catch the steer, immobilize him, brand him, doctor him, let him up to resume his eating. Justin McKee announces that it's still a part of the cattleman's everyday life, but I'm not so sure. When I was a kid in Oklahoma and working around cattle, I was always enjoined from chasing them. And roping them was a no-no, unless it was absolutely necessary. Keep them as tame as possible, don't make them afraid of human beings: That was the stockman's creed. A docile steer is easier to work with. Besides, a steer's value is in its weight at the marketplace—the more it weighs, the more meat it produces. Spooked beef cattle who are used to fleeing whenever people come around are going to be skinnier—and worth fewer dollars in the auction ring.

But it was different in the old days. During the heyday of the real cowboys, the cattle they worked with were anything but docile. Moreover, most of them would never wind up on a dinner plate somewhere. Before the 1900s, range cattle were valuable mostly for their potential as boots and saddles, not for their potential as prime rib. I've read some gruesome passages about cattle operations on the Texas coast. Near Rockport, tens of thousands of cattle were slaughtered for their hides, the bloody leftover carcasses hauled out into the Gulf on barges and shoved into water already foaming red from earlier trips. The Gulf became alive with sharks as the unwanted meat went overboard.

The cowboys working six-hundred-pound steers on the range couldn't handle them the same way you could a roped calf—pick it up, drop it to the ground, and tie its legs. A man who spent his days on horseback was going to be lithe, not nearly hefty enough to muscle around an animal of that size. So they developed a difficult yet effective technique for dealing with the steers. A mounted cowboy approached the running steer from the steer's right side and snared its horns with his rope. He then directed his horse to veer to the left, flicked his rope between the steer's hoof and hock, then jerked the steer to the ground. The idea was that the steer would have had the wind knocked out of it by the abrupt fall, leaving it stunned, temporarily immobilized. By the time the steer began to recover, the cowboy had dismounted and dashed to the downed animal to truss three of its legs with his pigging string. Then he was able to brand or do whatever else was needed to the animal.

Out of this grew steer roping as competition. Of all rodeo events, it has the greatest potential for injuring the animals. Broken horns, broken ribs, broken legs, broken necks. While these kinds of injuries were taken in stride in cattle country in the early days of rodeo, people in the East and other regions who had no idea of what occurred on the range, in the corral, and at the slaughterhouse were shocked at what happened to steers in the arena when they were roped. Even when the steer is uninjured, the "jerk" itself can seem violent to spectators, much like a sudden right cross that drops a heavyweight fighter. It was too much for the animal rights' activists of the early 1900s, and soon, in many states, steer roping as a sporting event joined cockfighting, dogfighting, and bearbaiting as an illegal activity.

But in cattle-country states like Oklahoma, Texas, and Wyoming, steer roping flourished as a sport. When I lived in Oklahoma, I knew many people who were obsessed with "steer jerkin'." In addition to ropers with ranching or farming backgrounds, no small number of white-collar types—doctors, lawyers, accountants—invest a lot of money in horses and trailers so they can take part in weekend steer jerkin' jackpots. Spending your weekend spare time roping steers strokes your macho pride just a little bit more than spending it on a golf course. While the event is divorced from all but a very few rodeos,* it thrives on its own circuit. Fans by the thousands pack arenas in places like San Angelo or my hometown, Guthrie, to watch the best steer ropers, most of whom come from Texas and Oklahoma. The best of them all is the cowboy who has won the most world championships in history. Guy Allen of Santa Anna, Texas, has racked up seventeen of them and has qualified for an incredible twenty-seven consecutive steer roping National Finals. Among ropers he is regarded with the kind of awe once reserved for Ike Rude—and the way he's going, Allen might be here at Cheyenne when he is in his seventies, trying to tag a steer. But outside the demimonde of professional steer roping, his name is hardly known at all.

The steer roping comes to a close just as chariot racing begins on the track. Justin McKee barely has a chance to announce the start of the chariot race before the first bareback horse of the day breaks out of the bucking chute below me. Then comes steer wrestling, followed by saddle bronc riding and calf roping. And then it's time for another event on the track, this one a matched horse race. The horses dart around the track, but suddenly there is a collision across the arena from me. Two horses lose their footing at full gallop, smash into each other, falling to the dirt, rolling over each other, and tripping a third horse. Three riders are on the ground with the writhing, kick-

---

*Steer roping is fully sanctioned by the PRCA, even if it isn't part of most PRCA rodeos. Rodeos like Cheyenne and Pendleton accord it reverence because of its cowboy roots, but the event does not appear at the National Finals Rodeo. The National Finals Steering Roping took place in Amarillo in the late fall of 2003, a couple of weeks before the NFR got under way in Las Vegas.

ing horses. The horses manage to rise to their feet again—miraculously—apparently unhurt. One rider manages to hobble to the fence. But two other men lay as motionless as discarded rags in the dust. I see no signs of revival as the medical crews work on them. Eventually the men are loaded onto stretchers and Justin McKee intones over the loudspeakers, "As I mentioned earlier, we're slow to change in the West, and we're not very politically correct. So I'm going to ask you all to lift up a prayer for these two riders." The riders leave the arena to the crowd's applause, neither showing any signs of life. I expect to hear the worst. But tomorrow I will learn that after spending the evening in the hospital, both men emerged with no serious injuries.

Meanwhile, another round of bull riding has started up in the bucking chutes. Then team roping, a competition for rookie saddle bronc riders, more steer wrestling, more bareback riding, even more steer wrestling. Now on the track are daredevil riders. One particularly gifted young man is dipping and twisting, and flipping himself from the saddle. I learn he is no other than John Harrison, Freckles Brown's grandson. John's full repertoire of stunt work includes Roman riding (riding two horses simultaneously by standing with a foot on the back of each horse) and maneuvering around flaming stakes. In addition, he is terrific at roping—something he's been doing ever since he saw a trick roper perform at a rodeo when he was six years old. Harrison leaves the track, and there's more saddle bronc riding, barrel racing, and a final round of bull riding followed by a wild-horse race.

I leave the arena thinking that the fans get their money's worth at Cheyenne, no question about it. By my count, more than two hundred cowboys and cowgirls participated in this afternoon's rodeo—and that doesn't include the people taking part in the horse races, chariot races, stunt riding, and so forth. Only a handful took home any money.

JACK KEROUAC was not impressed by Frontier Days. Riding on the back of a truck in the late 1940s, he came into town smack-dab in the middle of rodeo week. One of his companions, dubbed Slim in *On the Road*, exclaimed that it was Wild West Week, as the travelers dismounted from the truck.

> Big crowds of businessmen, fat businessmen in boots and ten-gallon hats, with their hefty wives in cowgirl attire, bustled and whooped on the wooden sidewalks of old Cheyenne; farther down were the long stringy boulevard lights of new downtown Cheyenne, but the celebration was focusing on Oldtown. Blank guns went off. The saloons were crowded to the sidewalk. I was amazed, and at the same time I felt it was ridiculous: in my first shot at the West I was seeing to what absurd devices it had fallen to keep its proud tradition.

Tonight I am walking the streets that Kerouac walked fifty-five years ago. There is plenty of bustling and an occasional whoopee. There are plenty of Western hats and boots, though cowgirl outfits seem a little rare. I don't see any wooden sidewalks and I'm having a hell of a time determining what he meant by "Oldtown" and "new downtown." Maybe he was writing about a replica of nineteenth-century Cheyenne built at the rodeo park in the late 1920s, replete with false-front saloons and dance halls, that has since been razed. Maybe not. But here in downtown I have seen fleshy men dressed up as gunfighters—or at least a Hollywood version of what gunfighters should look like. And I've seen them fire blanks at each other, some of them pretending to die. And I've seen tourists in flip-flops and baggy shorts and oversized T-shirts applaud them.

Not much of what I see tonight has to do with keeping the "proud tradition" of the West. No, Jack, you got it wrong. Or at least your alter ego, Sal Paradise, did. At Cheyenne, it has been about the tourists ever since the first Frontier Days. Not that there's anything wrong with that. "Ridiculous"? Yes, I suppose you could view it that way. *Absurd* might be a better term. Myself, I'm just amazed.

I've never been to a place that seems so obsessed with the outsized. While a parade is a standard feature in Western towns during rodeo time, Cheyenne puts on no fewer than *four* rodeo parades during Frontier Days' run: "The four CFD parades begin in front of the Wyoming state capitol building at 24th Street and Capitol Avenue with a cannon blast promptly at 9:30 A.M. The nineteen–city block parade features *one of the world's largest* collections of antique carriages and automobiles." Prescott has one rodeo-related pancake breakfast; Cheyenne has *three*. And they are so big that the organizers use a cement mixer to blend the batter. "This *phenomenal* feature of Cheyenne Frontier Days has attracted the attention of Civil Defense teams searching for ways to improve their methods of carrying out mass feedings . . . Cheyenne has this feat down to a science. The Boy Scouts and Girl Scouts chip in along with CFD volunteers to feed nearly forty thousand folks in six hours. That's 111 people per minute!" It is an astonishing thing to see a pancake cook flipping flapjacks over his back while a Boy Scout scurries about with a pan to nab them before they hit the dirt.

Nothing related to the Cheyenne rodeo is more deeply rooted in absurdity than the CFD nighttime concerts. These fill the grandstands with tourists willing to shell out even more money, after paying to see the afternoon rodeo. The first of these occurred in 1951 and the big star on hand to kick things off was—no, not John Wayne, not Gary Cooper, not Jimmy Stewart, not Roy Rogers, not Gene Autry, not even William

Boyd, but—Fred MacMurray! He was no slouch in terms of fame, but he wasn't exactly a living, breathing symbol of Western heroics, although he had acted in a few oaters by that point and would be in others later in his career. No, he was best known for devious, understated villains of the kind he played in Billy Wilder's *Double Indemnity*, or for his roles as the overwhelmed straight man in low-key comedies like *The Egg and I*. Not exactly someone you'd expect to see at a rodeo. Even more absurd than MacMurray was the act that accompanied him. No Hank or Ernest or Lefty—instead, Lawrence Welk and his orchestra.

Last night's concert was just as absurd, in its own way. The alternative metal bands Staind, Static-X, and Lo-Pro roared so loudly that the windows of my room vibrated in the Days Inn, across town. I don't know how good the turnout was for the LA headbanger bands. But I know tonight's Toby Keith concert must be a sellout.

Keith is the reigning king of the pop-country music coming out of Nashville, and seems to be a presence I can't escape out on the rodeo circuit. Since the early 1990s, he's turned out a string of hits while adopting the sort of stage theatrics that made a country music superstar of his fellow Oklahoman Garth Brooks. About a year after the terrorist attacks of September 11, 2001, Keith released a politically charged album called *Unleashed* that struck a chord with American conservatives. Rodeo contestants and fans are usually on the right side of the political spectrum, and *Unleashed*'s big hit, "Courtesy of the Red, White, and Blue (The Angry American)," started resounding through arenas across the country shortly after its release. Today, the song continues to elicit enthusiastic applause whenever it is played at a rodeo. With his long hair and beard, Keith looks a little like the pissed-off son of Hank Williams Jr. I've seen that image on T-shirts everywhere I've been today. So I'm sure the grandstands are packed for Keith's hyperpatriotic performance tonight. I really don't want to deal with a mob of that size, and I decide to stay away from the arena. Around midnight, I head back to the motel.

I ARRIVE AT THE arena a little after eight o'clock the next morning. If Cowboy Don were around, he'd look askance at what I'm up to. I'm here to attend Cowboy Church, set to get going around nine. Cowboy Don wasn't the sort to darken a church sanctuary, or to sober up enough to show up for a service at the rodeo grounds. Besides, in his day, praying and hymn singing weren't things rodeo cowboys did much of, at least not in public. But that's changed now. These days cowboy athletes are almost as prone to thank their lord and savior for an accomplishment in the arena as football players are to kneel and cross themselves in the end zone after scoring a touchdown.

I have no idea what to expect from Cowboy Church at Cheyenne. A friend of mine who rode bulls told me that most Cowboy Church events are very informal, with no designated leaders. They are opportunities for Christian cowboys to "witness" if they feel the call to do so. But, given that this is the Daddy of 'Em All, I suspect Cowboy Church at Cheyenne will be pretty well organized.

Several dozen people are gathering in the grandstand on the west side of the arena, opposite the bucking chutes. Most of the crowd seem older, dressed in Western attire, although there are a few people in T-shirts and shorts. A cluster of young men I recognize as rough-stock riders appear, clutching Bibles and dressed in the cleanest clothes they could dig out of their suitcases. A temporary sound system has been assembled in front of the grandstand, and music is playing as people take their seats. It's Christian music with steel guitars and fiddles. It's not quite Luke the Drifter, but it's also not soulless, synthesized contemporary Christian. I take a seat at the far edge of the crowd and respectfully remove my Resistol.

Leading the service is evangelist Susie Luchsinger from Atoka, Oklahoma, and her partner in Psalms Ministries, husband Paul Luchsinger, a former PRCA steer wrestler. Susie is a low-key, pleasant woman who seems to feel right at home in the arena. And she should. Her maiden name is McEntire, and her grandfather, John, won the steer roping here in 1934. Twenty years later, her dad, Clark, claimed the same title. Her brother, Pake, and son, E. P. Luchsinger, also have competed at Cheyenne. The best-known member of the McEntire clan, singer and actress Reba, has played night concerts at the rodeo maybe a half dozen times since 1985.

Susie begins singing, and like her big sister Reba, she has a big voice. As the sweet sound of "Amazing Grace" fills the soft morning air, some wranglers start to move a large group of horses from pens at one end of the arena to pens at the other. The song, the horses, and the setting all complement each other. Peaceful.

The service itself is steeped in Southern Baptist tradition. It's heavy on the witnessing. Barry Burk, a top calf roper in the '60s and '70s, takes the microphone to tell how he was involved with six other cowboys in the formation of the cowboy chapter of the Fellowship of Christian Athletes in Phoenix in 1978—a risky undertaking in what he calls those wild days of rodeo. "It was a rough, tough carousing bunch when I started back in 1963," he says. From small gatherings of cowboys around horse trailers in those days, Cowboy Church has grown to become a standard feature at rodeos. Which pleases Burk and the others who want to lead rodeo down the road of righteousness. Burk, an Oklahoman, waves the bloody shirt of the PRCA's decision to move the National Finals from Oklahoma City to Sin City, Las Vegas, twenty years ago. It was a contentious thing back then, and I'm surprised people still have strong feelings about it.

A tearful cowboy poet reads verses likening himself to an all-too-ordinary horse for sale. One buyer agrees to buy the horse after his little girl sees something special in him, just as Jesus sees something special in the cowboy poet.

Paul Luchsinger speaks longer than anyone else during the service, giving an account of his misguided ways as a father and husband. He describes himself as being narrow-minded and angry, at times abusive. And this was *after* he'd undergone a conversion to evangelical Christianity, conducted while kneeling in prayer and holding the hand of another rodeo cowboy: "You can imagine what a lot of people today would think about that, seeing two cowboys holding hands." His witnessing is pretty detailed, enough so that I'm squirming in my seat. "I was swatting the kids, swatting Susie." I guess witnessing is designed to make people squirm. He says he got so bad that Susie left him. That's when he saw the light.

Susie sings again, this time an achingly beautiful rendition of Carole King's "You've Got a Friend," which works as a religious song, though I'd never thought of it as anything but an overplayed love song from the '70s. As Susie sings the final hymn, some rodeo volunteers cross the arena with body boards to be used in case of accidents in this afternoon's rodeo. They stow the boards in the partially underground photographers' pit, in front of the west grandstand. A reminder that for all the peaceful, easy feelings in the grandstand now, rodeo is still a hard-assed business once the horses and bulls start coming out of the chutes.

I leave while Susie is still singing. I stop by the men's room. While standing at the troughlike urinal, I read a handbill posted on the wall. CFD IS WORTH CELEBRATING. GETTING AN STD IS NOT. STOP BY THE FIRST-AID STATION AND ASK FOR A "PACKET."

There you have it, I say to myself. Susie's songs about the love of Jesus, and a handbill about where to get free condoms: the yin and yang of rodeo.

SUNDAY AFTERNOON, the arena is awash with T-shirts from last night's Toby Keith concert. To the west and south are slender rain clouds, purple against the high blue sky. One directly west of the arena is dumping rain on the fifty miles of nothingness between Cheyenne and Laramie. Hard to tell if the showers will make it here or not. The storm is, however, positioning itself to block out the sun, at least for a while, and that's good. The crowd seems more festive than it was yesterday. Maybe they're happy about the shade, maybe they're still cranked up from Toby Keith, maybe some of the spirit of this morning's Cowboy Church has spread out among 'em. Whatever, the crowd is upbeat.

I walk up to the press deck on the east side of the grandstand and see a bearded man about my age who looks vaguely familiar. We talk for a while, then exchange names, and it turns out he is Chris Wall, a Grammy-nominated country singer and songwriter working out of Texas.

"Oh yeah," I say, "*I like my women just a little on the trashy side*. You probably get tired of hearing people say that, though." "Trashy Women" is a song he wrote that was a regional hit for Jerry Jeff Walker before becoming a big country hit for a band called Confederate Railroad in the early '90s. Wall has written better songs, like "I Feel Like Hank Williams Tonight," but the novelty tune "Trashy Women" seems to be the song he'll be best known for.

"Well," he says, "yeah, I do get a little tired of it—until the quarterly royalty check comes in. Then I'm not tired of it at all."

He tells me that he's helping out a Cheyenne radio station with its coverage of Frontier Days. Did he take in the Toby

Keith performance last night? He smiled wryly while shaking his head no. "I'm as patriotic as the next guy, but that's a little over the top."

I nod.

The rodeo unfolds today much as it did yesterday. As I watch, I decide that Flint Rasmussen is as big a draw as any cowboy competing here today. And maybe the best all-around athlete in the place. Rasmussen is a thirty-four-year-old barrel clown from Montana. As such, he doesn't get directly involved with handling the bulls during and after a ride, but leaves that responsibility to the two bullfighters—although he certainly gets involved if things get out of hand. His primary job is to entertain, and at this Rasmussen is probably the best clown that rodeo has known.

He traverses the arena during the entire rodeo, climbing walls, dashing up into the grandstand, flirting, teasing, and otherwise carrying on with the crowd. All of which is broadcast over the PA system by way of his wireless microphone. Announcer Justin McKee serves as Rasmussen's straight man. But Rasmussen and McKee have taken that age-old setup to a higher plane. They have worked together many times, and their timing is impeccable. Rasmussen improvises throughout the show rather than rely on moth-bitten gags. McKee keeps up with him. Rasmussen plays the freewheelin' rascal, as obsessed by the pretty girls he sees in the stands as Harpo Marx was in his movie bits. He chides the pick-up men, complaining that they wear the ugliest shirts he's ever seen. One of the pickup men plays along by lassoing Rasmussen. The barrel clown celebrates the sun's emergence from the clouds because it brings out two things he most associates with Frontier Days: halter tops and the smell of coconut oil. He dances like Michael Jackson, moonwalking to "Billy Jean" while wearing baggy clown pants. Later he performs a parody of Irish river-dancing stompers he calls "Lord of the Clowns." He doesn't seem to stop moving throughout the entire rodeo performance, which lasts for more than three hours. Rasmussen says:

> Contrary to what some people say, animals don't think like people or act like people. If they decide to lay down in the chute for three minutes, they are going to do that. This creates a dead spot. My goal is to have the people that paid . . . to get in not even realize that there was a dead spot. If the bull lays down I'm going to take over and entertain them. That's my role, the majority of what I do.

He's so gifted athletically he even fills in for a team roper— and so we see Rasmussen on horseback, hatless but otherwise in full clown regalia, spinning a rope. He misses his throw, but what the hell? He looks good doing it.

It's no wonder that the former schoolteacher has been awarded rodeo's highest honor as a barrel clown—he performed at the last five National Finals in Las Vegas, plus he has a passel of Coors "Man in the Can" awards. My guess is that he'll be back in Vegas again this December.

JESSE BAIL hasn't had the best of Julys, notwithstanding his winning the all-around cowboy award at the Navajo Nation's Fourth of July Rodeo. I'd like to report that he turns everything around at today's Frontier Days performance. Unfortunately, things don't go his way.

He rides his bull in the opening round of bull riding, scoring a 78. But that doesn't seem like a good enough score to get him into Sunday's short-go. But at least he fares better than eighteen-year-old Alfonso "Poncho" Limas, a native of Texhoma, Oklahoma, who is currently a freshman at Dodge City Community College in Kansas. Poncho is sucked down into the well almost as soon as his ride begins, and suddenly he's under the bull. As the clowns try to distract the bull, Poncho squirms to the left, then to the right, then to the left again, each time just barely avoiding a crushing blow from the animal's menacing hooves. Finally Poncho is up and scurrying to safety. Welcome to Cheyenne.

In the first saddle bronc riding event, Jesse rides his horse, but, again, his score—a 70—isn't likely to get him into the short-go. It's by no fault of his own, though. The horse isn't helping him. The shallow, spasmodic bucks it gives him aren't enough to rack up a good score. After Jesse climbs out of the arena, I head out to find him.

I meet Jesse outside the cowboy ready room. He's favoring his left leg as he moves toward me. We shake hands for the first time. In person, he's as friendly and unassuming as he's been on the phone. He's a big guy, as rough-stock riders go. He's just a couple of inches under six feet tall and weighs 180 pounds. He has dark hair and innocent eyes peering out from under the black brim of his hat. It takes about three lines of conversation to confirm he is a sure-enough cowboy.

"You've kind of had a rough summer," I say to him.

"Well, yeah—," he answers.

"You been hurt? Looks like you're limping."

"Oh no, no. I just haven't been riding very good."

Pure cowboy-code stuff. Don't blame injuries, even if injuries are the cause of a bad streak. No excuses. If you bear down and try hard enough, you can win even if you are banged up.

Jesse tells me he's taking part in the Professional Bull Riders event that night. I say I'll be there, wish him luck. Then he limps back to the ready room.

AT LEAST TONIGHT'S evening entertainment doesn't feature any washed-up '70s rock band or other mediocrities. Instead it features the rock stars of the rodeo world, the cowboys competing in the Professional Bull Riders tour. The major league of the PBR is the twenty-nine-city Built Ford Tough Series, at which forty-five riders compete. Tonight will be a performance of the PBR's Challenger Tour, more or less the organization's AAA minor league. Although some top riders, including Justin McBride, will ride tonight.

The PBR has trucked in its own stock and, in essence, its own portable arena, which has been erected facing the west grandstand of the arena, in the few hours between the end of the regular rodeo performance and the beginning of the start of the Challenger Tour event. It looks like a sort of miniature baseball outfield. The PBR has allowed me to get close enough to view the action at cowboy level. I'm standing next to a gate leading into the small arena. A film crew from the BBC is here as well. With its slick marketing machine running overtime, the PBR has been successful in positioning bull riding as the next "breakout sport." Meaning that its organizers hope it will enjoy the same meteoric rise in popularity that NASCAR enjoyed in the 1990s. The press has responded enthusiastically to the marketing blitz. Mainstream magazines like *Esquire* and *Men's Journal* have devoted features to the emerging phenomenon. Given Europe's seemingly ceaseless fascination with all things cowboy, it's not surprising that the BBC would dispatch a crew to follow the fortunes of Wiley Peterson, a twenty-four-year-old PBR cowboy from Pocatello, Idaho. Also shooting film is a crew from Japan, which is focusing on the entirety of Cheyenne Frontier Days, not just the bull-riding event.

Things begin with a video, shown on a JumboTron, to the tune of Toby Keith's "Angry American" while images of PBR cowboys in various military and patriotic settings flash by on the screen. The crowd shouts its approval with each phrase and especially whoops it up when the image of one of its favorite cowboys hits the screen.

Now it is time for the cowboys to make their entrance. They are announced individually and take their stances in a formation before some metal pillars that stand, for the time being, in the center of the arena. The music and the voices over the PA are deafening, much louder than at a concert I attended when I was fourteen that featured Black Sabbath and Mountain—which I thought was the loudest thing I'd ever hear. There are shooting flames from the pillars—I can feel the warmth where I'm standing—and other exploding pyrotechnics. Finally all the cowboys are in place, standing like gladiators facing the crowd, which is on its feet. The cowboys exit to more explosions, and a crew hurriedly removes the props from the arena.

I understand the appeal of the PBR immediately. The action is fast—no languorous stretches of roping. It mostly occurs in a relatively few square feet in front of the chutes—no saddle broncs straying out over the vast acreage of a big arena like Cheyenne's. It's perfect for TV. An eight-second ride that takes place in a small area, followed by shots of the cowboy exiting the arena, then a replay of the ride with expert commentary, then it's back to the chutes for a close-up of a rider pounding his bull rope. And the next ride begins. It's an energetic show, to say the least. The thudding music—some of it metal and techno that would have been unheard of in a rodeo event just a few years ago—never allows your adrenaline level to sag. The lights and the images on the JumboTron ensure you'll never nod off. As if you could nod off watching the best bull riders in the world competing in America's original extreme sport.

But for me, the fireworks and music and lights are just so much bullshit. I was prepared to dislike my first ever in-person PBR event. But as the riding gets going, I totally lose myself in it. Here is a whole generation of young Freckles Browns taking their cues from the master and approaching bull riding as a scientific thing. For years rough-stock riders complained about the quality of the stock available for draw at a rodeo—case in point, Jesse Bail's saddle bronc ride this afternoon. A terrific rider on a mediocre horse equals a mediocre score. But at a PBR event, you won't see mediocre *bulls*. These are the best and the brightest bovines, bred for what they do and costing upwards of a hundred thousand dollars. Bulls have become a valuable enough commodity to draw investors who've never worked cattle in their lives, people like Elton John's songwriting partner Bernie Taupin. The best riders, the best bulls—excellent ride after excellent ride. Make that astonishing ride after astonishing ride. Even the bullfighters are the best in the world—tonight accompanied by Flint Rasmussen, who works PBR events in addition to his PRCA gigs.

The first section of riders features Justin McBride, who rides a D&H Cattle Company bull with the innocent name of Hillside Strangler. Both rider and bull live up to their game, and after a showy backflip dismount, McBride leaves the arena with a score of 87.5. The next riders are not so lucky. Or maybe not so skilled. K. J. Pletcher of Ardmore, Oklahoma, is thrown by a bull named Speckled Bird; Pletcher exits slowly, holding his head. Another Oklahoman, Lee Akin, has a go on the Page/ Teague bull Crossfire Hurricane—annoying junk that most of the music is, whoever programs it has the good sense to play the Rolling Stones' "Jumping Jack Flash" while Akin soars off Crossfire Hurricane before the eight-second buzzer sounds. And on it goes. Until it's Jesse Bail's turn on a bull with the politically incorrect name of Tar Baby. Tar Baby is adequate enough, if not great, at spinning and bucking. Jesse gives him a first-rate ride, scoring an 87—good enough to get him into tonight's short-go. Jesse leaves hobbling and the announcer says he's suffering from a hip pointer. Injured, yet so far today he's ridden two bulls and a saddle bronc and has yet to be bucked off. His third bull of the day is coming up in a little over an hour.

During a break, I meet Justin McBride. He's a friendly guy yet he's not shy to speak up when asked his opinion. A bit of a character. I tell him I've read the profile of him and other PBR riders written by Chris Heath for *Men's Journal*.

McBride grins and looks over at the PBR flack accompanying him, who rolls her eyes. McBride nods in the woman's direction and says, "Well, they were a little upset about some of the stuff in that article." He tells me that Heath came to spend a day—McBride's birthday, as it turned out—on the McBride family's ranch outside Elk City, Oklahoma.

McBride took the British writer fishing, then treated him to a song: *I got a twelve-inch dick / a dozen roses / and a pickup truck, hubba-hubba-hubba,* explaining he never wrote more of the song because "I figured that's all I'd need." Some of McBride's cowboy friends showed up, and soon enough they were drinking beer, dipping snuff, and trying to catch the goldfish in the fishpond. As the evening progressed, Heath learned that McBride's last birthday party got a bit reckless.

"If you look on pbrnow.com, you will learn that Justin broke his hand at last year's Bullnanza," Heath writes. "This isn't quite the full story . . . most of the damage was done in Elk City late on his birthday night. Justin is reluctant to spell out too many details, but amid all the other fun, there was a fight. 'We were just being cowboys.'" A lot like the rough, tough carousing bunch Barry Burk described yesterday morning at Cowboy Church.

Heath didn't witness any fights at this year's party, but most of the cowboys were "joyously drunk" before sundown, when the serious drinking began. The next morning the cowboys snored away "comatose" on the living room floor of McBride's parents' house, with clothes scattered over the ground and in the bushes outside.

With the PBR pushing bull riding as family entertainment, I can understand now why eyebrows were raised at the organization's headquarters in Colorado Springs when Heath's article appeared. But the first time I read it, I didn't pay much attention to the antics he described. I remember my own birthdays when I was in my early twenties. Clothes in the yard? Bent Coors cans covering the grass? Yes. Part of being young. Hell, these guys are also cowboys. I'm surprised things didn't get more out of hand.

The thing I remember most about Heath's article is McBride's reasoning for why bull riders do what they do:

> The best thing I know to say is that it's the only thing we know how to do . . . You know, we grew up being cowboys. We loved old Westerns, John Wayne movies. We grew up being cowboys and then we found a way to be cowboys and still make a great living, and to be way cooler than anybody in the world. You show me a sport that challenges a human being against a two thousand–pound animal . . . You know, you might find a rich kid that rides bulls really good. But mostly we're all the same people. I mean, look at Tuff Hedeman. He's a poor kid growing up—an ugly, stupid idiot, and he'll tell you even worse just so it sounds good. He didn't have a shot at life other than working for eight dollars an hour—it was his best hope. And now he's one of the most popular cowboys who ever lived.

McBride and I make small talk for a while. Then he leaves me his phone number and invites me to visit his ranch outside Elk City sometime. He heads back to the chute area. The event continues to wind along its course, alternating between the absurd (the Wind River Native American dancers in traditional regalia, dancing to techno and lights—much more fit for a rave than for a rodeo arena) and the sublime (the rides themselves).

When the short-go comes around, both Bail and McBride are drilled by their bulls. (Brazil's Paulo Crimber will eventually win Cheyenne's 2003 PBR prize.) The event ends with a fireworks display, but I don't stick around for it. I find myself walking among the stock pens north of the arena. In one large corral, a couple dozen horses are frantically galloping in circles, spooked by the explosions. I head over to the encampment of RVs and travel trailers. Coming from a sound system somewhere in the jumble of grayish forms is a song I recognize, Ray Wylie Hubbard's "Screw You, We're from Texas." I try to find the source of the music, to no avail. Damn, you never know what you'll stumble onto up here in Cheyenne, at this biggest Daddy of 'Em All.

I sit on a fence rail not far from the museum, look out at the sprawling rodeo park in the darkness, and think back on the PBR event. Would Cowboy Don have liked it? Being of the generation he was, he would no doubt have hated the music and the lights. But I am sure he would have cherished standing in the spotlight, recognized as a stud bull rider. One thing I'm certain of is that he never felt like a "somebody" when he was young. Abandoned by his father. Raised by a mother with a history of unstable relationships. Hustling for work in the pool halls and bowling alleys of downtown Denver. Recognition of the sort the bull riders received tonight would have been some salve for his troubled soul. Plus it most likely would have won him a girl or two. He would have loved it.

⇥ 4. A LOT OF FLOURISH ⇤

Bullnan_a
Oklahoma City, Oklahoma—August 2003

DOWNTOWN Oklahoma City has changed a lot in the twenty-two years since I lived there. Urban renewal began draining away most of the city's soul when I was still in elementary school. Now there's scarcely anything left with a patina. Just boxy late twentieth-century office buildings, with a few attractions thrown in to draw tourists. I have an address scribbled down for an arena called the Ford Center. I have no idea what the Ford Center looks like. But it is on Reno Avenue, and I know for certain what Reno Avenue is. Or at least what it *was.* The Reno Avenue I'm driving on now bears scant resemblance to the one I knew when I was a kid.

Old Reno Avenue was the very embodiment of what Oklahoma City's Mason "Classical Gas" Williams once termed "the raw power of life caught in the act of being"—several blocks of ramshackle buildings housing pool halls and shoeshine parlors and barbershops and used-tire dealers and beer joints and greasy spoons and secondhand auto parts stores. I believe he was right: You could find anything on Reno Avenue. Need a wooden spool of cable? That was the place to go. How about a whore with prices that accommodated a workingman's budget? Head to Reno Avenue. Some older kids showed up at school one Monday with a matchbox of marijuana. Where had they scored it? Upstairs above a storefront shoeshine joint on Reno. Mason Williams's book *Flavors* contains a photo of Reno Avenue taken by Robert Howard in the mid-1960s. That photo captures the street exactly as I recall it. Beat-up brick sidewalk, grass invading the cracks. Barber poles. Bill's Café. Winos on the street, one heading toward a doorway beneath a sign that advertises both COLD BEER and BROOMCORN HANDS WANTED. And in the middle of it all, his back to the camera, strolling as if he owns it all is a cowboy in a straw hat and black boots. "I was afraid to go into most of those places," Williams writes. "I was afraid to touch anybody or anything." I understand what he means. I never got out of the truck when I went down there with Dad. But I was absolutely fascinated by what I'd see from behind the protection of the windshield. One of Cowboy Don's old cohorts once told me, "The last time I saw him must have been, oh, sometime around 1967 or so. He was drinking beer in one of those honky-tonks on Reno." No surprise there.

But now Reno shows no signs of its inglorious (or glorious, depending on your perspective) past. The street and the buildings that run beside it are well scrubbed and completely non-threatening. No winos, no cowboys. I spot the sign for the Ford Center up ahead. Modern and as clean as a suburban shopping mall. I try to remember what used to be where the center now stands, but I can't dredge up anything. Outside is an idling diesel truck with a Professional Bull Riders trailer attached to it. I go inside and walk up to the ticket windows to pick up my press credentials for tonight's Bullnanza. At the next window a middle-aged man in a straw hat pleads with the woman on the other side of the glass.

"You mean you can't find me three tickets that are together?"

"No sir. There just aren't any at this time. We're very close to a sellout."

"And in this section, you don't even have two together?"

"No sir. I have a single here and one here." She points at a seating diagram.

The man sighs mightily. "So if I want to sit with my wife, I'm going to have to sit up here?" He points to the nosebleed section.

"I'm sorry, but that's right sir. We're close—"

"I know, I know. You're almost sold out." The man turns to his wife, who is standing next to him. "Well, mama, what do you want to do?"

She shrugs.

He says, "If we sit up there, we won't be able to see shit."

She says, "I don't want to sit alone."

He sighs again and says to the woman at the window, "We'll take these two."

"And do you still want a third ticket?"

"No, we'll just tell him you ain't got any more tickets. He won't want to come if he sits by himself."

The man forks over some cash. Such is the burgeoning popularity of the Professional Bull Riders tour.

I leave the Ford Center and walk back to my SUV, its windshield well spattered with grasshoppers I hit while driving up from Austin, almost four hundred miles to the south. I leave Oklahoma City, the streets all but deserted at noon on a Saturday and head toward Guthrie, where I plan to spend the night with Mom and Dad.

I DON'T HAVE much spare time on this trip, but whimsy overtakes me as I approach the second Guthrie exit on Interstate 35. I pass it by and drive on another fifteen miles or so to the Mulhall exit. I take a left on Mulhall Road to get to Roselawn Cemetery. The cemetery sits on a rise a couple of miles above Beaver Creek. It is a nondescript plot of ground, surrounded on all sides by cow pastures and hay meadows. A hundred twenty years ago this was prime grassland, the only timber being cottonwoods, hackberries, some post oaks, and a few other varieties of trees along Beaver Creek and, farther to the south, the Cimarron River. But years of overgrazing and ill-considered tillage have destroyed much of the topsoil. Everywhere you look you can spot sandstone outcroppings and gashes in the red clay soil caused by erosion. They look inflamed, like massive abrasions. The poor soil conditions have fostered the growth of an opportunistic juniper that we called a red cedar throughout the countryside. So now when you take in the vista from the ridgetop where Roselawn sits, cedars dominate the view as much as anything. I used to take my maternal grandmother on drives through this area, the place where she grew up. Grandma would peer out the windows and say, "Land's sake, son, it pains me to see how the cedars have took over everything. This used to be good country."

I park my SUV outside the cemetery's fence and go inside.

When I was a kid, I used to go to Roselawn with my grandparents to put flowers on graves for what they called Decoration Day. At the time, three generations of Grandma's family were entombed in Roselawn's red clay, including her grandfather Jim Bell, who staked a nearby claim during the Great Land Run of 1889. Grandma would tell me stories as we made our way from grave to grave. We'd end up at the Mulhall family plot. There, encased in the red clay below the newly cut grass, were the remains of a family as responsible as anyone for rodeo becoming part of the national fabric: Colonel Zack Mulhall, the patriarch. His wife, one of his sons, his daughters. Especially his daughter Lucille, dubbed the First Cowgirl, an early twentieth-century celebrity and one of the finest athletes on horseback that the West has ever known.

ZACK MULHALL was born Zachariah P. Vandeveer in 1847, probably in Missouri, although he would later tell census collectors that his birthplace was Texas. Without question he spent his early childhood in Texas, living there until his mother died. Shortly thereafter, his father decided to move to Missouri with the boy. But they never got farther than New Orleans, where his father contracted yellow fever and died in 1855. Zack was reared by his aunt in St. Louis, and adopted her married name, Mulhall. The Mulhalls were Irish Catholics, and Zack attended Notre Dame for a few semesters and played professional baseball for a while. Eventually, he went to work for a railroad.

When he was twenty-eight, he married sixteen-year-old Mary Agnes Locke. Like Zack, she was an orphan who had been taken in by the Mulhalls. Zack and Mary Agnes were not related by blood, but his marrying his quasi-adopted sister (no records exist indicating that the Mulhalls actually adopted either child) was scandalous enough to cause tongues to wag when he eventually relocated his family to the Unassigned Lands. Zack did a lot of things in his long life that caused tongues to wag.

By 1889 Mulhall was an assistant livestock agent for the Santa Fe railroad, which had a north–south main line that pierced the center of the Unassigned Lands. "It was Zack's job to route the cattle and remove them from the train when cars were in short supply or when the cattle needed a rest," my old friend, the late Kathryn B. (Kay) Stansbury, writes in her biography of Lucille Mulhall; her book remains the most complete work about the family. Because Zack grazed cattle many times on the vast expanses of buffalo grass in this part of the country, he knew exactly which parcel of land he wanted to claim as his own. He was not a man to take chances, though. Long before the official start of the Great Land Run, he took steps to ensure he got what he desired. Stansbury writes:

> At this very moment his cowboys were camped on the banks of Beaver Creek near Alfred [a water station on the Santa Fe line] tending a herd of cattle. All of the cattle were not Zack's but belonged to various owners, and the herd was being fattened before being shipped to the East via the railroad to market . . . So the existence of the cattle camp was legitimate, but the presence of the cowboys, their shelters, and fences was questionable.

In fact, they qualified as Sooners—settlers who illegally entered the Unassigned Lands before the start of the land run, in order to snatch up the choicest claims. The tongue waggers would mutter for years that Mulhall got his choice spread only because he "Soonered up" on the property.

Even though he had his hands there already to secure his property, Mulhall was able to gallop into town on his horse ahead of all the other settlers. He staked a claim directly southwest of the Alfred water tower. A town sprouted up east of the water tower. Michael Wallis writes, "Immediately after erecting a temporary shelter on his homestead, Zack built stockyards and gave the railroad some land for right-of-way, and a train station. He built a big, rambling family residence just west of town that extended north into the Cherokee Outlet. When Mary Agnes and the rest of the Mulhalls arrived the following year, local citizens already had successfully petitioned the railroad to rename the town Mulhall in honor of Zack, the mayor at the time." I'm not sure if it was the railroad or the postmaster who ultimately determined the town's name, but if it was the former, it must have been a pretty easy decision, given Mulhall's association with the railroad's lucrative cattle-shipping operation.

Through land purchases and acquisitions of unclaimed homesteads, Mulhall built his ranch up to more than eighty thousand acres. He left the Santa Fe to become the general livestock agent for the Frisco Railroad. Between his personal holdings and his important position with the Frisco, Mulhall became one of the best-known business figures in Oklahoma Territory. With his walrus mustache and high-crowned Stetson, he cut an impressive figure on horseback, and he was easily recognizable. But Mulhall wanted more than mere recognition. He wanted to be a full-fledged celebrity, like Buffalo Bill Cody. He knew there were two ways to achieve that. First, make a name for himself in show business. Second, ingratiate himself with the rich and powerful.

Ten years after the Great Land Run, Mulhall—who was calling himself Colonel Zack Mulhall, though he had no military background—entered show business and began to promote roping and riding contests. He named the organization that staged these events the Congress of Rough Riders and Ropers. *Rough rider* was a common term at the time for horse breakers, but it also evoked images of Buckey O'Neill and the other colorful members of Teddy Roosevelt's volunteer regiment. Mulhall was not blind to that. In fact, he encouraged speculation that he had been among those who charged San Juan Hill, enough so that Hall of Fame roper Sammy Garrett, who got his start in Mulhall's show, stated in his autobiography that Mulhall had been a Rough Rider.

In 1899 Zack took his troupe to South McAlester in Indian Territory. Part of the show was a performance by a band that Mulhall had organized. There were also displays of trick roping and riding. Part of the show was a prototype for a rodeo. Prize money for this segment came from entry fees paid by cowboys wanting to compete in the bucking and roping contests—just like in modern rodeos. But there was one aspect of the contest that was *very* different from modern rodeos. One of the contestants was Mulhall's daughter, fourteen-year-old Lucille. Competing against seasoned hands, Lucille roped one steer in forty-three seconds, the next in seventy-one seconds, the next in a cool thirty seconds. When her three roping times were totaled, they were the best in the field, and Lucille took home a thousand-dollar purse.

The Indian Territory ropers must have been astounded by what they witnessed from this teenage girl. Lucille didn't give the appearance of being physically foreboding. In the words of a newspaper reporter:

> She has big, blue-gray eyes that look straight at you; a tanned smooth skin that shows the marks of the sun in sundry small freckles; a small mouth and teeth as white as a wolf's; a determined chin; and a forehead in which perception and reflection [are] both well marked. She is slightly above average height, and weighs one hundred thirty pounds. Her figure is symmetrical, and her every movement ladylike and graceful. She walks as lightly and as easily as she rides.

With her apple cheeks and her curls, she was considered a beauty by late nineteenth-century standards. Meeting her about a year later, a smitten Teddy Roosevelt called her "the golden-haired girl of the West." This golden girl could quote the classics in Latin—she attended school at a convent in Guthrie—and she could kill and skin a wolf, help a mother cow deliver her calf, and bulldog steers.

Although the crowd in South McAlester might have been shocked by her performance, people around the Mulhall ranch were not surprised at all by her cowboying acumen. Zack had his children on horseback as soon as they could walk, so the whole brood became accomplished riders. But Lucille also learned how to train horses, how to rope calves, and how to brand while most kids were still learning the alphabet. Kathryn Stansbury writes:

> The ability to throw the lariat was no longer a pastime; accuracy was necessary to catch the calves. Once she asked her father for some calves of her own, and he laughingly told her she could have all she could brand. That was a mistake. She had her own branding iron made with the initials LM and promptly set about branding.

Zack called the deal off after he saw how many calves were turning up with the LM brand.

Later in 1899 the Mulhall show arrived in St. Louis to play for a county fair. St. Louis was a sophisticated metropolis. Linked to the great cities of the eastern United States, it was a place where an entertainer could boost his or her career to continental prominence. So if you played St. Louis, you wanted to give it your all. That's just what Lucille did. Her performance there established the foundation of her national reputation. Appearing with her in the show was an unknown cowboy from Claremore, Indian Territory, named Will Rogers—the Cherokee Kid. Rogers also hoped to make a name for himself, but he came up short at the show. "I made the serious mistake of catching my steer and he immediately jerked me and my Pony down for our trouble," he wrote thirty years later in his folksy style, which included misspelled words, unusual capitalizations, and odd colloquialisms. But Lucille dazzled the audience. Rogers recalled:

> Lucille was just a little kid when we were in St. Louis that year, but she was riding and running her Pony all over the place, and that was incidentally her start, too. It was not only her start, but it was the direct start of what has since come

to be known as the Cowgirl. There was no such a thing or no such word up to then as *Cowgirl*. But as Col. Mulhall from that date drifted into the professional end of the Contest and show business, why Lucille gradually come to the front, and you can go tell the world that his youngest Daughter, Lucille Mulhall, was the first well-known Cowgirl.

In 1900 the veterans of Roosevelt's Rough Rider regiment planned a reunion in Oklahoma City over Independence Day. The committee planning the event hired Mulhall's Wild West performers and the Mulhall Cowboy Band. Roosevelt, who was running for vice president that year, was in attendance, and Lucille blew him away. He sought out Zack Mulhall and urged him to take her on a national tour. "It was the first time the Mulhalls met Theodore," Stansbury writes. "In newspaper interviews for the next twenty years, the Mulhalls told and retold the story, giving Roosevelt credit for their being Wild West show performers. In actual fact, they already had the urge to perform, but perhaps this high praise from such a prominent person gave them further incentive. This chance meeting was the basis for a friendship that lasted their lifetimes." Roosevelt didn't seem to mind Mulhall's positioning himself as a member of the Rough Rider regiment.

Roosevelt arranged for the Cowboy Band to march in the inauguration parade for William McKinley. With that, Zack achieved celebrity on a national scale as a show business star and as a friend of the rich and powerful. His Cowboy Band morphed into a promotional group for the Frisco Railroad. Soon the band and the Wild West troupe were appearing at festivals, conventions, theaters, and fairs across the country. Lucille was always the star of these performances, although Will Rogers and Tom Mix were also among the performers, as was the septuagenarian Apache war leader Geronimo.

Mix's involvement in the Mulhall troupe led directly to his becoming one of the biggest film stars of his day. Born and reared in Pennsylvania, he learned horsemanship from his father, a stable keeper. He arrived in Oklahoma as an army deserter in 1902 and took a job as a fitness instructor and boxing coach at the gym in the basement of the Carnegie Library in Guthrie. Later he became a bartender at the Blue Belle Saloon, where he came into contact with Zack Mulhall. Mulhall saw star quality in Mix. Soon, with the help of Mulhall and the territorial governor, Thompson B. Ferguson, Mix was the drum major of the territorial band, even though he didn't know how to play an instrument. Mulhall invited him to join his troupe, and Will Rogers taught him the elements of roping. Soon Mix was performing as if he had grown up at Buffalo Bill's knee, out on the range. No one would have guessed he was a Pennsylvania boy turned army deserter. Taking a cue from Colonel Mulhall, who seemed to have few qualms about reimagining himself, Mix began to invent a background for himself. His personal history grew more grandiose the more famous he became. By the time he was in pictures, he claimed to have been one of Roosevelt's Rough Riders, a mercenary in the Boer War, a frontier sheriff, a Texas Ranger, and a fighter in both the Boxer Rebellion and the Philippine Insurrection. There wasn't a lick of truth to any of it. Sure-enough cowboys who worked with Mix in silent Western films rolled their eyes at him and tried to stand clear when the bullshit started flowing. One of these, Yakima Canutt, a great rodeo star and the best stuntman ever to work in Hollywood, summed it up well: "Tom was the goddamnedest liar that ever lived."

Mulhall's group hit its peak as a Wild West show on April 22, 1905—exactly sixteen years after the Great Land Run—with a performance at Madison Square Garden. Coverage by the New York press corps was effusive. On the streets of Manhattan, the cowboys were as exotic as potentates from the Arabian Peninsula, and reporters dogged their every move. In the spotlight of this sort of media attention, an event occurred on the sixth day of the Mulhall performance at the Garden that forever changed Will Rogers's life. A steer with a five-foot horn span leaped over a gate as Lucille attempted to rope it. It climbed up an aisle, terrifying the crowd. One foolhardy usher grabbed it by the horns and was tossed over several rows of seats for his gallantry. Rogers roped the steer before any more damage could be done and received credit for saving the day. The publicity caught the eye of vaudeville promoters, who convinced him that a big-time show business career was in the stars. As the rest of the Mulhall troupe returned to Oklahoma, he remained in New York, soon to become a wealthy celebrity as a star of the Ziegfeld Follies, a top-bill movie actor, and a newspaper columnist.

As for Lucille, she continued to dazzle crowds as the "first well-known Cowgirl" with the Mulhall show through 1910, and she continued to amaze and frustrate male contestants against whom she competed in rodeos. She also gained a measure of notoriety when she killed a steer during a show at the Coliseum in Chicago. Steer roping almost always involves the animal being dragged after it is knocked off its feet. In Chicago, according to newspaper accounts, Lucille dragged her animal around the arena until it "gave a convulsive gasp and became unconscious," its neck broken. The crowd apparently reacted with disgust as the carcass was dragged out of the arena. Criminal charges were brought against Lucille, although the judge dismissed the indictment because he refused to believe it was likely that a slightly built woman like Lucille could kill an eight-hundred-pound steer.

Like most Wild West operations, Zack Mulhall's show ran into financial hard times—especially with the advent of silent

Western movies, some of which starred performers like Tom Mix, Will Rogers, Hoot Gibson, and Yakima Canutt, all of whom cut their entertainment teeth with Wild West shows headquartered in Oklahoma. The Congress of Rough Riders eventually disappeared from the entertainment scene, but Lucille spent years performing with other troupes, sometimes headlining her own show. She always received good press for her performances, but critics roasted the groups with whom she appeared as being second-rate compared to the top Wild West offerings, such as the Miller Brothers' 101 Ranch Show, headquartered near Ponca City, Oklahoma.

Her most interesting appearances at this time were at rodeos. The title generally accorded to her of being "the first cowgirl" is not entirely accurate. However, she was the first woman to prove to a national audience that women could successfully compete in all rodeo events, sometimes besting the top male cowboys while doing so. She participated in roping events at early Cheyenne Frontier Days, Calgary Stampede, Fort Worth Fat Stock Show, and Pendleton Round-Up rodeos. She inspired other ranch women to take up rodeoing, and women's events in roping and rough-stock riding became standard fare at many big rodeos—especially the Pendleton Round-Up—in the years before and just after World War I.

Lucille had a short-lived marriage to singer Martin Van Bergen at the peak of her Wild West fame. In 1919 she married Tom Burnett, the son of fabled Texas rancher and oilman Burk Burnett. Tom Burnett was a born-and-bred Westerner who spoke fluent Comanche and counted the old Comanche war chief Quannah Parker as one of his best friends. His experience as a cowhand led him to love cowboy contests. After he inherited a substantial part of his father's fortune, he began promoting rodeos in his hometown of Iowa Park, Texas, as well as in neighboring Wichita Falls. The marriage to Burnett seemed to be ideal for Lucille. She attached herself to one of the great cattle dynasties of the West by marrying him—for sentimental reasons, that must have pleased a lot of members of the Mulhall clan. But, more important, Tom had money, which the Mulhalls sorely needed. The ranch had dwindled to thirteen hundred acres by this point and was no longer a fully functioning cattle operation. Buildings were in disrepair, and the ranch was suffocating under a large mortgage. Kathryn Stansbury writes that Tom paid off the mortgage with the agreement that the ranch would be in his and Lucille's name. But Lucille and Tom both possessed strong wills, and the marriage lasted just a year. Lucille received the Mulhall ranch free and clear in the divorce settlement.

But financial hardships were now part and parcel of the Mulhalls' lives. In 1931 Will Rogers came through Oklahoma on a benefit tour. An elderly Zack Mulhall sought out Rogers at a stop in Stillwater. Rogers arranged a private meeting with the old man, on a fire escape. With tears in his eyes, Rogers pressed a roll of bills into Zack's trembling hand before saying goodbye for the last time. Zack lived only another seven months.

For the next nine years, Lucille lived on the ranch in Mulhall. She became a living embodiment of the old days for people around Oklahoma, and she appeared as grand marshal at Eighty-Niners' Day parades in Guthrie, and at other parades around the state. But her national fame eroded. The week of Christmas 1944, Lucille and three other people were returning to Mulhall from Orlando, the town a half dozen miles to the north where my mother used to attend rodeos on the Thedford Ranch. About a mile from home, the car in which she was riding was struck by a truck. Lucille died in the crash. The editorialists who noted her passing pointed out that it was an automobile—

emblematic of the mechanization of the twentieth century—
that had caused the doom of America's first cowgirl.

I DRIVE TOWARD Guthrie, taking the old route, U.S. 77, a narrow stretch of two-lane concrete. As I wind past Wild Cat
Curves, I remember Hump Halsey. For years Halsey operated
an Angus ranch on Wild Cat Curves. Hump was a sure-enough
cowboy and an all-around good guy. Mom always said of
Hump, "He made you smile whenever you were around him.
He was always so upbeat." That's how I thought of him, too. It
has been years since I saw him. I think about when it could have
been, and I remember.

My first wife and I were living in a trailer house on a patch of
land in the country outside Mulhall. I was unemployed, broke,
and writing and rewriting a coming-of-age novel full of high
school football and angst, which ultimately no publisher would
want to touch. The community of Mulhall was having some sort
of civic festival, and I drove into town to check it out. I ran into
Hump, who was with a man who appeared to be about ninety
years old, yet who seemed spry and lively. The old man turned
out to be none other than Sammy Garrett, the celebration's hon-
oree. Garrett was a street kid in Mulhall when he started hanging
out with the cowboys at Zack Mulhall's ranch. Zack took a liking
to him, as did Will Rogers, who taught Garrett the finer points of
fancy roping. Soon Garrett became one of the featured performers in Mulhall's Wild West shows. If there is little doubt that
Rogers was the greatest trick roper of all time, then there's also
little doubt that Sammy Garrett ranks number two on that list.
Garrett thrilled audiences with his lassoing feats at Wild West
shows, fairs, and vaudeville venues throughout America during
the first half of the twentieth century. He also performed fancy
roping in movies. Moreover, he was a champion rodeo competitor, especially good at bulldogging. He was named all-around

cowboy at the 1914 Pendleton Round-Up and received the title of world champion trick roper seven times at Cheyenne's Frontier Days. It didn't surprise me that Garrett was Hump's buddy. Hump seemed to know everyone.

Hump himself was a terrific roper and bullwhip artist—talents he displayed when he toured with the Oklahoma A&M Entertainers while attending college at what's now Oklahoma State University. He also bulldogged and took part in the roping events at rodeos. One of the Hump Halsey stories told around Guthrie concerned how he came to propose to his future wife, Eddie Lou Pritchett, a Mulhall girl who had been an Eighty-Niners' Day queen. He won enough money steer wrestling and roping at an Oklahoma City rodeo to buy an engagement ring. He then flew an airplane up to Mulhall and landed on the Pritchetts' back pasture. He climbed out of the airplane and announced his intentions—a grand way of doing so.

FOR TWENTY YEARS, beginning the year after the Great Land Run, Guthrie was the territorial, then the state capital of the state of Oklahoma. It was a community with grandiose schemes for itself. The town started as a collection of tents on the day of the Great Land Run. Soon wooden buildings began replacing the canvas structures. Next buildings made of native sandstone went up. Finally bricks gave Guthrie its dominant look. Dreamers envisioned Guthrie's becoming something like a San Francisco on the plains. Boosters touted its brick streets, electric lights, trolleys, and municipal parks every chance they got. It was home to literary societies and opera houses and several newspapers. But it was also home to brothels, casinos, and saloons. And it always was a cowboy town.

I take a drive through Guthrie's business district. It's a different place than it was when I was a kid. Much has been done to restore the Victorian buildings that give the town its character.

168 · W. K. STRATTON

Thirty years ago, they were all pretty run-down. I don't recognize the businesses I pass. The mom-and-pop stores downtown began to die off as soon as Wal-Mart opened its first store on the south side of Guthrie in the 1970s. The C. R. Anthony Store where Mom bought me my first pair of Levi's 501s is long gone, as is the Melba Theater, where Mom and I saw *Junior Bonner* all those years ago. The beer joint where the cowboy dressed like Paladin rode his horse through the door while I watched from my post in the Guthrie Junior High School band, is now the closest thing that the town has to an upscale bar.

It's all a little sad for me, so I think back to days before my days. When Lon Chaney worked as a stagehand at the opera house attached to the Royal Hotel. When Carry Nation smashed up saloons as she ran her temperance campaign; the newspaper she published in Guthrie was known as the *Hatchet*. When Tom Mix tended bar and taught boxing. When Lucille Mulhall turned heads when she left the ranch and paid visits to the big town down south.

I park my SUV near the offices of what used to be called the *Guthrie Daily Leader,* "The Oldest Newspaper in Oklahoma," where I got my first paying writing job the spring I was a senior in high school. I walk past people on the sidewalk whose faces I don't recognize as I make my way to the small sandstone building that serves as the box office for Jelsma Stadium. It's locked up, as is the chain-link gate to the stadium proper. I look through the links in the gate at the bleachers where for years I watched the "mighty, mighty Bluejays" of Guthrie High School take licking after licking.

I close my eyes and try to remember how it looked when Guthrie's Eighty-Niners' Day Rodeo took place here. The bucking chutes ran along the south end zone. And the grass on the football field would be plowed up. And an ambulance from one of the funeral homes would be backed in to the makeshift arena from a gate at the south end of the bleachers on the east side of the stadium. An improvised brass band would be set up to provide music to accompany the rides—for a year or two I pounded a drum as part of that ensemble. It all comes back to me. The bad stadium lights. The flea-bitten rodeo stock. The second- or third-rate cowboys: Guthrie's rodeo was not sanctioned by the PRCA in those days.

And out on Harrison Avenue, the carnival. It typically seemed to be a bit on the second-rate side, too. I learned early to be on my guard. In Guthrie during the relatively innocent 1960s, you could leave a lawn mower or something else of value sitting outside your house, and chances were that no one would bother it. But Mom always fretted at the first sign of the carnies, rolling into Guthrie. The third week of April meant locking up anything carnival roustabouts might see in the yard and deem worth stealing—or "kipping," as Mom put it. My stepbrothers and I were allowed to go to the carnival, but we were instructed to ride only certain rides. You couldn't trust the handiwork of the carnival roustabouts. The carnival midway was off-limits, no exceptions. All the games were crooked. The carnies would steal you blind if you gave them half a chance. Nearly four decades passed before it occurred to me that Mom might have had other reasons for wanting to keep me away from the midway.

But the games of chance didn't really interest me much. My favorite thing to do was ride the Ferris wheel. I loved it when the wheel stopped with my car at the top. I could glance over at the upper rooms of what was once the Royal Hotel, now known as the Avon. From my Ferris-wheel perch, I could see men hunched over card tables in those shabby rooms. I could see the pool halls where you could buy illegal liquor. And I could look to the right and see Jelsma Stadium under its bad lights and watch some of the rodeo.

I GO BACK TO my SUV and start driving down Harrison Avenue toward my folks' place on the far-east side of Guthrie, but I remember something else I wanted to see. I take a couple of left turns and drive back toward downtown on Oklahoma Avenue. The building that housed Colonel Bailey C. Hanes's Singer sewing machine store and pawnshop has changed, like nearly everything else in Guthrie. When I was a kid, it was a dark place loaded with cheap musical instruments, jewelry, the odd set of golf clubs, woebegone radios and TVs, and just about everything else that could be pawned. My boyhood buddy Vic Fey and I hit Hanes's shop regularly, generally annoying Hanes or his wife by asking to examine things we had no money to buy or by asking to pawn worthless watches we'd dug out of trash cans or found on the sidewalk. Hanes would indulge us for a while before running us out of the shop. Vic and I assumed Hanes was just another merchant in town. We had no idea that he was the closest thing Guthrie had to a working author as well as an amateur rodeo historian.

At the time Hanes was spending his hours away from the shop collecting material for what would become a landmark book. He'd already written a guide to raising bulldogs and a book-length study of the pistoleer Bill Doolin. In 1977 the University of Oklahoma Press published his biography, *Bill Pickett, Bulldogger,* the first book to deal with the African American Wild West and rodeo star. When Hanes began his project, Pickett was still a mostly obscure figure who'd only recently been elected to the Cowboy Hall of Fame. Tardy recognition for a man who can be spotlighted as the single-handed creator of what has become a standard rodeo event.

"Bill Pickett may have been slow," Hanes writes in the prologue of his Pickett biography (the "slowness" he refers to is in reference to Pickett's best time compared with the best times of bulldoggers of the 1960s and '70s),

> but he did more for rodeo bulldogging than any other man. In every respect, he was a working cowboy (the only Negro in the five-hundred-member Cherokee Strip Cowpunchers Association) and a performer (universally recognized by the fraternity as the progenitor of the only standard rodeo event that can be traced to a single individual). He has been cited as the inventor of rodeo bulldogging, and he was the first cowboy to bulldog more than five thousand head of cattle in the arena and on the range. Were it not for Pickett, the development of steer wrestling in rodeo might have come along much later.

If it had come along at all.

In late 1870 or early 1871, Bill Pickett was born in north-western Travis County, Texas, maybe twenty miles from Austin. He was the son of freed slaves. He was also a member of a family who were among the hundreds of African Americans working as cowboys during the halcyon days of the cattle industry in Texas—one report I've read estimated that as many as one-fifth of all cowboys who drove the herds north out of Texas and across Indian Territory to Kansas were black men.

In Austin, Pickett had many opportunities to observe real working cowboys. Hanes writes, "Columns of bawling, cowboy-directed cattle were familiar sights on Congress Avenue, [Austin's] broad main street. Austin matrons were angered often by invasions of stray steers that devoured their flowers and shrubs. Farmers cursed because hitching posts, erected for their wagon teams, were monopolized by cow ponies. Cattle buyers and sellers thronged the avenue to arrange lucrative trades usually sealed by word and handshake." Young Pickett was mesmerized by the horses, cattle, and cowhands. There was no question about what he wanted to be when he grew up.

Indeed, when he grew up, he was one of the finest cowboys that ranchers in Texas and Oklahoma ever had the opportunity to work with, but the thing that made him stand out was a skill he first started developing when he was ten years old. Ranchers and butchers used cow dogs to help them control cattle. In those days, the bulldog expert Hanes notes, the typical cow dog was at least half English bulldog and weighed around sixty pounds. These dogs could render a thousand-pound steer helpless by chomping its lip and clamping down. The steer would not move as long as the dog maintained its grasp. Pickett saw these dogs at work, as cattle moved through Austin, and he marveled that an animal could master another animal, one more than ten times its own weight, with such a simple maneuver. He inevitably decided to try it himself. He grabbed a calf by the ears one day. The calf struggled to escape, but Pickett held firm to its ears until he could bite it on the lip. Once his teeth were sunk in, he let loose of the calf's ears. The calf became docile. Pickett flipped his own body to the ground and, just as he thought it might, the calf went tumbling with him. Soon he offered to show a group of Littlefield Cattle Company cowboys how he could control a large calf. The cowboys gave him that opportunity with a large calf that they were branding. Pickett clamped down on the calf's lips and it lay still, even while the cowboys branded it. Hanes writes, "The cowboys were amazed and soon spread the word around Austin that the Pickett kid could bulldog a calf while it was being branded. Thus began a legend that was to grow into one of the most colorful realities of the sports world in the twentieth century."

By the time Pickett was in his teens, he was earning money around Travis and Williamson counties in Central Texas by riding bucking broncs and giving demonstrations of his bulldogging techniques, which he executed on steers, adding the feature of impaling its long horn into the earth when he flipped it to the ground to further immobilize the animal. While living in Taylor, Texas, he formed his own small rough riders troupe with his brothers. By 1903 he teamed up with rodeo promoter Dave "Mr. Cowboy" McClure, who booked Pickett to perform at the Prescott Frontier Days that year. It was from Prescott that his nationwide fame began to spread. The next year, he bull-dogged at the Daddy of 'Em All, and the *Wyoming Tribune* exuberated:

> The event par excellence of the celebration this year is the great feat of [Bill] Pickett, a Negro who hails from Taylor, Texas. He gives his exhibition this afternoon and twenty thousand people will watch with wonder and admiration as a mere man, unarmed and without a device or appliance of any kind, will attack a fiery, wild-eyed, and powerful steer, dash under the broad breast of the great brute, turn and sink his strong ivory teeth into the upper lip of the animal and, throwing his shoulder against the neck of the steer, strain and twist until the animal, with its head drawn one way under the controlling influence of those merciless teeth and its body forced another, until the brute, under the strain of slowly bending neck, quivered, trembled and then sank to the ground, conquered by the trick. A trick perhaps, but one of the most startling and sensational exhibitions ever seen at a place where daring and thrilling feats are commonplace.

A writer for *Harper's Weekly*, the best-known national publication of the time, wrote of Pickett's performance with the same kind of zeal.

Pickett startled the young world of rodeo all right. Soon other cowboys were attempting to match his bulldogging prowess. By the early 1910s bulldogging had become a standard rodeo event. In 1912 the great rodeo cowboy and future silent-movie star Art Acord won the bulldogging title at the Pendleton Round-Up. Two years later Sammy Garrett claimed the championship at the same rodeo. In 1914 Cheyenne Frontier Days added the event to its lineup. A year earlier, Prescott had staged a bulldogging competition at its Frontier Days.

In 1905 Pickett performed with Geronimo, Sammy Garrett, Tom Mix, Lucille Mulhall, and a host of other Western luminaries at a blowout for the National Editors Association convention at the fabled Miller Brothers' 101 Ranch in northern Oklahoma—a mile-long parade of performers stretched out from the entry gates to the arena. The annual convention brought together newspaper editors by the hundreds, and whoever shined for them during the entertainment would certainly receive press coverage nationwide. So all the entertainers were at their best. The acts ranged from the sublime to the hideous—Geronimo killed and skinned a bison in what was billed as the slaying of his *last* buffalo. In fact, as an Apache from the desert, the old warrior might have never hunted buffalo in his life, so he could well have killed both his first and last buffalo. Geronimo also was photographed driving a Cadillac on the ranch. By Hanes's account, Pickett's bulldogging was the most thrilling event of the day. A month later, Pickett bulldogged at the Calgary Stampede to great acclaim, thus becoming an international star. Theodore Roosevelt became a fan and urged the Millers to include Pickett at the show they staged at the 1907 Jamestown Exposition in Virginia. Pickett would be associated off and on with the Millers for the rest of his life, moving his family from Texas to a home he bought in Ponca City not far from the 101 Ranch.

The Miller Brothers' 101 Ranch Wild West Show became the biggest, gaudiest extravaganza of its type. All manner of Western celebrities took part in its shows over the years. In fact, perhaps inspired by the success of Broncho Billy Anderson's *The Great Train Robbery* two years earlier, the Millers shot film of Tom Mix on the ranch the day after the 1905 show for the newspaper editors. (Eventually Mix and the Miller Brothers parted on bad terms, with the Millers pressing charges against him for stealing horses, although Mix was never convicted.) But no one drew bigger applause from the crowds than Pickett. He was a full-fledged star.

His celebrity damned near got him killed when the Millers arranged for him to attempt to bulldog a fighting bull in a ring in Mexico City. Pickett fought the bull for more than half an hour—his beloved dogging horse Spradley suffered a near-fatal goring during the bloody combat—before exiting the arena in shame, pelted by bottles, fruit, and even knives from the bullfighting fans. Pickett spent weeks recovering from his injuries.

One thing Hanes missed in his biography of Pickett was an important, if mysterious, contribution Pickett made to film. In the early 1920s, after years of performing at rodeos and Wild West shows, Pickett traveled to the all-black town of Boley, Oklahoma, to film *The Bull-Dogger* for the Florida-based Norman Film Manufacturing Company. Norman also shot enough footage of Pickett to include him in a second film, *The Crimson Skull*. The films were among the first with all–African American casts, and Norman attempted to portray African Americans without stereotyping. Black Americans had certainly heard of Pickett for years, but few actually had seen him perform. The color line was unbending at many rodeos. Pickett might be on the bill, but African Americans weren't allowed to sit with the white folks in the stands at many rodeos. The same was true for many of the big venues where the Miller Brothers' show played. In communities where racial barriers weren't so tight, the cost of tickets prohibited many African Americans from attending shows. But by the 1920s, movie theaters catering exclusively to black audiences were sprouting up all across America. Admission cost just a few cents, and African Americans by the thousands watched Pickett on film. *The Bull-Dogger* in particular made Pickett a heroic figure among African Americans of the early twentieth century.

Sadly, if prints exist of *The Bull-Dogger* or *The Crimson Skull*, they haven't turned up. Few film companies saw the need to keep prints or negatives of movies once they'd had their run at the theaters. At the *Ponca City News* in the mid-1980s, I wrote a feature story about a museum curator's search for copies of *The Bull-Dogger*. She had no more luck in finding *The Bull-Dogger* than anyone else. "Scholars believe the last complete celluloid print burned or disintegrated years ago," the *Los Angeles Times* reported in 1996. "What remains is the poster, which includes a color illustration of Pickett, leaning against a post, a cryptic smile curling across his craggy face." Copies of the film's lobby poster have been a steady seller for movie poster vendors and have made his face and smile a familiar image. Too bad the United States Postal Service can't take credit for making his face familiar to even more Americans. The post office decided to issue a stamp honoring Pickett—a good thing—but when the stamps went on sale, people who knew of the legacy of Bill Pickett recognized that it was his brother's portrait instead of Bill's gracing the stamps—a very bad thing, one that prompted an African American friend of mine to quip, "I guess the post office thinks we all look alike, too."

Pickett's star eventually faded. He lost his wife, and, though he was over sixty, he had to turn to ranch work to make ends meet. In March 1932, he was halterbreaking horses in preparation for a sale on the 101 Ranch—whose own star had faded from the glory days of the early 1900s, into bankruptcy. A chestnut gelding kicked Pickett in the head as he tried to subdue it in the pen. Hanes writes, "Pickett quickly got up and stood hunched over with his hands on his knees, blood gushing from his mouth, nose, and ears. Walton Lewis jumped from his horse and ran to Bill's aid, arriving just as Pickett lost consciousness and collapsed in his arms." The ranch cowboys rushed Pickett to the hospital in Ponca City, where he lingered for days. The doctor who treated him announced, "Ah, hell, it's Pickett. He'll live." But the old bulldogger died on April 2, 1932. Zack Miller—not to be confused with Zack Mulhall—ordered the 101 Ranch blacksmith to build a simple wooden coffin, and planned to bury Pickett without much fanfare. But the receiver of the bankrupt 101 intervened and agreed to pay for a full-fledged funeral for Pickett.

He was buried on the ranch near the monument built to memorialize the great Ponca chief White Eagle. When I tromped up across some pastureland to find Pickett's grave several years ago, I was a little stunned by what I found. His grave was marked by no more than a simple sandstone tombstone that had been paid for by the Cherokee Strip Cowpunchers Association—a far cry from the more ornate tombstones for the Mulhalls in Roselawn Cemetery. A few other African Americans associated with the 101 Ranch are also buried in this area, including Henry Clay, who taught a young Will Rogers how to do rope tricks. Legend has it that Pickett's fabled doggin' horse, Spradley, is buried nearby as well.

Upon Pickett's death, Rogers wrote that he considered Pickett to be a close friend and that he valued the times he spent with Pickett and his family at their home. Dozens of mourners turned out for his funeral, the great majority of whom were white. Lucille Mulhall called him a straight shooter who had saved her life in the arena many times. Zack Miller tried to make appropriate tributes to the man who had been the star of his Wild West troupe, but he was so bound up in the racism prevalent in those days that he wound up insulting the man instead. In one of the pieces about Pickett's death, a *Ponca City News* reporter quoted Miller as saying, "Bill's hide was black but inside he was pure white." Miller apparently liked the line and changed it a bit to include in a poem he sent to many of his friends: "Bill's hide was black but his heart was white." He also told people that if ever "there was a white Negro, it was Bill." A couple of Pickett's fellow Wild West performers were even less polite—"If ever there was a good nigger, it was Bill Pickett." And so it went. Nearly lost in all this racist blather is the accurate assessment rendered by Western writer Homer Croy: "Everyone treated Bill Pickett with great respect, for he was not only a good man, but he contributed more to rodeo entertainment than any other one person."

Pickett had a hell of a life, far too much of it marred by ignominy. He starred at venues that prohibited African Americans from being part of the audience. At times promoters dressed him up in toreador's duds in hopes that the spectators might think he was Mexican instead of African American. Often he wasn't even billed by his name; instead, he appeared on programs simply as the Dusky Demon. Barred from hotels where other performers stayed, Pickett sometimes had to sleep with the stock on train cars. Even ostensibly laudatory newspaper and magazine accounts turned out to be insulting. The *Harper's Weekly* article that gave Pickett his first national exposure referred to him as a "darky." When my grandfather first read about Pickett in Frederick Bonfil's *Denver Post*, he encountered horribly stereotyped dialogue: "Yessah. Ah t'rows dem wif mah teeth." "Ah's tellin' yo' de truf-shore." "De rope's jes in the way." And worse.

A LOT HAS BEEN written about Pickett since Hanes published his book in the 1970s. Cecil Johnson's *Guts* is, in ways, a better biography of the great bulldogger, although Hanes's book has been a steady seller for the University of Oklahoma Press since its publication. You have to respect Hanes: He was a white man of a generation and of a place that not only accepted but also fostered racism. When Hanes began his Pickett research in the 1960s, Guthrie still had "white" and "colored" designations for restrooms at the county fairgrounds, a pretty well defined color line that separated north Guthrie from south Guthrie, and restaurants with signs reading WE RESERVE THE RIGHT TO REFUSE SERVICE TO ANYONE posted in their windows (translation: no blacks better try to eat here). In his book, Hanes seldom called out the racism that Pickett endured, yet he did not shy away from reporting the second-class treatment and the stereotyping and degradation. Writing the book must have been an interesting journey through the soul, a journey Hanes would not have undertaken had Pickett not been a great rodeo cowboy, maybe the best ever.

I ARRIVE AT my parents' house on a tributary of Bird Creek. Though it's now more than thirty years old, I still think of it as the new house—ranch style, low-slung, an early '70s dream home. To the west is Dad's old shop, now rented by my stepbrother.

I get out of my SUV and survey the five-acre tract of land. I feel haunted, as I always do when I first arrive here. I remember old friends and relatives I've not seen in decades, beloved dogs long dead and buried in the red clay along the creek. "Everything flows on and on like this river, without pause, day and night," Lun Yü reports Confucius saying as he stood on the banks of a stream. Just so. That river has removed most of what I knew from my childhood.

I carry my bag inside, where Dad greets me. I am unnerved when I see him. At times my life has brought me into close contact with professional football players, an NBA star or two, a few competitive bodybuilders, rodeo cowboys (of course), and more than a couple of mean-assed barroom bouncers. But I've never been around anyone as physically intimidating as Dad was when he was a young man. He stood right at six feet tall and weighed over two hundred pounds, with a barrel chest and biceps the size of cantaloupes, and he was easily the strongest man I'd ever known, doing the kinds of things you see on ESPN's strongman competitions, as part of his everyday job. I never saw him ride a horse or wear cowboy boots or a Western hat, but he had a lot of cowboy in him in terms of attitude. Independent as hell. Strictly adhering to a highly personalized moral code. Tough and stoic. Fearless. Unwilling to take shit off anyone. The hard work and hard knocks he endured as a young man have taken their toll. He walks slowly, hunched, and it occurs to me that he's like an old bull rider who just keeps going in spite of crushed bones, arthritis, cancer, or whatever else has been thrown at him. The only difference is that he was damaged battling oil-field riggings, big trucks, and a steady assault of automobiles over the years instead of taking on bulls.

"C'mon in, fella," he says.

I take my bag back to my old bedroom. I return to the living room and Mom has arrived. We hug and I sit down. She wants to know if I'm hungry. Soon I'm munching on a chopped barbecued-beef sandwich, heated in the microwave, and potato chips. Mom and Dad fill me in on the comings and goings in Guthrie—too many of them goings, deaths of people I knew growing up. Mom asks if I had any problems finding the Ford Center in Oklahoma City and I say, "No, but Reno Avenue is sure different from what I remember it being." I tell them I ran up to Roselawn Cemetery, and we talk for a while about Mulhall. Then Mom gives her opinions about the PBR so far, who's doing well, who's injured, whom she likes to see ride. That leads to a conversation about rodeoing around Guthrie.

Mom says, "Yeah, they've really fixed up the Roundup Club grounds nice. They've been having quite a few little rodeos out there."

"That's good," I say.

She tells me about a teenage boy who was killed somewhere in Oklahoma during a rodeo and about fund-raiser rodeos that have been held for him. She tells me about the teenage girl who was killed during barrel racing—where was it?—she thinks it was over around Shawnee.

She says, "What happened was, this girl was racing and after she came around the last barrel, her horse got away from her. This other girl was out of the way, sitting on her horse, watching, when the racer's horse collided with her. Her horse went down and rolled over her, and that's what killed her. You don't think about things like that happening in barrel racing."

Dad is watching us talking, a sort of bemused expression on his face. He always looks that way whenever Mom gets excited about rodeo.

We talk about the Mulhalls and Sammy Garrett and Hump Halsey. I mention Chester "Chet" Byers, the world champion from Mulhall who literally wrote the book on trick roping, back in 1928 (it's still in print with its original introduction by Will Rogers), a rodeo star up until his death in 1945, one of three people from Logan who are in the National Cowboy Hall of Fame (Lucille Mulhall and Garrett are the other two). We talk about Lucille's great-niece Juliana Swanson and Hump and Eddie Lou's daughter, Lisa, both of whom were schoolmates of mine at Guthrie High School. We talk about the Thedford Ranch.

"It wasn't much," Dad says of the Thedfords' rodeo grounds. "I remember it being just the arena and one section of seats. But I never went up there for rodeos. Just remember driving past it."

"Well, that's just about what it was," Mom says. "That's where the young guys would come who'd want to learn to rodeo. They just jackpotted. You know, they'd throw however much into someone's hat and when it was over, the winner took the money. It seems to me that the Thedfords had stock, but sometimes some of the big rodeo stock contractors would bring their stock in to buck 'em out. You can't let your bucking stock go too long without bucking 'em out or else they'll lose their will to buck."

I ask her about the Thedford brothers that she knew and whether any of them are still around. "The last I knew, one or two of them were up somewhere around Enid. I knew Darrell the best of them. He was a character. He was one of your wild and crazy kind of cowboys." She smiles at some recollection from long ago. "He used to date one of my best friends. He was a mess."

"Did you know a roper from around here named Dennis Musil?"

"I sure did," she says. "He was from Crescent." Crescent, located about fifteen miles west of here on the other side of the Cimarron River, is the second-largest town in Logan County behind Guthrie. Crescent lived through a period of some notoriety in the 1970s and '80s as the location of the Kerr-McGee nuclear plant where Karen Silkwood worked. But in the 1950s, it was maybe best known as the home of Musil, who was quite a rodeoer.

Mom continues, "Yeah, I knew Dennis. I ribbon roped with him up at Thedford's."

"Is that right?"

"Sure did. He had a girl he was dating, but for some reason she couldn't make it one night when he was roping. So he asked me if I'd ribbon rope with him."

Ribbon roping is an event you can still find at small rodeos. In it, a roper (usually male) and a runner (usually female) form a team. A small herd of calves with ribbons attached to their tails is turned loose in the arena. The mounted ropers attempt to rope a calf. If a roper snags one, his teammate rushes to the calf and unties the ribbon. She then races to a finish line. The first runner to cross the finish line wins.

"Did you ribbon rope much with Musil?" I ask.

"Oh no, just the one time. I did ribbon roping quite a bit, but just once with Dennis."

There is a lull in the conversation. Then Mom says, "You remember Myrt down at Doctor Petty's office, don't you?"

Of course I do. Never mind that I wore boots and a hand-tooled Western belt when I was young, I wasn't a very tough kid. In fact, I was sickly and I spent a lot of time at James Petty's clinic. Petty was an unusual doctor for his day. Other physicians were ready to yank out a kid's tonsils with relatively little provocation, but Petty wouldn't do it unless absolutely necessary. "The Good Lord wouldn't have given you tonsils if he didn't mean for you to have them," he'd say. "They'll save your life someday." So my tonsils remained in place, but keeping them came with a price. I suffered through horrible bouts of tonsillitis—high fever, vomiting, endless chills. Petty got me through them with injections of penicillin given to me by his nurse, Myrt—Myrtle Trapnell.

I ask, "What about Myrt?"

"Well," Mom says, "her husband, Fred Trapnell, he announced a lot of rodeos around here."

"I remember that name, Fred Trapnell."

"I don't know," Mom says. "I guess he had a job somewhere, but I just remember him at the rodeos."

Dad perks up. "Fred Trapnell?"

"Yes, you know, Myrt's husband."

"Well," Dad says, "he worked at C. J. Nelson's Oldsmobile at the parts desk. But he was gone as much as he was there." Off rodeoing.

I look at Mom, whose face says *that's right,* even if she doesn't utter a word.

I eat the last of my potato chips and check my watch. I need to get back to Oklahoma City for the PBR event.

As I'M DRIVING down Interstate 35, I pass the exit for Edmond, home of my alma mater, one of those colleges that big-time college football coaches dismiss as a "directional school." In my lifetime, it's had three different names. Currently it is called the University of Central Oklahoma, but when I went there it was Central State University. Before that, it was Central State College. I can't think of Central State without remembering my college mentor, an English professor named Harry Ebeling. Good old Harry. I have fond memories of sitting in a windowless beer joint with Harry and listening to him hold forth on Hume or Mailer or Dr. Johnson or Joan Didion or Jim Harrison or Edward Abbey to the accompaniment of Conway Twitty on the jukebox and the clacking balls on the coin-operated pool table.

My college reading lists included works by Saul Bellow and Philip Roth, Ralph Ellison and James Baldwin, N. Scott Momaday and Leslie Silko. I'd consume those books and admire their ethnicity. These writers had *cultures* to write about. As for me, I was just a white-bread American, generic as all get-out. But now I am thinking that I was the product of a culture, a culture that was far removed from Ward and June and the Brady kids, though it was hard for me to see it at the time. Kicker culture.

Guthrie may have had grandiose designs for itself early in its life, but ultimately it could not escape its destiny as a shitkicker town. Those of us who come from there or from places like it can never honestly deny that some elemental part of our souls is pure kicker. The biggest celebration in town? Eighty-Niners' Day, of course, with its rodeo and its parade chock-ablock with Roundup Club riders. The biggest social event of the year? The fall county fair and livestock show, in particular the auctioning of the grand champion and reserve grand champion steers. Second place? The spring livestock show. Another big social event was the annual Future Farmers of America Calf Fry, which featured deep fat–fried calf testicles served with baked beans and coleslaw. People lined up in droves to take part in that "feed." In high school, I was most likely to be seen wearing a blue chambray work shirt over a tie-dyed T-shirt with faded blue jeans. But the most honorable uniform to wear in the school halls was the dark blue corduroy FFA jacket with Levi's 501s and a pair of Tony Lama boots. To be sure, being named football homecoming queen was a big honor for a girl at Guthrie High School, but FFA Sweetheart was a crown of nearly equal standing. My battered Ford Galaxy in the school parking lot bore a GOOD OL' GRATEFUL DEAD bumper sticker and a faded McGovern bumper sticker, but a much more common vehicle was a Ford or Chevy pickup with a GOAT ROPERS NEED LOVE TOO bumper sticker. I played in a rock band that fancied itself as something of a cross between Neil Young's backup group, Crazy Horse, and the Dead. We had a following, sort of, but it was nothing like the enthusiastic fans of Ricky and the Raiders, a clean, tight band that aped the twanging Telecaster sound of Buck Owens and His Buckaroos.

Even if I was a bit of a hippie constantly in trouble with school officials about the length of my hair, my own kicker roots were never buried very deep. I was a fool for Gram Parsons when virtually no one else in Guthrie knew who he was, even if the fiddle player on his studio albums, Byron Berline, was an

Oklahoma boy whose father-in-law was the doctor who delivered me. The emblem of cool for me was not the Beatles so much as Clint Eastwood in the "Man with No Name" Westerns of Sergio Leone, just as the emblem of cool for my stepbrother Elden had been Paul Newman in *Hud*. I used to stand in front of the mirror in our bathroom and try to scowl like Clint. Enchiladas and barbecued ribs and chicken-fried steak were my favorite foods. I smoked Marlboro cigarettes. I drank Coors beer. I might as well have had *kicker* pasted on my forehead.

Independence is the most valued trait for an honest-to-goodness shitkicker. A kicker will tell someone to piss up a rope before he'll compromise. Punching a time card, drawing wages—these are the marks of surrender. A kicker has free agency in his blood. The best life for a kicker is one lived largely outdoors, preferably on privately owned land, with cattle as the primary focus. At the livestock shows at the Logan County Fairgrounds, young kickers who won prizes for their hogs and sheep gathered a measure of respect. But it was nothing like the prestige accorded to the owner of the grand champion steer. A high point in my stepfather's life came in the 1940s when he showed a prizewinning steer not only at the county and state fairs, but also at Kansas City and Chicago. The honors he won gave him standing in the community, which in turn helped him years later when he went into business for himself.

Rodeo is a strong magnet in kicker culture. For a lot of cowboys, it offers the chance to make some money, maybe enough to set up a place of one's own, cattle of one's own—the chance to be able to boast of never having to punch a time card. Or at least that's the motivation a lot of books and movies like to present. And maybe that's true for some cowboys. Maybe some of them feel a connection to the Old West when they put on their boots and spurs, and that's why they do it. In fact, most of the cowboys I've known haven't given much thought to the future or to the past. The qualities necessary for rodeo include independence, skill, animal know-how, and a sort of balls-to-the-wall, I-ain't-scared-of-nothin' panache. Those were the qualities that drew my schoolmates Flipper Ellison and Curtis Watts into trying their hand at it. They're the qualities that caused Guthrie's wrestling coach to make a stab at riding bulls at the Eighty-Niners' Day rodeo when I was in high school—he limped around the school halls for a week afterward. They are all qualities prized in kicker culture, the culture that produced most of the bull riders I'm getting ready to watch at the Ford Center tonight.

Yet there's no better way to elicit a look of sadness from a kicker mother than for her son to tell her that he's going out on the rodeo circuit. She may love rodeos herself, but she'd just as soon her boy not become part of it. He'll be gone for a lot of the year. Chances are he'll be living a pretty reckless lifestyle. He'll risk injury or death every time he comes out of the chute. He'll be lucky to make much money at it (even in this time of greatly inflated rodeo purses), yet he won't be content to consider it merely a hobby. The Academy Award–winning actor Ben Johnson—a real cowboy, product of the fabulous Chapman-Barnard Ranch in the Osage, son of a world champion steer roper, Ben O. Johnson—took a year off from the motion picture business to go on the circuit as a team roper. He returned to Hollywood as a world champion, but as he liked to tell people over the years, a world champion with no money in his pocket, a worn-out car, and an angry wife. He hung out at rodeos for the rest of his life, but he knew his job was making movies. A lot of cowboys never figure that out. Rodeo gets in the blood, becomes addictive. It's difficult to pull the plug on it even when all the signs are there that your career is over. The great Donnie Gay says he gave up drinking and smoking, both hard things to do. But nowhere nearly as difficult as trying to hang up his bull rope.

I smile as I ponder all this. I think about Harry Ebeling and the first time I met him. In a classroom in the Liberal Arts Building at Central State, he gave a lecture that included both Norman Mailer and Johnny Cash. He also called Kris Kristofferson one of the finest poets of our time. He wore Levi's and a pair of custom-made cowboy boots. A kicker with a literary bent, much like me. As I came to know him, I learned he had a whole lot of cowboy in him, at least in terms of attitude. Maybe too much cowboy for his own good.

No wonder we bonded.

DOWNTOWN Oklahoma City is crowded now. I find a parking garage three or four blocks from the Ford Center and pull inside. It seems odd to be dealing with congested streets and parking tickets in connection with a rodeo (although I've dealt with these kinds of things at urban rodeos in places like Fort Worth, Houston, and San Antonio). Or odd for a bull-riding event, to be more precise. I've been used to parking near stock barns or out in open grass fields. I'm wearing my trusty Lucchese boots. After Cheyenne, I'd spent an hour or so cleaning and polishing them, reviving them after their exposure to the dust and horse-shit of the Daddy of 'Em All. I'm guessing they'll hardly be smudged after my evening in the Ford Center—unless, of course, they get stepped on by some fans.

As I approach the Ford Center, there is a blaring of car horns and several high school students climb out of cars to join other teenagers on the sidewalk. Signs appear. The kids start passing out placards. I realize I'm in the midst of a protest—of all things. In the middle of Oklahoma City, arguably the most conservative city in America. You just don't expect to find protesters here. I'm wondering if this is a pro–animal rights rally of some sort. But, no, actually the demonstration is aimed against the PBR for allowing big tobacco—in particular U.S. Smokeless Tobacco—to sponsor its events. A young man with a face littered with pale pink acne hands me a small orange flyer: BULLNANZA . . . SPIT OUT BIG TOBACCO! RODEOS ARE FOR FAMILIES, NOT TOBACCO. I look up after reading it and say, "Protesting tobacco?"

"Well yeah—," he says, as if I'm some sort of dunderhead.

"Why?"

He grimaces and explains that he and the other kids here tonight are part of an organization called OKSWAT (Oklahoma Students Working Against Tobacco), whose goal is "to empower and unite youth to resist and expose big tobacco's lies while changing current attitudes about tobacco."

"These guys are the worst," he says, nodding toward the arena.

"The PBR?"

"Them and the other rodeo stuff, yeah."

"Why do you say that?"

"Well—look at this."

He shows me an ad for Copenhagen—one of the best-known snuff brands of the U.S. Smokeless Tobacco Company—from the PBR's magazine. It shows Ty Murray on the back of a bull with a quote: "Out here, we enjoy our tobacco. But the only thing we light up is the arena."

He says, "A lot of kids think someone like Ty Murray is pretty cool. He shouldn't be saying it's okay to dip snuff. Doesn't he know about the cancer?"

A car loaded with other teenagers comes around the block and honks, and the kids on the sidewalk yell back at it. I wish the kid good luck and start back toward the Ford Center.

By the time I reach the entrance, the crowd is shoulder to

shoulder thick. I show my wristband to the ticket taker. "Let me see that again," he growls.

I stop and hold up the wristband again. "I'm with the press," I say, somewhat meekly.

"You need to give a man a chance to see these things plain," he says. "Go on in."

I head down to the arena floor.

I station myself near the steps leading to the platform that overlooks the chutes. The Ford Center opened in 2002, and it looks none the worse for wear after a year's worth of use. One of the primary functions of the twenty-thousand-seat arena is hosting the home games of the Oklahoma City Blazers, a minor-league hockey team that has had a solid, sometimes fanatic following over the years in this Sunbelt city far removed from the frozen North. It's also home to the Yard Dawgz, Oklahoma City's arena football team. For the Bullnanza tonight, the PBR has had the arena's floor circled with what look to be two-by-twelve boards. These boards cup truckloads of dirt that have been dumped onto the floor. The dirt has been harrowed into a fine riding surface for the bull riders.

From the arena floor, the Ford Center's seats rise up in bland circles to the high ceiling. I remember the NFR events I attended at the old Fairgrounds Arena. Somehow it seemed to be much cozier than this place. I think about Freckles Brown and Tornado, and smile. Almost thirty-six years ago.

Tonight's Bullnanza has its roots at the Lazy E Arena outside Guthrie. By extension, the PBR itself can be traced back to the Lazy E. The Lazy E began back in the 1980s as the brainchild of Ed Gaylord, a steer roping fanatic with an unlikely pedigree. He was not raised a kicker. Instead, he grew up in one of Oklahoma's wealthiest and most powerful families. His grandfather, E. K. Gaylord, bought the *Daily Oklahoman* at the turn of the twentieth century and built it into the state's largest newspaper. In the process, he became the most controversial person in Oklahoma, championed by many, despised by many. He created a media empire of newspapers, radio stations, and television stations that he lorded over until he was more than a hundred years old. When his son Edward L. Gaylord, Ed's father, took over, the empire continued to grow, expanding into entertainment and acquiring the Grand Ole Opry, among other things. Ed grew up in Nichols Hills, home of Oklahoma City's old money. But he wasn't exactly your typical Nichols Hills kid. Back in the mid-1980s, Ed told me that he had been obsessed with rodeo, in particular roping, since he was in high school. He and some of his like-minded Nichols Hills chums would escape the well-mannered neighborhoods every chance they got, to go to steer roping jackpots. Eventually he bought a ranch among the blackjacks—the scrub oaks that are part of the ancient forest known as the Cross Timbers, which stretches from Kansas across Oklahoma and into Texas—where he raised horses and practiced steer roping. He named the ranch the Lazy E. Eventually he decided to build a covered practice arena. "At the time," he told me, "the PRCA was looking for a home for the National Finals Steer Roping. One thing led to another and we ended up building the arena." The Lazy E Arena, which opened in 1984, ended up being a seven-thousand-seat venue that could be used for a lot more than just the annual steer roping championship. It became a favored site for horse shows and other events. At one point in the mid-1980s, when my career had bottomed out and I'd been forced to take a job with a weekly newspaper in Guthrie to pay the bills, I received a call from the arena's manager, A. G. Meyers, who said that Stephen Stills had been in the night before, during a horse sale. In the Lazy E's cantina, Stills produced a guitar and performed an impromptu concert for the astonished patrons. Stills's surprise appearance added to the Lazy E's quickly growing reputation. Everybody who was anybody in the worlds of rodeo, cutting horses, or quarter horses seemed to go out of the way to make a stop at the Lazy E. Then, in 1989, the Lazy E sponsored the first Bull-nanza, then called Bullmania, and the history of rodeo changed. The event was designed to be a tribute to none other than Freckles Brown, whose reputation had only continued to grow in the years since his death. The idea was to bring together the best bull riders in the world to honor the consummate bull rider. And it would be nothing but bull riding—no bucking broncs, no bulldogging, no roping, no barrel racing. Just bull ride after bull ride. That prototype of the Bullnanza was successful beyond the dreams of anyone at the Lazy E, even though the February weather was about as bad as it had been that December night more than twenty years earlier when Freckles rode Tornado. Subsequent Bullnanzas proved to be the richest and most popular competitions of the arena's production company, illustrating to the world that a lot of money could be made from bull-riding events. The success of these events directly influenced the formation of the PBR. And in conjunction with the PBR, the Lazy E has taken its gem on the road. Four of the stops on the PBR's Built Ford Tough Series are Lazy E Bullnanzas—one at the arena in Guthrie, one in Reno, one in Nashville, and tonight's in Oklahoma City.

The seats of the Ford Center are filling quickly. I watch people getting settled with their nachos and their beer and their officially licensed PBR paraphernalia. Loud music plays over the sound system. The bulls seem restless in the pens behind me. I close my eyes and think about a hot summer afternoon almost twenty years ago.

JUNE 1984: The wind does not sweep down the plain in Little Dixie because plains are pretty damned scarce in the southeastern corner of Oklahoma. Instead, haunting hills and mountains, dense forests, and slow creeks and rivers rule the landscape. In summer, the heat and humidity combined with the dead air can steam the last drop of ambition right out of you. The best thing to do is to find a roadside tavern, pull over, and sip icy Coors beer while waiting for the day to die. But I am speeding along crooked two-lane highways in a borrowed Cadillac with a busted air conditioner, and I have work to do. So no beer for me. Plus I'm on my way to meet Freckles Brown. You don't want beer on your breath when you're going to meet someone you consider a hero.

I've cranked down all four windows. Hot, damp air roars into the Caddy, threatening to blast the stack of papers beside me into the already well-littered countryside. I keep a hand on one particular piece of paper as I drive, the page torn from a legal pad with the sweat-smeared directions to Freckles's ranch. This is Indian Country, the Choctaw Nation, and I am looking for the peyote church outside Soper, where I'll make a turn onto a county road that will lead me to a crook in the Muddy Boggy River called Kelly Bend. It's not far from where the Muddy Boggy slithers into the Red River.

I make the turn at the Native American Church and ponder the Red River as I head down the county road—it's a mythic river, John Wayne and Montgomery Clift on the trail, head 'em up and move 'em out. The Red River was the nemesis of Texas cattlemen attempting to drive herds to railheads in Kansas in the decades following the Civil War. No telling how many people, horses, and cattle lost their lives to its floodwaters, shifting channels, and quicksand during the heyday of the trail drives. There's no more apt place to meet up with a heroic cowboy like Freckles than here.

I think about those gallant black-and-white images of Wayne and Clift that Howard Hawks captured in *Red River* and about how they're essential to American culture. I wonder if an image of Freckles as portrayed by Willie Nelson will become essential as well. That's the big news in these parts this summer of 1984—a movie deal is in the works that will have The Red Headed Stranger play the Ageless Wonder from Soper. A couple of weeks earlier, country singer Red Steagall told me, "The idea for the movie came up a few years ago when Willie and I were flying to New Orleans to play in a celebratory golf tournament for Bum Phillips. He and I got to talking about Freckles, and Willie says, 'You know, Red, we oughta do a movie about him.' It takes a long time to pull something like this together, but it looks like we'll get a movie made." Based on this information, I wangled an assignment from the editor of the *Tulsa World* Sunday magazine for a profile of Freckles. And so I am parking the borrowed Cadillac beneath a shade tree on Freckles's Kelly Bend Ranch, ready to record the musings of someone set to be blessed by the golden touch of Willie Nelson.

I'm not sure what I expected. Maybe somebody like Sonny Steele, the Robert Redford character in the film *The Electric Horseman*, which came out in 1979. A fast-living, hell-raising, Cadillac-driving, heartbreaking cliché? A Wild Turkey–sipping guy living in a sprawling ranch house with pet longhorns grazing in the front yard? Would he be a great bullshit artist, able to spin a yarn as long as the Red River itself? I didn't know much about his character at the time. Only that people who knew him loved him. Everyone seemed to be rooting for him back in '67 at the National Finals, so I figured he was a good guy. But other than that, he was a mystery to me.

I climbed out of the Cadillac and walked up to the house, where Freckles's wife, Edith, greeted me. "Freckles will be right down," she said. "We had some hay we had to get in and he's been working up in the meadow all day. Can I get you something to drink?"

I thanked her, thirsty after the hot drive. She brought me a cool glass of well water, which I gratefully gulped. Freckles arrived in a few minutes, offered me a handshake and said, "Glad to meet you." He spoke quietly but earnestly. I never doubted for a moment that he really was glad to meet me. Freckles invited me inside.

The house was nothing at all extravagant. A simple ranch house—a real ranch house as opposed to the ranch-*style* houses that had been sprouting up in suburbs across America for years. This was a place designed to provide basic shelter for people who were drawing their livelihood from the land. Comfortable enough, but not an ounce of ostentation. A little on the rustic side, with unfinished tree trunks serving as the support columns for the gallery porch. Eventually I learned that Freckles and Edith had in essence built the house themselves. We walked into a dark living room, not air-conditioned (or at least the air-conditioning wasn't running), and Freckles sat down on a couch across from me. It could have been any of about a hundred living rooms in country houses around Oklahoma and Texas I'd been in. About the only thing that distinguished it from all those other living rooms was a coffee table that doubled as a display for some of Freckles's most valued trophy buckles. Freckles took off his hat and there was an impression in his hair where the band had pressed into his head. I'd seen that look on countless men who'd been working hard outdoors in the heat. I felt myself relaxing. Freckles was an ordinary guy, an ordinary guy who'd done great things. He answered my questions in a soft, calm voice, his eyes crinkling and his mouth spreading into a broad grin when he said something funny.

Like when I asked him about Willie Nelson.

"I don't know him. I know a lot of people who do know him, and they tell me he's a real good guy. Now Edith, she doesn't want to have anything to do with Willie. I told her that he'd been around forever but wasn't making any money until he grew his hair out like that and started dressing the way he does. Still, she doesn't seem real taken with him."

He looked over at Edith, eyes crinkling, grinning. Edith gave him a good-natured grimace.

We talked about his life—the sugar beets and the cow milking and the rodeoing in China, all of that. He told me about his involvement with the Cowboy Turtles Association, the precursor to the PRCA. "I always wondered why you guys called yourselves the Cowboy Turtles," I told him.

He replied, "They called us that because we were so slow to get organized." Crinkled eyes, broad grin.

We talked and talked, talked about everything except the prostate cancer that he apparently whipped the year before. Then came a lull in our conversation. He leaned forward and touched the coffee table. "You know, that bull's hide got as hard as this table before the gate opened. He knew what was going to happen and he knew what he was supposed to do."

I hadn't brought up Tornado. But Freckles knew I'd want to hear the story. And he told it. Jim Shoulders running into the arena. Clem McSpadden telling Freckles to go back into the arena to receive even more applause. All of it.

"I was there," I said when he finished.

"You were?" he said.

I told him about our trip down from Guthrie through the icy weather. Freckles nodded as I spoke. I guess he'd been listening to people tell their stories about that night for years. Probably a story or two from people who claimed to have been there but who in reality were not. Clem McSpadden once said that if everyone who claimed to have been there really had been there, the Fairgrounds Arena would have had to have held a hundred thousand people. But Freckles believed me. "That was some night, wasn't it?"

"Sure was," I said.

Yeah, it sure was some night, I'm thinking now. I left Edith and Freckles's place a little bit later and drove back up the road toward the Native American Church. I've talked to a lot of people over the years—musicians, actors, rich folks (including a couple of billionaires), authors, scientists, big-name athletes and coaches, politicians (including one president of the United States), but I've never been as impressed by anyone I've met as I was by Freckles. The cancer that Freckles thought he had defeated came back to kill him in 1987. Delivering Freckles's eulogy at the funeral, McSpadden said he never knew what the term "beautiful human being" meant until he met Freckles. Exactly. A beautiful human being. And a quality human being. Just being around him made you feel good about yourself.

THINGS GET rolling at Bullnanza.

As bull riders wearing shirts emblazoned with the dot-com addresses of their corporate sponsors scurry around the chutes, the voice of an announcer reverberates and growls across the arena. I don't know who the announcer is, but his voice has none of the honey of a Cy Taillon or a Pete Logan or a Clem McSpadden. Instead it sounds more like the barking of a hyperkinetic WWF announcer. Then comes a video to the tune of Toby Keith's "Courtesy of the Red, White, and Blue." Images of PBR riders interspersed with shots of military equipment and President Bush. The crowd is wild in its approval. As the video comes to an end, I see the men on the platform behind the bucking chutes stuff their fingers into their ears. I'm thinking it's a humorous sight—guys in Wranglers and Western hats and boots with their fingers in their ears. But I understand why they are doing it when the explosion of fireworks begins. It is so loud that it jolts my body and causes my ears to ring. There is a shower of fire ahead of me, like a thousand sparklers erupting simultaneously. If the Toby Keith video made the crowd wild, the pyrotechnics have sent it to the edge of delirium. But things quiet down when the announcer says it's time for "The Star-Spangled Banner." Singing it is an Oklahoma Highway Patrol trooper, and he does an admirable job. As soon as the national anthem ends, I look to my right and see the BBC film crew I'd met in Cheyenne. We exchange smiles and hellos. They're filming Wiley Peterson, who is going through a routine that looks as if it's been choreographed by the Village People—but he's actually just loosening up to get ready for his ride. I notice the cowbell attached to his bull rope. It bears a cross.

The rides begin, one after another: outstanding bulls, outstanding cowboys. The crowd loves it. There is little doubt who the favorite is tonight: Justin McBride. That's to be expected, since he comes from Elk City, just over a hundred miles west of here on Interstate 40. McBride has been in close pursuit of tour leader Chris Shivers of Jonesville, Louisiana, for most of the season, and the partisan fans here would like nothing more than to see McBride win tonight. Shivers hasn't had the best event so far, so McBride has a chance to make up ground.

McBride scores on his first ride and makes the same sort of spectacular catapult to dismount that I first witnessed in Cheyenne. But this time he lands hard on his back. The crowd groans. McBride hobbles back to the chutes from the arena. He's bent over from the waist and seems to be hurting. But shortly after he makes it through the gate, he spits out his mouthpiece, stands, and grins. Everything's okay.

But there's not a lot of grinning going on among the riders in the ready area. This is the most intense set of cowboys I've ever come across at a rodeo-related event. They are focused, edgy. If a rider racks up a good score, he comes through the gate beaming. But if he's thrown before the buzzer, he exits with eyes burning, angry at the world. To get to the passageway leading to the locker room, the riders have to step down onto a stretch of bare concrete. The no-scores inevitably slam their bull ropes onto the concrete so that the cowbell clatters as they make their way to the passage. The rattling of disgust.

At one point, I notice some commotion to my right and I see two riders, one from Oregon, one from New Mexico, stomping around near the pens.

"You don't need to get pissed off," one says.

"You're just saying I don't know what the fuck I'm doing out there."

"No, I didn't say that. I got nothing fucking against you."

"You think I can't ride worth a shit."

"Listen, you asked me to tell you what went wrong, and I'm just trying to do that."

"Well, you don't know what the fuck you're talking about."

"Well fuck you!"

"Fuck you, too!"

If these guys are more than a little testy, I understand. The stakes are high. At the end of the Bullnanza, and at the end of any PBR event, the five riders with the lowest season point totals will be dropped from the forty-five-man roster of the elite Built Ford Tough Series. The top five point holders in the U.S. Smokeless Tobacco Challenger Series will move up to take their spots. So PBR contestants can't really afford a slump. Beyond that, excelling in the PBR offers rewards unheard of in the PRCA. Earlier this year, the riders had a chance to qualify to win a million dollars for one eight-second go on the back of a bull, which would have boggled the mind of a Junior Bonner.

Ford and Budweiser ponied up funds for the so-called bounty bull competition. The average winners of the first three

PBR events broadcast on NBC faced off for the bounty bull qualification in Greensboro, North Carolina—also televised by NBC. The rider leaving Greensboro with the highest aggregate score got to face the next hurdle. Chris Shivers turned out to be that rider. At the PBR open event in Anaheim, California, Shivers managed to ride a selected bull picked specially for this ride, which qualified him to take a shot at the million-dollar bull ride in Colorado Springs on April 12, 2003. Unfortunately for Shivers's bank account, in Colorado Springs the bull emerged victorious, and the bull's owner received a fifty-thousand-dollar bonus because he bucked Shivers off.

Not that Shivers will face the poorhouse anytime soon. Even at this point in the season, Shivers is already well on his way to topping $2 million in career earnings. Moreover, he's arguably profited from commercial endorsements as much as anyone in rodeo history. He's commercially branded all the way down to his bull-riding glove. Before a ride begins, the TV broadcasters always like to show a close-up of a cowboy's riding hand as he's adjusting his bull rope. Shivers's glove is emblazoned with a Jim Beam insignia, which gets nationally televised as Shivers gives his bull rope a final couple of slugs with his free hand.

Shivers is emblematic of the new breed of bull rider, who'll pick up a dollar at virtually any opportunity. When I attempted to set up an interview with Shivers, Denise Abbott of the PBR relayed a response from Shivers's professional representatives, Cowboy Sports Agents, located in Yukon, Oklahoma, saying that he would be available only for a fee. I've never paid for an interview, believe it's unethical to do so, and I didn't pursue it. I ran into the same kind of thing when I attempted to interview Ty Murray. His agent told me that the all-time record holder for all-around cowboy titles was under exclusive contract to a book publishing company and therefore couldn't talk to me because I was writing a book to be published by a different company.

Don't get me wrong. I think it's wonderful that these cowboys have the opportunity to make this kind of money. For generations, even champion bull riders often found themselves ending their careers broke and permanently injured. They often ended up living out the rest of their lives scraping by, doing whatever they were able to do to earn a buck.

Rough-stock riders in general and bull riders in particular often carried around a lot of resentment about the way rodeos were set up. Bull riders were the main draw, the real crowd-pleasers, yet they usually had one of the smallest winning purses at a rodeo. The ropers' purses were bigger simply because so many more contestants entered roping events. These purses also gave ropers an advantage when it came to competing for the all-around cowboy title, which was and continues to be determined by dollars won at rodeos. And because ropers tended to be injured less often than rough-stock riders and usually competed in multiple events (calf roping, steer roping, team roping), they had another leg up on the rough-stock riders. Moreover, there was a class distinction between ropers and riders—"ropers and roughies" as my friend the former bull rider Louis "Bubba" Murphy calls them. The late rodeo historian Willard Porter once told me that he considered old-time steer ropers like Ben O. Johnson—father of the actor Ben Johnson—of the Chapman-Barnard Ranch in the Osage as the princes of the sport. "They had the best horses and the best equipment," Porter said, "and they traveled in style." Apparently they considered themselves princes as well, looking down on the rough-stock riders, who were apt to hitchhike or hop a freight to get from one rodeo to the next. Finally, rough-stock riders never believed they got their due from the rodeo promoters and their stock contractors, in terms of the consistency of the quality of bucking horses and bulls at rodeos. In the old days, a rider might have been on a good streak when suddenly he would hit three or four rodeos at which he drew mediocre bulls that didn't perform well enough to give him the chance to rack up a good score. *Sorry, son, them's the breaks.*

But the PBR has changed all that. These guys can make a lot of money, in and out of the arena. They ride bulls bred especially for bucking and spinning and giving a rider hell, so they never have to worry about mediocre stock. They have investments and insurance and outstanding medical care. Bubba Murphy is in his thirties now, but his X-rays show the skeleton of an old man. A lot of these PBR riders will probably end up in the same shape, but at least they'll have nest eggs. Ropers might still consider themselves the better of rough-stock riders. They might still think of themselves as the princes. But the PBR has made bull riders the rock stars of the rodeo world, sure-enough celebrities.

And I'd take being a rock star over being a prince any day.

As I watch Shivers fail to score high enough to get into tonight's short-go, I think about Freckles. In 1967, the year he rode Tornado, he won the bull-riding competition at the NFR—and collected twenty-three hundred dollars for his efforts. The year before, when the Houston rodeo first moved into the Astrodome and became the richest rodeo on the circuit, he won the bull riding there and received a check for thirty-five hundred dollars. "At that time," Freckles told me, "it was unheard of for a fella to win that much money in an event at a rodeo." I'm guessing some of these PBR cowboys will spend thirty-five hundred dollars on good times between performances in Vegas, at the World Finals this coming November. When Freckles was ill at the end of his life, he didn't have enough money to cover his medical bills, so Clem McSpadden and other friends raised funds for him. I doubt that any of these guys I'm watching tonight will have to worry about winding up in that kind of situation.

I don't know what Freckles would have thought about all the commercial endorsements, the glitz, and the loudness of these PBR events. But I know he would have relished the opportunity to ride bulls of this caliber, to compete against riders of this caliber. Freckles would have made one hell of a rock star.

THESE GUYS ARE intense, but they allow some room for humor, too. Wiley Peterson has a terrific ride, scoring a 91. He comes through the gate sweating but smiling. As the score is announced, a round of applause comes from the crowd. Peterson smiles even bigger. As Peterson bends down to tend to his bull rope, another rider strolls up to him, straight-faced, and starts making clucking sounds. Peterson's smile disappears. He looks perplexed. *Why are you calling me chicken?* Smirking, the other rider says, "Why didn't you try spurring?" Peterson continues to look perplexed for a moment, then realizes he's being bullshitted and his smile returns. The other rider grins, too, and slugs Peterson playfully on the shoulder.

In the end, it is not Justin McBride's night. Or for that matter, Wiley Peterson's night. In the short-go, Gilbert Carillo, a thirty-one-year-old rider from Stephenville, Texas, who competes on the PBR circuit with his twin brother, Adam, scores a 94 on the Page/Teague bull named Crossfire Hurricane. And that is good enough to win the Oklahoma City Bullnanza title. "I'm shocked," Carillo says, looking truly dumbfounded. "I only got to be here because one of the bull riders in the event, Spud Whitman, was hurt and couldn't ride. I would've never got the chance to do it if it hadn't been for that." Carillo receives a check for twenty-nine thousand dollars because of the opportunity Spud Whitman opened up for him. McBride finishes second, picks up fifteen thousand dollars, and moves upward toward Shivers in the PBR standings.

I leave the Ford Center, my ears ringing from the noise. I spend quite a bit of time stuck in traffic. Then I'm on Interstate 35, back to Guthrie, back to my parents' house. Mom and Dad are in bed by the time I get back. I go to my old bedroom, undress, and climb in bed myself.

In the darkness I find myself thinking about Zack and Lucille Mulhall, Bill Pickett, Sammy Garrett, Will Rogers, Chet Byers, Tom Mix, and the other greats who once cowboyed in and around Guthrie. And about Hump Halsey and Dennis Musil and Fred Trapnell. The whole tradition of rodeo in my hometown. The marketing minds running the PBR are doing their best to distance bull riding from old-fashioned rodeo, which they consider to be hokey and out of touch with the entertainment demands of modern Americans. They want to "position" bull riding as an extreme sport, the original American extreme sport, not as a rodeo event. They're after the big money they can get from full arenas in cities on the East Coast and good ratings on TV. They want an audience that far exceeds people with backgrounds like mine, shitkickers from small towns in the West. Not surprisingly, the success of the PBR has caused some rankling among rodeo people with a more traditional mind-set.

But in fact the PBR is a bigger part of that tradition than it might seem to be. Zack Mulhall staged Wild West shows to make money. Some of his greatest successes came not in the West but in places like New York and St. Louis. A lot of what his daughter Lucille did could be considered early twentieth-century extreme sport. So the PBR essentially is doing nothing different from what Zack Mulhall, Pawnee Bill, and the Miller Brothers—not to mention the king of them all, Buffalo Bill Cody—set out to do: staging an exciting show with a lot of flourish that pleases the fans and rakes in some money.

⊰5. Lettin' 'Er Buck⊱

Pendleton Round-Up
Pendleton, Oregon—September 2003

COWBOY DON left no impression at all on rodeo tradition in and around Guthrie. As far as I can tell, he was only in Guthrie for the Eighty-Niners' Day celebration, when he met my mother. Then he was back on the road, and I don't know that he ever came back. He certainly impressed no one in Guthrie who saw him at the rodeo. He struggled to master bull riding. Once he was in Kansas, working with rodeo stalwart Gene Peacock and some other cowboys who were trying to help him with his bull-riding skills. He climbed onto a bull in a chute at a practice pen and gave a nod for the gate to open. The gate opened, the bull charged out, but Cowboy Don never made it out of the chute, bucked off before the bull even hit the gate. He whacked his head on one of the boards constituting the sides of the chute and was out cold when he hit the dirt. It took several buckets of water to bring him around. Cowboy Don finally stood up, soaking wet. He stepped out of the chute in a daze, stopped, took off his boots, and dumped the water out of them. Then he put his boots back on and limped out of the practice pen.

However, his short time in Oklahoma allowed him to hook up with a legendary figure in rodeo, Cecil "Mr. Rodeo" Cornish. Maybe Cowboy Don's biggest contribution to rodeo came when he worked as part of Mr. Rodeo's crew.

Cecil Cornish's dad, Dick Cornish, was one of the real cowboys who drove herds up from Texas to the railheads in Kansas. The Chisholm Trail crossed an expanse of grassland, in what is now northwestern Oklahoma, known as the Cherokee Outlet. When Dick Cornish moved cattle up the trail, he developed a special liking for the land in the outlet and decided that if it ever became available for settlement, he wanted a piece of it. In September 1893 he got his chance. He took part in what's become known as the Cherokee Strip Land Run, riding a roan horse named Hornet. He staked a claim near what would become the town of Waukomis.

Like much of the rest of Oklahoma and the Indian territories in the late nineteenth century, Waukomis was a wild place that saw the occasional shoot-out. It also boasted of being home to the world's tallest man, Lewis Wilkins Jr., who stood eight feet two inches tall and weighed more than 350 pounds. Fitting, a big man in big country. Dreams were also big in that area. Cecil Cornish was born there in 1910. He had cowboy dreams, big cowboy dreams.

Thumbing through my copy of Robert Gray's short biography of Cecil, *Mr. Rodeo, Himself*, the pictures interest me most. Here's a photo of Cecil with Lynn Beutler, the famed stock contractor, and Gene Autry. Here's a photo of Cecil with Tex Ritter and Roy Rogers. A few pages more, and here's a photo of Cecil with western swing master Bob Wills and Bob's brother Johnnie Lee. A few pages further, and here's a photo of Cecil with the great Warren Oates on the set of John Milius's 1973 film *Dillinger*. Oates played the Depression-era bank robber; Cecil, in his only film appearance, played a jail guard. The western swing singer and actor Jimmy Wakely, who acted in more than fifty films and composed music for about twenty-five movies, once tried to get Cecil to consider a career in Hollywood. "Ah, I'm just an Oklahoma farm boy," he told Wakely. "I don't belong in movies."

He did belong in rodeo arenas.

In the mid-twentieth century, Cecil was one of the most respected specialty acts in big-time rodeo. No one was better as a trick rider. Here is a photo of him Roman riding two horses, and another of him riding standing up with a foot on the back of each horse. But he's doing so while the horses are leaping a fence. I've never seen anyone do that in person. I can't even remember ever seeing a picture of it before. It must have been a spectacular thing to witness. But Cecil didn't need to ride two horses to be spectacular. He could amaze you on one horse, gliding around an arena at top speed, performing gymnastics on the saddle. But like John Payne, the One-Armed Bandit, Cecil's greatest achievements came not in the arena but in the practice ring. Cecil was a great animal trainer.

"I don't really know why I got started," he told Robert Gray. "My father was a cowboy and I guess I was just born that way. I had an interest in animal training ever since I was a youngster. I was always training horses to lie down or something like that . . . I seemed to have a natural way with horses and cattle."

Did he ever. Here is a photo of Cecil with his Liberty horses, six matched golden palominos. Beautiful animals. Cecil had them trained to waltz, kneel, and lie down. In the photo they're doing their signature move—all six of them rearing back simultaneously to stand on their rear hooves, while Cecil is posed in front of them, his arms raised like an orchestra conductor. I flip a few pages in the book and I see a photograph of a white Brahma bull. I've never seen this particular photo, but I recognize the bull. Its name was Danger, and he was one of Cecil's stars. Danger could jump over a car and through a flaming hoop, all to the squeals of approval from children in the rodeo audience. Here is another photo of Danger—in this one, Cecil is riding the bull and has brought him to rest in a position like the horse in the famed statue *The End of the Trail*. How Cecil was ever able to train a bull to do these things confounds me.

I put down the book and open my desk drawer. I pull out a worn envelope and thumb through a stack of photographs until I come to one of Danger, one that's not in the book. In this photo Danger is standing placidly while a small boy straddles him just behind the bull's distinctive Brahma hump. The boy seems to be about six years old. The expression on his face is a curious one, a combination of joy mixed with apprehension. But he has nothing to fear. There is a man standing behind him holding the reins attached to a halter on the bull. The boy's name, Lee Voyles, is scrawled in Cecil's handwriting across the top of the picture, as is the location where it was taken, Belle Fourche, South Dakota. The name of the man holding the reins is not written on the picture. He is rail thin and tall and he has a winning grin. He wears a black felt Western hat. He is my father: Cowboy Don.

There's not much detail to the photo—it was snapped with a Kodak Brownie; the print was tiny, with serrated edges. I always feel a ticklish sensation at the base of my stomach whenever I look at this picture. It was the first photo of Cowboy Don that I ever saw. An old friend of his mailed it to me when I was in my mid-thirties.

I put the photo back into the envelope and return to Gray's book. I turn to the middle of the small paperback to the pictures of Smokey the Wonder Horse. Terrific as the Roman Jumping Team, the Liberty Horses, and Danger were, it was Smokey who made Cecil a star.

Smokey was a particularly handsome paint, born to a Morgan mare on Cornish's place outside Waukomis. Cecil thought the colt was particularly intelligent, and when it was no more than two weeks old, he began training it to do simple tricks. Smokey's repertoire of tricks grew, and the tricks themselves became more complicated. Soon Cecil had Smokey performing at small-town rodeos around Oklahoma. Smokey's reputation grew until the horse became, as Gray notes, the most famous horse in the Southwest, next to Roy Rogers's Trigger. Indeed, Trigger's trainer, Glenn Randall Sr., who also schooled the horses for the Charlton Heston version of *Ben-Hur*, once told Cecil that Smokey was the best-trained horse he'd ever seen. Gray writes, "Smokey's act through the years consisted of a variety of tricks. They usually entered the arena with Cecil riding and Smokey dancing to the music. They would put on a pantomime and some other tricks. Cecil says that Smokey was a real show horse, reacting to the music as well as the cues from him." More bluntly, Cecil said Smokey was a real ham. Of course Cecil was a real ham, too.

"Smile, Smokey," Cecil would say. And Smokey would raise his head and bare his teeth to the crowd. Then they would play dead, rider and horse each lying on the dirt, not twitching a muscle. They'd play catch. Smokey would sit on the ground like a dog. Cecil would throw a bandanna in the horse's direction, and it would snatch the bandanna from the air with its teeth. Smokey on a pedestal—the horse would stand with one of its front hooves on a small platform and the other front hoof raised in the air while waving a small American flag with its teeth. And then there was the famous broken-leg routine. Gray writes:

As the announcer dramatizes the scene, Smokey "breaks" his leg and his rider [Cecil] is injured in the fall. The rider, seeing his mount in pain, draws his gun to put him out of his misery. But at the instant Cecil is to fire, Smokey raises his head, giving his master a pleading look that "saves" him. Then the horse gets up and the injured rider lies across his back. Smokey limps a few paces before assuming the *End of the Trail* pose while Cecil sits upright as the forlorn rider. Seldom would there be a dry eye in the stadium.

Okay, there probably were plenty of dry eyes in the stadium, but it was still an impressive horse-and-rider act. People clamored to see it. Cecil got paid $150 to take Danger down to the Eighty-Niners' Day Rodeo in Guthrie one year and have the bull jump over a roadster. But when Smokey and Cecil performed in their prime, Cecil got paid as much as fifteen hundred dollars for an appearance by the wonder horse.

I look again in the envelope of photos. I search until I find another Brownie shot, taken in South Dakota. Cecil must have been behind the camera. In the picture are his son, Wayne, and Cowboy Don. Cowboy Don looks even skinnier than he did in the photo with Danger. His Levi's and Panhandle Slim shirt are loose enough to flap in the wind. His pants are stuffed into his cowboy boots and his black hat is pushed back on his head. He has a goofy smile, almost a caricature smile, too big for his face. Behind Wayne and him is the rig used to transport Smokey.

I put up the photos and Gray's book. I think back to the late 1980s when I worked on the *Tulsa World*. I had lunch one day with an editor I didn't know well. He was a good reporter because he got me to talk about my personal life in ways that I normally wouldn't around someone I didn't know well. He asked me about some people he knew around Oklahoma named Stratton—*was I related?* I answered that I didn't know. I told him my father was a runaway dad, that I knew almost nothing about his family or him except that he rodeoed. *"Rodeo?"* His eyes lit up. "You should give Cecil Cornish a call. He knew everyone who rodeoed in the fifties."

Maybe I would call him, I said. And I thought that would end it. I'd always been curious about Cowboy Don, but at the time, I'd never given any serious thought to finding him. We went back to the office and I sat down at my desk. Within five minutes, the editor was at my desk with a piece of paper in his hand.

"Here's Cecil's phone number. Give him a call."

"Okay," I said. "I will."

He continued to stand at my desk and I realized that he meant *give him a call right now.* I picked up the phone and punched in the numbers. The editor stepped away from my desk as I did.

Cecil answered with a gravelly hello and I stammered something about being a reporter in Tulsa looking for a fellow named Don Stratton, a fellow who might be my birth father. "Well," Cecil said, "the only Don Stratton I knew was the one who worked for me back in the fifties."

"Yeah?" I said, feeling a drop of cold sweat slide down the side of my face.

"Yeah, he tried to cowboy some. He knew carnivals real good. His mom owned one or something."

Carnivals—yes, I'd heard about that connection. "I think this is the guy."

Cecil laughed. "Oh, Don had a son? Well, that's news to me." He laughed again. "Your daddy was a character."

"Is that right?"

"Oh yes," he said.

"You know what became of him?"

"Don? I haven't seen him in years. Let me think. Yes, it was 1962. He quit me in the middle of a rodeo I was doing in Memphis in 1962. He left to go work with his mother on the carnival

circuit. Yes, that's right. It was 1962 in Memphis. Never saw him
again after that. You might call my son Wayne. He knew Don
pretty good. He might know what became of him." He gave me
Wayne's number, which I scribbled down.

"When did he start working for you?"

"Well, let's see, that would have been in nineteen and fifty-
five. Yes, that's right. We were going up to South Dakota to
work rodeos. I used to hit the Black Hills Roundup in Belle
Fourche. They still have it, but back then, it was one of the
biggest Fourth of July rodeos around. It's not anything like it
once was."

We talked for a while longer. Then I called Wayne Cornish.
He seemed to be as flabbergasted as his dad that someone would
call out of the blue asking about Don Stratton. He, too, laughed
as he remembered him.

Wayne said, "Don never seemed to be the sort who'd have
a family."

"Well," I said, "he really wasn't. At least as far as I'm concerned. My mother split up with him before I was born and I
never knew him."

"Yeah, I can see that," Wayne said. "You know, the first
thing that comes to my mind about him was the carnivals. All
those rodeos had a carnival set up with them. And Don and I,
we'd go walk through the midway. Don knew how all the games
were rigged, you know, so they could cheat the people. But Don
would go up and start beatin' 'em at their own games because he
knew all their tricks. You should have seen the expressions on
the faces of those carnies when Don would start winning."

I asked him about the time frame when Cowboy Don
worked for Cecil. "Yeah, that sounds right. Dad said he left us
in Memphis in '62? Yes, that's about right. He was off and on
with us back then. Not all the time. Yeah, Mom didn't like it
when Don would show up."

"Is that right?" I said.

Wayne hesitated. "Kip, I hate to say this stuff about your dad, but he was a drinker. A heavy drinker."

"That doesn't surprise me," I heard myself say.

"Well, Don would come around, and he and Dad would get to drinking together, and Mom hated that."

"I can imagine," I said. And my mind conjured up the voice of Billy Joe Shaver from his first album on the old Monument label: *Three fingers whiskey pleasures the drinker/Movin' does more than the drinkin' for me . . . Movin's the closest thing to being free.* "Do you know where he is?"

"Goodness, I'd have no idea. It wasn't too long after he left us that he sent Dad a postcard saying he married a woman with some land and that he finally had some good horses. It surprised us where it came from. It seems like it was on one of the coasts, but then again maybe not. Maybe Florida? But that doesn't seem right, either. I'd have to see if I can find it. I came across some pictures that had Don in 'em the other day. Maybe that postcard is in with them."

He's dead set on ridin' in the big rodeo . . . Willy keeps yelling, "Hey gypsy, let's go."

I said, "I'd like to see those pictures. I've never seen him. Not even a picture of him."

"You've never even seen a picture of him?"

"No."

Reckon we're gonna ramble till hell freezes over.

"Well, let me see if I can find 'em and I'll send 'em to you. You can take 'em to one of those places that copies pictures, then send 'em back to me. And I'll look for that postcard."

"And that was the last you heard of him, that postcard?"

"You know, I did see him one more time. It was several years later. I was working a rodeo in Estes Park, Colorado. The Rooftop Rodeo, ever hear of it? Anyway, I was walking along

and I come across Don, who had a camera. I asked him what in
the world he was doing with that camera and he said he was
a rodeo photographer now and he was taking pictures of the
rodeo. He was the last person in the world I expected to find
there. And you wouldn't expect him to be a rodeo photographer
or anything like that. But I never saw or heard from him again."

"Do you know when that was?"

"Let me think. Yeah, it was 1970, no, 1971, I believe."

Wayne never did find that postcard, but he did send the pictures. He was right about Cowboy Don heading out to one of
the coasts, but it turned out not to be the East Coast or Florida.
In fact, it was about as far from Florida as you can get in the
lower forty-eight states. Cowboy Don found the woman with
the ranch and the good horses in Oregon.

I AM ON A Southwest jet that is plowing through low gray
clouds as it approaches Portland. It's been five years since I was
last here. It was an entirely different sort of day, completely
clear, and below us was a spectacular view of the Columbia
River. It's been a long time since I've been able to see the
ground on this trip. I'm not sure exactly where we are.

I look down at the book that I've been reading since I left
Austin early this morning. It's a handsome volume published by
G. P. Putnam's Sons more than eighty years ago, with Putnam
himself writing the introduction. No one prints books of this
quality anymore. The glue of the binding has not cracked. The
pages have scarcely yellowed. The title is deeply etched in gold
leaf across the top front cover: *Let 'Er Buck*. Below it is a photograph of a rough-stock rider on a bucking bronc, hat raised
in his right hand in the classic pose. He is wearing chaps that appear a bit odd to my eye, which has been trained in the warm
weather of the Southwest. I think of chaps as leather leg pro-
tectors, originally designed for southern Texas cowboys work-

ing scrub brush. A couple of styles developed: shotgun chaps, which were tight and which you stepped into like you were putting on a pair of pants; and batwing chaps, the most familiar kind, with long flaps of leather that are fastened with snaps and rings, the standard chaps worn by rodeo cowboys. But when cowboys made their way with herds to Wyoming and Montana and Idaho and eastern Oregon, they discovered that they didn't need chaps for protection from brush as much as they needed them to keep their legs warm. Someone got the idea to make chaps with long Angora-goat hair, and soon these woolly chaps became the most distinctive item of apparel worn in the West. I've never seen anyone buck out a horse wearing angora. It must be quite a sight to watch a cowboy spurring while wearing them.

Below the picture of the cowboy in the woolly chaps is the author's name, also etched in gold leaf: CHARLES WELLINGTON FURLONG. Furlong is largely forgotten today, but he lived a singular American life. He was born in Cambridge, Massachusetts, in 1874. After graduating from college, he spent the better part of a decade teaching at Cornell, after which he embarked on a career as an adventurer. He is credited with discovering the wreck of the U.S. frigate *Philadelphia* in Tripoli harbor in 1904. Three years later, he became the first American and the second white man to explore the interior of Tierra del Fuego. In Patagonia, he lived among the primitive Ona and Yahgan tribes. In 1909 he took time to write his first book, *Gateway to the Sahara*, based on his explorations in North Africa, then returned to South America, where he traveled extensively. In 1915 he sailed a schooner from the United States to North Africa, where he took a position as correspondent covering World War I. Eventually he joined the army and became an aide to President Woodrow Wilson during the Paris Peace Conference. After the war, he traveled to the West, where he lived the life of a

cowboy. In New York, he and G. P. Putnam were driving together in the countryside beyond the city. Putnam looked over
from the steering wheel and said he believed the Pendleton
Round-Up, held each September in eastern Oregon, merited a
book. Furlong agreed: "Of course. And I'm going to write it.
You publish it." The two men made a deal, and Furlong set out
for Oregon. A year later, *Let 'Er Buck* appeared.

In subsequent years, Furlong became a colonel in the army
reserve, hunted treasure on the Sacambaya River in Bolivia, recovered relics of Sir Henry M. Stanley from East and central
Africa, served on the commission that settled the boundary dispute between Chile and Peru, and held a position in military intelligence during World War II. Eventually, his papers wound
up at Dartmouth, the Hoover Institution at Stanford, and at the
University of Oregon, where scholars continue to mine them
for research projects. But for all he accomplished, he treasured
as much as anything the times he would go to Pendleton for the
Round-Up. He saw it as being the very embodiment of what
made America great.

"The Great Epic Drama of the West," he writes, "the
Round-Up, is but an atomic episode in the modern, forward-
moving West of today, but a drop of the red blood that surges
through the great throbbing heart of America, but it helps us to
understand its pulsing. If there was never another rounding-up
of the range clans in Pendleton, its Pageant has already been a
rich contribution to the Spirit of America."

That was in 1921. Sixty-five years later, Oregon's most famous author, Ken Kesey, who first started going to the Round-
Up when he was fourteen, would write:

It has become a spiritual gathering place. Those ancient
salmon dries, these stories and ceremonies and celebrations,
the stomp dances and the punkin rollers, the old-fashioned

back-lot bucking contests before a couple dozen idlers, and now the modern harvest festivals that every year attract forty, fifty thousand excited spectators plus millions of *Wide World of Sports* viewers across the nation . . . all twining together, blossoming full into that Blue-Ribbon American Beauty Rose of Rodeo—the Pendleton Round-Up.

The Round-Up meant a lot to Kesey, enough so that he and his longtime collaborator Ken Babbs worked on a screenplay during the 1970s about the epic confrontation involving George Fletcher, Jackson Sundown, and John Spain at the 1911 Round-Up. Babbs told me that the idea was to pitch the movie with, you guessed it, Willie Nelson cast in the role of John Spain— seems like a lot of people thought a rodeo movie starring Willie Nelson was a great concept back in the seventies and early eighties. Babbs said a deal never could get made for the movie—the screenplay ended up in the archive of Kesey's papers at the University of Oregon—so eventually he and Kesey recast the project as a book, a modern-day attempt at a dime novel that appeared as *Last Go Round* in 1994. It turned out to be Kesey's last book.

The section of *Last Go Round* I liked best is Kesey's introduction, in which he tells how he, his dad, his brother, and a hard of hearing family friend got caught up in Round-Up traffic while they were attempting to reach the Ochoco Mountains to hunt elk. That night, around a campfire, the elder Kesey told Ken and his brother about the Fletcher/Sundown/Spain confrontation for the first time. The tale, along with his father's descriptions of the wild and woolly events that occur at the Round-Up every year, prompted Kesey and his brother to implore their dad to take them to the rodeo, which he did a couple of years later. Later, as a junior at the University of Oregon majoring in radio and television, Kesey received an assignment to complete an outline for a documentary screenplay. The Round-Up immediately came to his mind, and he drove his Rambler to Pendleton. In the park adjacent to the arena, he befriended a member of the Umatilla tribe named David Sleeping Good, who invited him to spend the night in the family's tepee. The tepee was one of the hundreds of lodges that sprout up between the rodeo arena and the Umatilla River each year during Round-Up, and spending the night in it was something of a spiritual experience for Kesey—it also gave him his first taste of fry bread and honey and his first glimpse "into the dry, ironic world of Indian wit." When his host removed his shirt, Kesey saw he had a hand-carved prosthetic arm: "A tree limb was harnessed to the shoulder, the rough pine bark still on it." Later that night, Sleeping Good told Kesey his grandfather's version of the Fletcher/Sundown/Spain battle: "His granddad's tale was very much like my father's. Grander, even, inside a flickering tepee. More wonderful. More . . . powerful!"

Furlong's book is hard to describe. It's sort of a forerunner to the New Journalism. It is highly personalized in places, yet some parts read like a college history text. Some parts read like a dime novel, such as the section on the murder of the famed Umatilla County sheriff, Tillman "Til" Taylor, killed by desperados: "Like a flash, Owens, with the movements of a cat, grabbed the sheriff's gun, attempting to turn it on his captor; but he did not count on the power of Taylor's grip." Other parts read like a travelogue. Others, like a promotional brochure distributed by the local chamber of commerce. Some are marred by Furlong's surrender to the racial stereotyping of the time: He actually quotes the fabulous Nez Percé horseman Jackson Sundown as saying "Ugh." Some parts of the book are bold and innovative, such as Furlong's foray into participatory journalism some forty years before George Plimpton or Hunter S. Thompson gave it a try. Furlong agrees to take part in the bull-riding competition. It is a very different sort of bull-riding event than that at modern rodeos. The bull is saddled "far back where he can concentrate his strongest buck, the saddle skids with his hide over his backbone, he concentrates a tremendous amount of energy in a buck, and his movements are hard to anticipate." There is no halter rope, but "you are welcome to take hold of anything you can get." Furlong draws a notorious bull named Sharkey. "There was nothing, from volplaning to tailspin, that Sharkey couldn't do—an airship run loco had nothing on that jerked fresh beef." And Sharkey was huge, weighing a ton and a half. Furlong's account of his ride seems very much like a precursor to Tom Wolfe's prose style:

> Buck! the great mountain of concentrated extract of beef—buck!—beneath me—buck!—did gyrations that for rapidity and variety—buck!—buck!—would make a whirling dervish—buck!—giddy with envy—buck—buck—buck! No! my joints weren't—buck—coming apart—buck—they—buck—just—buck—buck—felt—buck—that way—buck. I was—buck—holding a ton, weight—BUCK—by the saddle horn—buck—buck—with my left hand—buck! It suddenly shifted — buck—and I held a ton in my right—BUCK—by the strap behind—buck—BUCK! I felt like an animated—buck—walking beam—buck—of a ferry boat with the engine gone crazy—buck—BUCK—BUCK!—but my fingers held—buck—buck—He's only jumping now,—but nearly ran down a herder who sprang aside—jab! went his goad—only the herder—jump—knows why or how and perhaps he doesn't—but jab went the point into Sharkey's flank—He wasn't expecting it—BUCK—neither was I—buck—I was slightly off balance, which an animal detects instinctively—I could feel the play and concentration of his great muscles—BUCK—something hit me under the saddle—BUCK—pulled out my

spine then jammed it together like an accordion—BUCK—
something else hit me under the chin—BUCK—something
else on top of my head and slammed my t-t-t-teeth t-t-t-
together—BUCK—my joints really were coming apart—
BUCK!—BUCK!!—BUCK!!! I looked down and saw—
way, way far down below me—my saddle—that's the last I
remember until I dug my way out of the dirt—only a wrist
broken.

Furlong won the bull-riding competition and was awarded
the mythical world championship title by the Pendleton judges.
Now *that* was participatory journalism. In 1966, at age ninety-
one, Furlong returned to Pendleton to ride at the head of the
Westward Ho! parade, billed as the largest parade in the world
without any motorized entries. Furlong rode at the head of a
column that included 2,145 people, 512 of whom were Native
Americans; 662 horses; twenty-three mules; more than a hundred ponies; twelve burros; nine oxen; and three dogs. The old
man never had a prouder moment.

The jet lands in the rain. I gather my baggage and pick up
my rental car. I load my suitcases into the trunk, climb into the
car, stick an old Uncle Tupelo disc into the CD player, and head
east on Interstate 84 into the wonderland that is Oregon, the
rain spattering on the windshield.

I HAVE NO IDEA what first brought Cowboy Don to Oregon
in the early 1960s, when he found a wife and good horses. It's
easy to understand what kept him here, though. Mountains, an
ocean, great rivers, stunning forests, desert land. Even now,
forty years after he came here, Oregon retains a sense of freedom about it that has disappeared from most of America. Or so
it seems to me. Among its other virtues, horse farms and
ranches are easy to find once you stray from Portland. And the

state has a terrific rodeo tradition, with great rodeos in towns like Saint Paul and Molalla and a number of all-Indian rodeos. Not to mention the Round-Up in Pendleton. So it's not a surprise that Cowboy Don stayed here, even if he did tell his friends out on the circuit that he wanted to live in Mexico again once his rodeoing days were behind him.

Cowboy Don lighted outside Estacada, a town that proclaims itself to be the Christmas Tree Capital of the World. It is southeast of Portland, just a short drive from Molalla. The woman he married was older than he was and they settled in on her ranch. Don and Dorothy were regulars at the St. Paul Rodeo, the Molalla Buckaroo Rodeo, and the Pendleton Round-Up, and they frequently traveled to Ellensburg and Puyallup, Washington, and to other rodeos around the Northwest. Cowboy Don worked as a horse trainer and a farrier, though if the truth be known, he was living off Dorothy's good graces and money as much as anything.

Eventually, Cowboy Don came to realize he was going to have to start working like "normal" people—stop hanging out at rodeos, get a job. That must have been a very difficult realization for a man who'd spent so many years drifting from rodeo to rodeo and from carnival to carnival. He met a man named Frank Blair who was in the heavy construction business—road construction, mostly. Dirt work, paving, asphalting. Cowboy Don signed up for a paycheck and bought a lunch box. He gave up cowboy boots for practical work shoes; jeans, for looser-fitting, more comfortable pants. When he worked for Cecil Cornish, he approached his job like it was part of a big prank. One day at a rodeo in Mississippi, Cecil paid Cowboy Don to tend to his animals while he and Wayne left for a while. Cowboy Don pocketed the money. He then "subcontracted" the work to some Mississippi locals—telling them that Cecil would pay them when he returned. Laughing to himself, Cowboy Don headed to the closest honky-tonk with Cecil's money in his shirt pocket. "He was just a rodeo bum. That's what he was," Wayne said, exasperated, as he told me the story, told me how Cecil showed up to find the locals expecting to be paid for work he'd already paid for once. But there was no pranking for Cowboy Don in construction. For the first time in his life, he had a boss who kept an eye on him at all times and wasn't about to cut him slack when it was time to work. Cowboy Don lived this kind of life for nearly twenty-five years.

And yet . . . he wasn't exactly walking the straight and narrow. Cowboy Don wasn't built for the straight and narrow.

He drank as much as ever. Beer remained his beverage of choice, and he'd down the better part of a case of Hamm's in a day. And he continued to smoke heavily, two or three packs a day. He knew those places that boasted of dim lights and thick smoke, and he relished being in them. He could chuck some change into a jukebox, pick out a few Merle Haggard tunes, and squint until his eyes adjusted to the dimness. If there was a woman there who seemed available, he'd drift in that direction. One thing never changed about Cowboy Don. He wasn't able to really make, let alone keep, commitments to women.

"He was something," Frank Blair told me. "One day I had him flagging traffic on a highway job. I don't remember what we were doing, but we had to stop traffic for quite a while. Well, Don noticed that there was a woman driving the first car in the line. So he walks up to the car and she rolls down the window and they start talking. When it was time for him to move the traffic forward, they'd already agreed to meet that night at a tavern. So Don starts seeing this gal, and he's still married to Dorothy at the time. I remember one time we were sitting in this café—Don has this woman with him—and Dorothy came in and like to tore that place apart."

Not surprisingly, Cowboy Don and Dorothy's relationship headed south. Under cover of darkness, Frank helped Don retrieve as many of his personal belongings as he could from Dorothy's house. Until then, Frank never realized the full extent of Cowboy Don's cowboying experience. There was a lot of Western gear—hats, boots, his horseshoeing equipment, a saddle or two, some rodeo memorabilia, and a smattering of trophies and trophy buckles. Cowboy Don looked it over and decided to leave it all behind. He stuffed some clothes into a bag and left with Frank in the rainy Oregon night.

Cowboy Don soon became involved with a woman from Beaverton named Ruby, again older than he. Ruby had a good job at the Beaverton electronics company known as Tektronix. Ruby owned property, had savings, was established. Soon they married, and Cowboy Don made his boldest stab at respectability. The work with Frank Blair fluctuated from contract to contract, so Cowboy Don took a job on the Washington County road crew. A regular paycheck, benefits, the works.

I'm looking at his Washington County employee ID card and the mug shot on it. He's no longer the sharp-featured, skinny man he was in his late twenties. No question about it, it's the same face, but softer, maybe a little bloated. He looks deadly earnest—no ear-to-ear grin. But the eyes haven't changed, still improbably dark, piercing, as if he were staring right through the person behind the camera. He carried this card in his wallet until he died, but I don't know how long he kept his Washington County job.

I know he worked some other jobs while married to Ruby. One of his half sisters visited him and Ruby and she remembered him going to work one day with a thermos of orange juice and vodka in his lunch pail. He was working on a bridge spanning the Columbia, and his boss had gotten onto him for showing up with beer on his breath. Cowboy Don's solution was not to go to work sober. Instead, he decided the boss wouldn't be able to detect vodka on his breath as easily as beer. He was wobbly by the time he made it to the construction site, and hits from his thermos didn't help matters. Before the day was through, he slipped and plunged into the Columbia's icy waters. He damned near drowned before his fellow workers fished him out. The brush with death combined with the cold river water sobered him instantly. He always was afraid of water after that.

On another occasion, he got a job working on a crew, cleaning towering grain silos. The scaffolding Cowboy Don was standing on collapsed, leaving him hanging by a safety line, high on the inside of a silo. He was stuck there for a long time before rescuers were able to get him down. After that, he was afraid of heights.

If I had gone through either of those experiences, I probably would have ended up scared of water and heights, too. Life-threatening experiences will do that to "ordinary" people like me. But it's interesting that Cowboy Don ended up that way. Here was a guy who, when he was younger, put his life on the line every time he stepped into a chute at a rodeo. Maybe getting away from the rodeo left him less foolhardy.

Or maybe not.

One time he encountered some difficulty with the cops in Alameda County in California. He was released and left in his pickup, but the Sheriff's Department impounded a trailer he was pulling. He got back to Oregon and persuaded some friends to make the drive down to the San Francisco Bay with him. Have a good time, maybe party a little on the way. They arrived in Oakland at midnight, paid whatever charges they had to pay to liberate the trailer, hooked it to the hitch on his pickup, and started north. At the time, Coors beer was not readily available across America. You could buy it in states that bordered Colorado, and in California, but not in many other places. Cowboy Don, being a true son of Colorado, loved Coors beer and didn't want to waste the opportunity to stock up on it. So he pulled over at a store, bought a few cases of Coors and stacked them in the bed of the pickup, iced down a couple of more, then hit the road again. There were four of them on the trip, two men, two women, sitting on the single bench seat in the cab of the pickup, drinking Coors as they traveled the 625 miles up Interstate 5. And when the ice chest ran low, Cowboy Don pulled over and cracked open a new case in the bed. They tossed the empties through a rolled-down window into the bed of the pickup and rumbled on through the night and through the morning and into the afternoon of the next day. The other man in this quartet had passed out by the time they reached Beaverton. Once the pickup had rocked to a stop, he woke up, blinked in the sunlight, and climbed out of the pickup. He glanced into the back. The cases of Coors were all gone.

"The bed was just about filled to the brim with those damned empties," he told me, shaking his head at the memory. "Of course it took us forever to get back from Oakland. Don used to tell me that he'd been a truck driver." True. He drove for Cecil Cornish and, before he came to Oklahoma, he held a membership in the Teamsters for a year and drove a truck for a circus. "But I sure couldn't tell he was much of a driver. He was the slowest guy behind the wheel that you could imagine. It took him a long time to get *any*where." Of course he drove slowly. One of a drunk's oldest tricks. Keep well below the speed limit so you won't attract attention. You don't want to get pulled over for speeding and have the cop smell alcohol on your breath.

THE RAIN continues as I drive along Interstate 84. I'm now in the Columbia Gorge, and the landscape is dramatic. The river is huge. The mountains are huge. The boulders are huge. The trees are huge. This is a good highway to drive along when you're feeling particularly full of yourself. Witnessing the majesty of everything surrounding you out here deflates the ego and puts you in your place in a hurry. I'm not even a third of the way to Pendleton, and I'm feeling pretty insignificant right now.

This rain must be welcome because it's apparently been a dry season in this part of Oregon. I keep smelling the distinctive odor of wildfires, and every so often I come across a patch of timber and grass burning, with firemen hosing the flames while rain falls at the same time. Strange.

The traffic thins out as I proceed toward the east. And slowly the landscape begins to change. I round a curve and notice that the hillside across the wide Columbia is devoid of trees. A tug tows a lonely barge down the middle of the river. A few more miles and the hills seem to become smaller, rounder. Trees are more scarce. The highway veers away from the river. The clouds break. The windshield wiper blades squeak on glass that's no longer very wet, so I switch off the wipers. I top a hill and suddenly it's sunny and the landscape widens. It's still hilly, but the hills are relatively small, rolling. Sort of like they are in southeastern Wyoming near Cheyenne. This is not the country most out-of-staters envision when they think of Oregon.

COWBOY DON could be charming and likable when he was deep in the sauce. But sometimes drinking brought out the horseshit in him. He could tell you about his "career" in rodeo and it would sound pretty grand, when, of course, it was anything but grand. Sometimes he claimed to have worked on Westerns in Hollywood. Hell, he knew all those guys, he'd tell you. Yakima Canutt, Ben Johnson. Why, he and Charlton Heston were buddies there for a while. Sometimes, when he was pretty far gone and in the right mood for it, he'd tell you about his two birth certificates and his two Social Security cards. There was the real Social Security card, the one based on his real birth certificate, reflecting that he was born in Denver in 1930. But then he'd show you the other set, the set that suggested he was born on the East Coast on June 22, 1930, the secret set. Why were they secret? Well, that's because they proved his true identity. And what was his true identity? Shssh, don't tell anyone, but he was in reality the kidnapped Lindbergh baby. In 1973, when he was drunk in the woods near Estacada, he came face to face with a Sasquatch. Yes, Bigfoot. The creature was five feet tall and "very broad." It was digging in the rotten stump of a large tree. Cowboy Don did his duty as a citizen and reported his sighting. It's been duly noted in *The Bigfoot Casebook* and you can find a few Internet pages containing his report without searching very hard.

Sometimes things went beyond horseshit to pure ugliness when he was drunk, though. When his half sister visited him and Ruby in Beaverton, she was shocked and appalled to see Cowboy Don lose his temper and slap his wife. The half sister cut her trip short and left Oregon as soon as she could. Yet people who knew Cowboy Don and Ruby at that time thought they were an ideal couple, perfectly suited for each other. When Ruby found out she had cancer and knew she was going to die, she set up a good portion of her savings into a trust fund for Cowboy Don. That she did this showed that she loved him. That she set up a trust fund for him instead of leaving him cash showed that she understood his essential nature. Had she left him a chunk of money instead, he would have pissed it away as quickly as he and his friends went through those cases of Coors he bought in California.

After Ruby died, Cowboy Don started dating another woman. This time he became involved with a woman who was younger than he. The marriage lasted for several years, but it was tempestuous. "What got Don into trouble was that he wanted to get all the attention from the women he saw," Frank Blair told me. "He never learned that you can't come between a woman and her children. He would get jealous of the attention that got paid to the children. You see, when the daughter of his last wife came home from the hospital after she had her baby, Don kicked her out of the duplex where they were living. That was pretty much the end of the marriage."

I'm remembering that conversation with Frank as I approach Pendleton. Frank had no idea of what Cowboy Don's childhood had been like in Denver. Frank didn't know that his friend had been neglected emotionally (as well as in other ways) by his own parents and, as a result, craved attention. All those years of womanizing fed that craving. As did the notice he received whenever he came to town as part of the rodeo.

"WHAT!" Charles Wellington Furlong writes in *Let 'Er Buck*.

> You don't know this country—never saw that marvelous view from pine-clad Cabbage Hill in the spring, that wonderview on the new highway of the Old Oregon Trail? Spread over the lap of the Umatilla Valley, nestling on the gently undulating bosom of its hills, lie the cultivated lands . . . Journey now by aeroplane over this huge, earthen bowl called the county of Umatilla . . . Hover now over the Round-Up City, Pendleton, the trade emporium of eastern Oregon.

The "trade emporium" of eastern Oregon is indeed in something of a bowl, with hills rising on all sides. The Umatilla River cuts through here, and Pendleton sits on its banks. I check into my motel to dump my luggage. Then driving around town, I can understand Furlong's enthusiasm for both Pendleton and the surrounding countryside. Downtown still has some kick left to it—reminding me of the small towns I knew while growing up in Oklahoma, before the advent of the Wal-Marts, when mom-and-pop businesses still flourished. It is a sure-enough Western town, pierced by railroad tracks, with cowboy bars that serve the drinks stiff and straight up. Its best-known employer, Pendleton Woolen Mills, manufactures the famed wool blankets prized by Native Americans throughout the West since the 1800s.

Finally I drive to the Round-Up grounds. A true Western relic, it is a sprawling structure of wood, maybe a little ramshackle, but completely soulful. I park on the street and maneuver my way around horses and pickups to get to the rodeo office in back. I pick up my press pass and foolishly ask if there's somewhere in particular I should park when the rodeo begins in earnest tomorrow. This elicits howls of laughter from the people in the office. "Hell," says one guy, "I'm one of the few people who has a parking spot and I never get to park in it. Somebody's always there. You just find yourself a place out here on the streets. You're gonna have to walk a ways, wherever you end up parking. I'd recommend getting here early." The people in the rodeo office laugh to themselves again, enjoying a little bit of a greenhorn's innocence. *Hey, we had us a guy in here today had nerve enough to ask about parking! During the Round-Up! Pretty obvious he's never been here before.*

No, I've never been to the Pendleton Round-Up before.

I leave the rodeo office and cross a muddy alleyway to the arena itself. I know the Round-Up blows the sides off this town each summer when it comes around, and has ever since the first Round-Up took place way back during the administration of William Howard Taft. These days, Pendleton has a population of 16,354. The Round-Up sucks in about fifty thousand more people every September. They fill up the few motels along the interstate and downtown in a hurry. In fact, Round-Up fans who have motel rooms frequently make their reservations for the next year's Round-Up as they're checking out of their motels. It was only thanks to the grace of some generous cosmic spirit that I happened to call the motel where I ended up just moments after someone else had called to cancel a long-standing reservation. And this was two months before the Round-Up began. If I hadn't had that stroke of good luck, I would have ended up among the folks who pitch tents along a grassy finger of land across the river from the state prison. Or on a school playground—the schools are dismissed during Round-Up. Or in the Safeway parking lot. If I didn't want to sleep under stars, I could have done what shelterless Round-Up fans by the hundreds do: rent a room in a private residence. "We have a lot of widowed women who look forward to Round-Up so they can make some money renting out rooms," a woman at the chamber of commerce told me. That, or I could have rented an entire house. A number of Pendleton residents don't want to deal with the noise and congestion that the rodeo brings to town, so they pack up and leave. Many do so after arranging to rent out their houses to Round-Up fan families. Even better than renting a room or a house would be stumbling onto the deal that Ken Kesey got all those years ago—an invitation to spend the night in a Umatilla tepee next to the river.

On this day before the rodeo begins, you can see caravans of people moving in. RV drivers are trying to wedge their massive rigs into impossibly small spaces. Tents are going up. Pickups loaded with lawn chairs and barbecue grills and ice chests prowl the streets. You sense that you're witnessing a gathering of tribes, a kind of Woodstock for my shitkicker brethren in the Northwest. You see license plates from Oregon, of course, but also a lot from Washington and Idaho and Nevada and Montana and Utah and Wyoming and California. But there are even plates from such faraway locales as Texas, Oklahoma, and Arkansas.

I enter the arena, which is about as far removed from the shiny new Ford Center in downtown Oklahoma City as you can imagine. It has been patched together over the years, wooden planks here, plywood patches there, aluminum bleachers across the way. I climb to a seat at the top and sit down. The day has grown hazy and cool. The steep hills surrounding Pendleton are softened by the sunlight filtered through the haze. Down below is the fabled grass on which the Pendleton Round-Up takes place. Surrounding the grass infield is a short white fence. A racetrack runs outside it.

Roping slack is taking place. As at Cheyenne, there is no roping chute. Instead the calves are herded through an open passageway. The old way of doing it. They start at a speed barely above a stroll, then break away just before they cross the line that begins the time clock. Ropers sit on their horses in the arena on either side of the passageway and the competitors box, casting their ropes onto the ground, then reeling them in. There's an informal feel to it all, just as there is to the old arena itself. On this mild day I can't think of any place I'd rather be.

If there is a sanctified place in all of rodeo, the arena at Pendleton has to be it. There's endless debate about how much similarity there is between the real cowboys of the late 1800s and the cowboys competing in rodeos and bull-riding events today. *Not much* is the consensus among most historians. To me, similarities are not as important as lineage is. There's something akin to apostolic succession in the rodeo arena. Today's ropers will be roping against older competitors who roped against ropers who roped against ropers who roped against ropers who roped in a cowboy contest against a trail hand or two who once drove a herd from southern Texas across Indian Territory to the railhead at Dodge City, Kansas. That continuity appeals to me.

Continuity—yes, that's what's important about the dirt down there below the grass. The Pendleton Round-Up got its start with a small bucking and roping event on July 4, 1909. Just a year later, it had become something entirely different, a large Western extravaganza with excursion trains hauling in thousands of people from as far away as Spokane and Portland. A thousand fans came from Walla Walla, Washington, alone. Pendleton forever staked its claim to being *the* Round-Up. And that second year the slogan "Let 'Er Buck" appeared on buttons worn by the fans and became synonymous with Pendleton. What a legacy the arena soil holds. Lucille Mulhall roped here. Bill Pickett dogged bulls here. Art Acord became a movie star largely because of his achievements here. As did Hoot Gibson and Yakima Canutt, both of whom won all-around cowboy championships at Pendleton. Chet Byers performed fancy roping here. Sammy Garrett bulldogged here and claimed his own all-around title. Ike Rude roped here, as did both Ben Johnsons—father Ben O., the ranch foreman, and son Ben, the movie star. Jim Shoulders in the 1950s and Larry Mahan in the 1960s each won both bareback and bull-riding championships here, as well as all-around titles. Lane Frost rode here, as did his mentor Freckles Brown. They've all been here.

More than any other rodeo, the Pendleton Round-Up has an appreciation for its heritage. When I first contacted Terry Murray about getting credentials for the Round-Up, she asked if I'd ever been before. I said no. "Well, you are in for a treat," she said. "With just a few minor changes, what you'll see inside the arena is just what your father saw when he came here in the 1960s." She was right. No commercial advertising is allowed inside the arena. Thank god. You can enjoy the rodeo without being constantly visually assaulted by marketing messages. There's no JumboTron to show replays of the rides. Thank god again. Just honest rodeo in an honest arena, which is all rodeo ever needs to be. Sadly, Pendleton is the only place remaining in America where you can see a big-time rodeo in such a sincere setting.

I watch a calf scurry across the grass after it has been untied. But my mind is not on the calf-roping slack. I let my eyes wander to the peaks of the tepees in the distance. In 1910 the organizers of the first full-blown Round-Up invited the members of the Umatilla, Cayuse, and Walla Walla tribes. According to Furlong's rendition, no one was sure whether the Indians would participate. Eastern Oregon, and Pendleton in particular, did not have a good reputation when it came to race relations in 1910. But shortly before the Round-Up began, the noted Umatilla leader Gilbert Minthorn led hundreds of Indians from different nations into town, where they set up tepees in the cottonwood trees between the river and the rodeo grounds. They've been coming back ever since. And not just as guests. Indian dancing and horsemanship contests are mainstays of the Pendleton Round-Up. Moreover, some of the best rodeo contestants in the Northwest are "Indian cowboys," a number of whom have shot out of the chutes at Pendleton on bucking stock. One of my favorite Indian cowboys who lived in this part of the country was the great Will Sampson, who played Chief Bromden in the film version of Kesey's *One Flew Over the Cuckoo's Nest*. Sampson was born in Okmulgee, Oklahoma, a member of the Creek Nation, where he started riding bulls when he was fourteen. Rodeo cowboy went on his résumé, along with painter (his works are included in the Smithsonian's collection), oil-field roughneck, and forest ranger, as he migrated from Oklahoma to the Northwest. Sampson stood six feet nine inches tall and weighed well over 250 pounds when he played Chief Bromden. I've tried to imagine what it must have been like to watch someone of that stature ride a bull. I can't picture it. It had to be an astonishing sight. He once told the *New York Times,* "When you're an Indian at fourteen, you have a lot of anger, and rodeoing is a way to dispel a lot of it."

I wonder if Jackson Sundown had a lot of anger.

THERE IS A story told about the Nez Percé leader Tuekakas, also known as Old Joseph, and the treatment he received at the hands of white people—even after he was dead. Old Joseph's band lived in the Wallowa Valley of Oregon and prided themselves that no Nez Percé had ever killed a white man. They were content in the beautiful valley, raising cattle and horses, living in comfortable lodges, dealing with white traders for the things they could not find in the valley. But over the years, more and more white people moved into the area and began to cast envious eyes on the Wallowa Valley. By 1863 the federal government demanded that Old Joseph sign a treaty relinquishing the valley. When he refused, the government reacted by convincing Nez Percé chiefs who had never lived in the Wallowa Valley to cede it to them by signing a treaty, Old Joseph be damned. When Old Joseph learned what had happened, he showed his rage by shredding a Bible that a white missionary had given him in an attempt to convert him to Christianity. But Old Joseph never left the valley, and when he died in 1871, his people buried him between the forks of the Wallowa and Lostine rivers. Within a few years, pressure from white settlers grew to the point that the government acted to force the Nez Percé—now led by Old Joseph's son, Heinmot Tooyalaket— to leave the Wallowa Valley. Heinmot Tooyalaket, better known as Chief Joseph, would eventually lead his band against the whites in the famous war that bears his name. In the meantime, white men entered the valley, stealing Nez Percé horses and cattle. But they weren't satisfied to stop with theft. When they found the grave of Old Joseph—the man who'd stood up to their demands for his people's land, the man who had torn up a Bible to show his contempt toward white avarice—these white plunderers dug up his bones and hacked his skeleton to pieces. One of the grave desecraters was a dentist, who claimed Old Joseph's skull as a prize. He displayed it for years in his office in Baker, Oregon.

And so, if you were an Indian in eastern Oregon in the late nineteenth and early twentieth centuries, well, you would run into people who seethed at you simply because you existed. Damned if those Texas cattlemen who drove the herds up this way didn't bring with them that notoriously virulent Lone Star racism. Not a good thing to be an Indian—damn, those Texans hated Indians.

And not a good place to be as an African American.*

Say you're George Fletcher. You were born in the Midwest, but your parents brought you here, way out in the middle of nowhere, to a place that's not even half settled by any civilized standards. You look around at this small town, Pendleton, and you have a hard time finding many other ten-year-old boys who look anything like you do. Your stepfather has a job as railroad porter for the Pendleton Hotel and your mom is working as a domestic around town. You live with them in a tiny shack the hotel owns, down by the railroad track. Things don't work out very well for you and your family, and before too long you're on your own. You have a job—transporting beer and whiskey from the saloons to the thirsty and horny patrons holed up in

---

*Chinese Americans also felt the brunt of racism in Pendleton: They were prohibited from even showing their faces on the streets, so "underground Pendleton" came into being. The tunnels and remnants of the subterranean shops now comprise one of Pendleton's tourist attractions.

the whorehouses. This line of work brings you into contact with all manner of Pendleton society, from cowboys and wheat farmers to lawyers and doctors. These people get to know you and they profess to like you and they give you a nickname— these people who *like* you—that you'll carry for the rest of your life in this part of the country: *Nigger George*. Call you that to your face when you're just a teenage kid coming into the brothel with drinks to quench the thirst of the sweaty patrons, parched from humping whores. Call you that to your face when you're an old man still crippled up a little from the injuries you received while fighting overseas for your country in World War I . . . *Nigger George*.

I wonder if George Fletcher had a lot of anger, too.

NOTHING that has occurred down there on the arena floor throughout the fabulous history of the Pendleton Round-Up carries more symbolic importance than the buck-off for the saddle bronc championship when the Round-Up was just a year old. Sundown, Fletcher, and John Spain were the three finalists in 1911—very real human beings who, through the telling and retelling of the story about that buck-off, have become mythic figures in the Northwest.

Thirty-year-old John Spain was a white man living in Telo-caset, Oregon, which is located in Union County about eighty miles southeast of Pendleton. The Spain family was well known in ranching circles at the time, and John had the reputa-tion of being one of the finest cowboys in the Northwest. "John was big and stout," his nephew, King Spain, told Doug and Cathy Jory, authors of *An Oral History of Rodeo: From Pendle-ton to Calgary*. "He wasn't a pretty rider, but they couldn't buck him off." He was tough, too. King Spain said, "John was riding the stagecoach once at the Pendleton Round-Up, and he was hanging from the side. I don't know who was driving the coach, but it upset right on [John], on the side he was on. Everybody in the crowd just gasped, afraid he was killed. He come up on the other side after the dust cleared and waved his hat at the crowd. He wasn't hurt a bit, but it was a spectacular wreck." A few months after the 1911 Round-Up, Spain lost a hand in a roping accident, but he hardly let that slow him down. He was back riding saddle broncs in Pendleton in 1912. Spain's career expanded beyond Pendleton to include appearances in rodeos as far away as Madison Square Garden, and stops on the vaudeville circuit.

At Pendleton in 1911, Spain did all that was expected of a rodeo cowboy—he gave it his damnedest effort and had some good rides. Unfortunately for him, he took part in an event that wound up being about more than just great riding, an event that ultimately carried the weight of history with it. As a result, Spain has ended up with a shadow cast over him and the role he played that year at the Round-Up—through no fault of his own.

Originally named Waaya-Tonah-Toesits-Kahn, Jackson Sundown was of Flathead and Nez Percé heritage. Chief Joseph was his uncle, and Sundown, born in 1863, grew up in the paradise of the Wallowa Valley. When he was fourteen, he participated in the war named for his uncle. He was among the teenage boys assigned to tend to the warriors' horses at night and to move the herd of spare horses whenever the Nez Percé decamped in their flight toward Canada; after humiliating the U.S. Army in battle after battle, the Nez Percé were finally bested by troops of General Nelson "Bear Coat" Miles in the Bear Paw Mountains of Montana. This defeat prompted Chief Joseph to deliver his eloquent "I will fight no more forever" surrender speech. But not all the Nez Percé surrendered. Sundown was among a group of fighters, led by White Bird, who escaped the bluecoats and managed to cross into Canada.

Shortly after they made it across the border, they were approached by Native Americans on horseback. These riders turned out to be a band of Lakota led by Sitting Bull. The Lakota welcomed the Nez Percé into their village, and Sitting Bull himself invited Sundown to live in his lodge.

Sundown lived among Sitting Bull's people for two years before stealing back into the United States, crossing the border into Washington. He managed to evade the white bounty hunters, who were being paid for the scalps of renegade Nez Percé, and made it to the Flathead Reservation in western Montana. He married, fathered two daughters, and started to call himself Jackson Sundown. He also began to get a reputation as one of the best horsemen in the region. In 1910 Sundown relocated to Idaho, where he married again—I'm not sure what became of his first wife—and lived at Jacques Spur and later, Culdesac.

After moving to Idaho, Sundown acquired a reputation as an outstanding rodeo performer. He was a tall man, lean, with a face that would have been ideal for engraving on a coin. He wore angora chaps and a large sombrero-like hat. He kept his long hair in braids, which he would tie under his chin before a ride. Seeing him on the back of a bucking bronc was a thrilling sight for those early-day rodeo goers. He was a poetry-in-motion kind of rider. His braids came untied after the second or third buck and began to move in perfect synchronization with the rising and falling of the horse's mane and tail, and the long hair on his chaps. He held his big hat high above his head, maintaining perfect form no matter what challenges the horse presented him. He was a confident rider, too. So much so that he would place dimes in his stirrups as he saddled a horse; once his ride was complete, he'd remove the dimes from the stirrups— evidence that he was in such control of the ride that even a dime couldn't slip out of a stirrup. Fifty years and more after his death, old-timers who saw him ride would swear that they never witnessed bucking horse rides anywhere close to the quality of Jackson Sundown's.

Unless the rider was George Fletcher.

Fletcher was rescued from his life working in saloons and brothels by a Presbyterian minister. The preacher pastored a church out on the Umatilla Reservation, and he moved Fletcher there, away from the vices of town. He saw to it that the young man received an education. The Umatillas took a liking to Fletcher. To the white men in Pendleton, he might have been Nigger George, but on the reservation, he was treated as an equal and was adopted by the Indian people as one of their own. He was taken in by several of the leading Umatilla families, including the Wildbills. Many years later, filmmaker Cedric Wildbill would say he considered Fletcher as family, as "Grandpa George." This relationship inspired Cedric and his wife, Tania, to film the superb documentary, *American Cowboys,* which remains the definitive account of the lives of Fletcher and Sundown, and of their participation in the 1911 Round-Up.

In terms of horsemanship, the Umatillas' reputation rivaled that of the Nez Percé. Fletcher was schooled in the art of training horses by some of the best riders in the Northwest. He learned how to break a horse without breaking its spirit. Soon Fletcher had a reputation of his own for his brilliance on the back of a horse. No one on the reservation or in Pendleton itself could name a better rider than George Fletcher.

Fletcher proved how good he was at the early rodeos held in eastern Oregon. But the white men who organized the rodeos treated him with contempt, even if he was the best rider to take part in their events. King Spain said, "They wouldn't even give poor Nigger George a number to put on. I don't think they were about to do a Negro any favors in those days. They was pretty tough."

As a black athlete, Fletcher no doubt was caught up in the backlash against Jack Johnson, an African American from Galveston, Texas, who shocked white America in 1908 when he captured the world heavyweight boxing title. At the time, the heavyweight championship was the most prestigious sports title in America. Even more shocking was Johnson's humiliating defeat of the former champion, Jim Jeffries, on July 4, 1910. Jeffries had come out of retirement to reclaim the title that he and his backers believed rightfully belonged to the white race. Rioting broke out in parts of America after the famed Great White Hope was so easily beaten by the skilled black fighter. That Johnson was the champion was bad enough in the eyes of white America. But what was truly infuriating was his refusal to play the role of "the good nigger." Johnson refused to defer to anyone; he was not about to "stay in his place." He was boastful and loved attention—unacceptable qualities for men of color at the time. Worst of all, he liked to keep company with white women. That in itself was enough to send white men into paroxysms of pure rage.

So it was against this backdrop of racial outrage that Sundown and Fletcher competed against Spain for the mythical world championship of saddle bronc riding in 1911. In that last go-round, Sundown rode first. Virgil Rupp writes in his history of the Round-Up, "His mount was Lightfoot, the fierce little bucker on which Bert Kelly won the 1910 bucking title. Pitching, sunfishing, twisting, Lightfoot did his best to dislodge Sundown." In the ancient film footage of the event that Cedric and Tania Wildbill discovered in the basement of Pendleton's library, Lightfoot is shown doing its best to twist its head back far enough to bite Sundown's leg. But to no avail. Sundown rode as gracefully as ever. "Then he scraped against a judge's horse," Rupp continues, "and Sundown, with a foot out of the stirrup, was thrown on the next leap. He was carried from the arena on a stretcher." Sundown, who was then forty-eight years old, was badly shaken but escaped serious injury. Except, perhaps, to his pride. He could now do no better than third place.

Spain went next. Rupp notes that Spain rode his bronc, Long Tom, in the "approved buckaroo style." Long Tom crashed through the wooden fence that separated the infield from the track in those days, but Spain was unfazed. Maybe. Some people in the crowd believed he touched his saddle when the horse went through the fence, which would have been a disqualification. But others agreed with the judges that he completed a solid ride on a good bucker.

Then came Fletcher. His first draw was Dell, a horse that scarcely bucked, so Fletcher was awarded a reride. Now he was on a horse called Sweeney, and Sweeney gave a bucking exhibition the likes of which no one in Pendleton had seen before. Yet Fletcher stayed on board, raking the whole time. Newspaper reporters said it was easily the "most showy ride" of the rodeo, and Fletcher received a huge ovation from the people in the grandstand. "The crowd shouted itself hoarse," Rupp writes. Fletcher's skill on Sweeney overcame whatever racial prejudice the fans might have had, whatever anger they might have felt toward Jack Johnson. Fletcher was the hero of the rodeo, and the crowd let him know it with their cheers. Now all that remained was for the judges to make it official.

The judges took a long time tallying their score. Finally the announcer shouted into the megaphones what the decision would be: John Spain was the saddle bronc champion of the 1911 Pendleton Round-Up.

The crowd was stunned.

A standard feature in rodeo is the disappointment the fans feel whenever a ride they like receives a low mark from the judges. The explanation is always that the judges have eyes trained to take in every nuance of a ride, that they note things that the average fan never sees. Rupp writes that Fletcher was perceived to be a "sloppy rider." In the words of a newspaper reporter: "He is as limber and relaxed as a rubber band and sits in the saddle so loose that his body flops about with every plunge of the bucker until it seems impossible to keep his equilibrium." That style didn't sit well with judges who believed a cowboy should be in control of his ride. Or at least that's what defenders of the judges have maintained through the years. It's hogwash, of course. Said longtime Round-Up official Jack Sweek about cowboys of color competing in early Pendleton rodeos: "For several years, those fellas weren't allowed to finish better than about a third." The color line was firm, never mind how well Fletcher rode.

Spain took the victory lap.

The crowd gave Spain respectful applause as he rode around the track on the trophy saddle. But when Fletcher rode around the track as the runner-up, the crowd went wild with applause. Sheriff Til Taylor decided something needed to be done to try to right the injustice. So he caught up with Fletcher and asked him for his hat. Taylor then cut the hat into pieces and "sold" the felt strips to Pendleton men of means who agreed something should be done to honor Fletcher. When he'd sold enough pieces of the hat to pay for a saddle, Taylor ordered a duplicate of the champion's saddle and presented it to the man whom many people still called Nigger George.

In a fairy-tale world, Fletcher would have gone on to have a stellar rodeo career, receiving the honors he was due as one of the West's great horsemen. That did not happen. Word of his skills as a rider spread after the 1911 Round-Up. The evidence suggests that the men running rodeos didn't want to chance that he might show up a white rider again. In the next few years, he found himself shut out by the big rodeos. When he paid his entry at smaller rodeos, white riders let it be known they would not compete against him. After he was injured in World War I, a career in rodeo was a moot point. He lived the remainder of his years on the Umatilla Reservation, a beloved and honored man who continued to train horses in the old way, without breaking their spirit.

Things might have ended that way. But five years later, Pendleton found a way to redeem itself. Against all odds, Jackson Sundown made it into the short-go with Rufus Rollens and Bronco Bob Hall. Sundown was now fifty-three years old—an incomprehensible age to be competing in a bucking event. He was twice as old as Rollens and Hall. He hadn't even planned on being involved in the 1916 Round-Up at all; after finishing third in 1915, he'd told people that would be his last appearance as a contestant at Pendleton. But sculptor Alexander Phimister Proctor, who was creating a statue of Sundown, convinced the old rider to give the Round-Up one more try and offered to pay his entry fee. So here was Sundown, riding against these two young riders—both white men. Some two hundred Nez Percé had joined the Umatilla, Walla Walla, and Cayuse in the encampment between the arena and the river, so many of Sundown's people watched as he saddled a wild bucker named Angel—he always insisted on saddling his rides himself—and prepared to ride. With his medicine pouch tied behind his ear, his long-haired orange chaps on his legs, and his braids tied beneath his chin and stuffed into the front of his shirt, Sundown mounted Angel to begin his attempt at the championship. Some of the cowboys helping to prep the horse offered advice. Lee Caldwell said, "Scratch 'em from the start. Make a ride in the first three jumps and then clamp down on him and get set for the rest of your ride."

Sundown told Caldwell and the others that he was riding Angel "for everything." Win the event or get bucked off trying.

As the ride began, Angel nearly "bent in two"—in the words of a newspaper reporter—trying to throw Sundown. But Sundown persevered and soon had a long, graceful "lick" going—spurring from Angel's neck down to the cantle of the saddle, over and over, with an almost dancelike elegance. His clearly was the best ride of the short-go. Some old-timers would claim that no one before or since ever had a better ride at Pendleton.

Now it was time for the judges to tally the score and pick a champion. It was a tense moment. Would the best rider receive the trophy saddle? Or would the old racial barriers be respected as they had so many times in the past?

An amazing thing started happening with the nearly all-white audience in the grandstand. These people were only a generation removed from Chief Joseph's War; some of their relatives were no doubt involved in the desecration of Old Joseph's grave. Their grandparents accepted the relegation of Chinese Americans to the underground of Pendleton. These were the same people who called Fletcher "Nigger George" to his face. And yet . . .

They were on their feet, shouting, long before anyone set out to ride around the track in victory. Letting the judges know that a repeat of 1911 was not going to be accepted. Some of these white people ripped up boards from the arena; others pried seats from their moorings. They waved these pieces of the grandstand in the direction of the judges. The message was clear. As an old Sioux cowboy named Phil Lane told Cedric and Tania Wildbill: "Those officials realized that doggone wooden stand was gonna go down to the ground if justice was not done. It was justice, you see. *Justice!*"

Finally the word came over the announcer's megaphones. Jackson Sundown was the saddle bronc champion of the 1916 Pendleton Round-Up and, by extension, the unofficial world champion. Not only that, he was named the rodeo's 1916 all-around cowboy. Sundown grinned, then threw his familiar sombrero high into the air. No one ever took a victory lap in Pendleton in greater triumph.

Sundown never competed at Pendleton again. Nor did he seek the limelight elsewhere. His last public appearance occurred a year later on behalf of Idaho Governor Moses Alexander, the first Jewish governor in the United States. Just seven years after his triumph at Pendleton, Sundown died of pneumonia and was buried near Jacques Spur, Idaho. Inscribed on the stone monument marking his grave are these words: IN 1916 HE WON THE WORLD'S CHAMPIONSHIP AT PENDLETON AND AN OVATION NEVER BEFORE EQUALED.

THE SLACK continues. Now it's steer wrestling. As the men on the field grapple with their steers, a woman climbs the steps and spreads out a quilt on one of the bleachers a couple of sections over from me. She slips out of her street clothes to reveal she's wearing a two-piece bathing suit. She stretches out on her belly, adjusts her sunglasses, and opens a paperback novel. It's that sort of afternoon—relaxed—the exact opposite of what tomorrow will be like when the rodeo proper gets going. Down on the field, a bulldogger charges after a steer and misses it completely. The dogger tumbles head over heels across the grass while the steer trots away. The announcer mentions something about a rider-only hoolihan. The ropers and doggers sitting on horses on either side of the box laugh. In unison, several of them shout, "Let 'er buck!" And they hoot at the cowboy, who hobbles over to retrieve his hat, then trudges back toward the box.

I watch for a while longer, then decide to explore more of Pendleton. As I stop at a train crossing, I find myself haunted by the memory of a dream, a dream I used to have about finding Cowboy Don.

It went something like this: I'd travel to one of those places dominated by open spaces, a big sky, a long horizon. Desert country, usually—though not always. Arizona or New Mexico, although sometimes it was West Texas or a remote town in Southern California. Once or twice it was Montana, the fast-flowing Missouri River nearby, a purple etching of mountains in the distance.

I'd drive a rental car up to a tavern made of cinder blocks, although I remember one fanciful version of the dream in which the tavern was adobe. I'd walk into the tavern and blink until my eyes adjusted to the darkness. For some reason, it was always late morning in the dream, and the bar would be nearly empty, Merle Haggard singing from the jukebox. Always Merle Haggard.

I'd spot him on a stool—no mistaking him. Sweat-stained Resistol cowboy hat, pearl-snap cowboy shirt, Levi's or Wranglers faded to the color of Paul Newman's eyes. In every version of the dream, he'd look just like the actor and rodeo star Ben Johnson. Not Ben Johnson as the dashing young Sergeant Tyree from the John Ford cavalry trilogy, but the wizened Ben Johnson from the Peckinpah years or from Peter Bogdanovich's *The Last Picture Show*. A man with a lot of hard times on the road engraved on his face—wrinkles, a couple of weeks' worth of sparse beard on his cheeks. He'd be bantering with the barmaid, eyes mischievous, smile flashing.

Then he'd look over at me.

In the moment of recognition, the repartee would come to an abrupt halt. An uneasy minute or two of no conversation, Merle singing about white line fever in the background. Then a handshake, a clasping of shoulders, a *let me buy you a beer*. We'd talk for a couple of hours, catching up on each other's lives. As we'd talk, we'd relax, realizing we were not headed for conflict. No recriminations. Just good talk, getting to know each other. A little.

Finally, we'd talk ourselves out, a row of dead longnecks on the bar in front of us, labels peeled off by nervous fingers and wadded into ashtrays. I'd get up to leave, a little unsteady from the beer. We'd walk out of the tavern together, into the blinding sunlight. A few words of parting, an embrace and a smile, the aroma of leather, old denim, beer, cigarettes, and sweat coming off him. I'd go to my car, he'd climb into his decrepit pickup with the beat-up shell camper.

And that would be it.

We'd leave knowing there'd be an occasional phone call, an occasional Christmas card, but we'd never see each other again. No need for it. We had just come together to fill in some holes, and now the work was done.

The last car of the train clatters past and jars me back to reality. The ringing of the bell abruptly ceases as the crossarm rises. I drive onward, thinking to myself that Pendleton would have been the perfect setting for the dream. Too bad it never came true.

I GO TO MY motel room and sit at a rickety table next to a window. I can smell curry cooking. The motel is operated by a family originally from India, so I guess that explains the curry. Still, it seems like the last fragrance you'd expect to find in a place as isolated as Pendleton. I close my eyes and ponder the dream and think back to the first time I came to Oregon.

It is five years earlier, in Portland. The sun-dappled campus of the Oregon Health Science University is far removed from any rodeo arena. No cowboys up here on Portland's Marquam Hill—called Pill Hill by the locals. I haven't seen a single Western hat. Mostly there are just people half my age in lab coats scurrying from building to building. A huge white marble head—that's the landmark I've been told to look for. It doesn't take too long to find it. I enter the building adjacent to it and go to the offices of the medical school's cadaver donation program. A few minutes later, I leave the building with a shoe box–size cardboard container wrapped in white paper. On one end is a label: CREMAINS OF ID:128295/SSAN: 524-22-8036/DEATH DATE: 10-7-92/CREMATION DATE: 8-1-94/COMMENTS: OHSU TO DISPOSE. That last line has been scribbled over with red ink now that I'm here to tend to Cowboy Don's ashes.

"Well, ol' 128295," I say aloud, "I guess I finally caught up with you."

A woman in a lab coat standing next to the big white head looks up at me from her notebook. Then she seems embarrassed that I caught her looking. Her eyes dart back to her notebook. I tuck the box back under my arm. In a few minutes, I'm on the interstate, headed for Salem.

DAMN, I'm thinking as I sit in the shadowy motel room in Pendleton, five years later. *Damn, damn, damn.* I wish it hadn't been that way. The fantasy of meeting a real-life cowboy who's a Ben Johnson look-alike in a beer joint was, of course, immeasurably better than what I got: a bag of gray powder finer than talcum, stuffed into a shoe box. On the other hand, finding Cowboy Don at all, even after he was dead, was no easy task. It took about six months and required the help of a mystery man I never met in person.

I started looking for Cowboy Don in earnest in January 1997. I had just started a new job. I had an office in the hills that abut Lake Austin. A beautiful area. But a particularly hazardous area to navigate whenever Austin gets its once-every-six-years ice storm. Two weeks after I started my new job, just such a storm hit, encasing buildings, trees, power lines, lawns, and especially roadways in an icy Saran Wrap. Because I'd just started the job, I felt obliged to make it to work in spite of the dangerous driving conditions. As it turned out, only one other person in the entire building had the same sense of foolhardy dedication that I did. I sat down at my desk and started my computer. I didn't have any work to do, so I began surfing the Internet. For some reason, I ended up at a missing-persons Web site, and on a whim, I decided to post an inquiry about Cowboy Don.

Before the day was through, I received an e-mail from a man in Denver offering to help. Because of his own family situation, he'd taken it upon himself to help relatives get together. Over the next few months, he did a lot of footwork in Denver. He sent me photocopies of information he'd found in city directories as well as a few public records. We continued to communicate until the summer. Then one day he sent me an e-mail saying that while he couldn't say so for sure, he believed Cowboy Don was probably dead. He recommended that I do a Web search for the Social Security Death Index. Check the names, he advised.

I found the Social Security Death Index on a genealogy Web site, searched for Don Stratton, and located a record that most likely was his. It showed that he had died not quite five years earlier, with Aumsville, Oregon, as his last address of record. Hoping I might be able to get a death certificate to shed light on the mystery of Cowboy Don, I searched for contact information for Oregon death certificates. I wrote down the phone number and other details on a legal pad. And then I did nothing more about it for a year. The legal pad lay on my desk, and I'd look at that number every day I was in the office, but I couldn't bring myself to call it. Killing a dream is a hard thing to do.

The next summer I finally called the number on the legal pad. I gave the man on the other end of the line my Visa credit card number and requested that the certificate be shipped by Federal Express. Two days later, I nervously opened the packet. Lung cancer—that's what killed him. He'd died in a nursing home in Salem, just up the highway from Aumsville. No next of kin were listed. Instead, Frank Blair's name appeared. Whoever typed the form x-ed over the word *relative* and typed *friend* in its place. The name of the funeral home that took charge of the body was listed. And that's about all.

I picked up my office telephone and called the funeral home, explaining that I was inquiring about the funeral for my runaway father. The woman I spoke to put me on hold to pull some files. When she came back on the line, she told me no funeral had occurred. Cowboy Don's body had been donated to the medical school in Portland. His friend Frank Blair said that had been Cowboy Don's wish. Did I have Frank Blair's phone number?

After I hung up, I took a deep breath and called Frank. We talked for more than two hours.

That night I told my wife what had happened that day.

"You should call the medical school," she said. "They might have his ashes. Sometimes they do that with a cadaver once they're finished with it—in case the family might want to have a service of some sort."

The next day, I telephoned the Oregon Health Sciences University. Don Carlos Stratton Jr.'s cremains were in storage. If I wanted to claim them, I could do so.

A week later, I was on an America West flight for Portland, my instructions for finding the gigantic white head scribbled on a wad of paper stuffed into my pocket.

I'M STANDING outside the grandstand before the start of the first full day of the 2003 Pendleton Round-Up. I see Justin McKee climbing the steps to the announcer's booth, and I'm glad he'll be calling the rodeo. A few moments later, I run across Flint Rasmussen in his clown paint. Good, he'll be performing here, too. I'm looking forward to hearing a continuation of the repartee between McKee and Rasmussen that I heard in Cheyenne. I move to an unshaded platform, adjacent to the track, that is reserved for the press.

As I watch the grand entry into this ancient arena, I decide that the Pendleton Round-Up is going to be the finest rodeo I'll see this year. The six hundred or so contestants will include the top-ranked riders, ropers, and bulldoggers on the PRCA circuit. So there's no question about the quality of the competition. The grand thing is that they will be competing here in this old arena in front of people who cling to something indefinable yet important—call it quality—at a time when the rest of the country seems to be willing to flush it away.

The grand entry is a long procession featuring all sorts of honorees, including representatives from the Happy Canyon pageant, which takes place next door to the rodeo arena—"The colorful night show takes you into the past to relive the lives of our forefathers . . . the story begins with the Indians in their native surroundings, highlighted by their colorful dress and a portrayal of their early American cultures . . . the emigrants come—they fight—then peace, and the scenery changes to a brawling frontier town." The Native American princesses from Happy Canyon are elegant in their regalia, even the one young woman who wears a pair of Nike soccer slides over her moccasins, which have intricate white beadwork.

The highlight of the grand entry is the appearance of the Round-Up royalty. Led by queen Darla Severe, the five women jump their horses over the fence, separating the track from the infield, while bearing flags. As they race around the arena, they elicit rousing applause. The royalty at Pendleton has a rich tradition to draw upon. Joan Burbick writes in *Rodeo Queens and the American Dream:*

In the 1910s, the roundup introduced rodeo queens from varied backgrounds. In these early years, queens included movie stars such as Mary Duncan and Josie Sedgwick, the famous rodeo cowgirl Mabel Strickland, and daughters of local businessmen and ranchers drawn from both the Indian and white communities. In that period, rodeo queens could also be rodeo cowgirls. They rode trick horses, roped, raced, and competed with bucking horses and bulls. Mabel Strickland was a good example. Queen of the Pendleton Round-Up in 1927, she had petitioned the rodeo board to compete directly with men for the title of all-around rodeo cowboy. She was refused.

I don't know how well any of the present royalty would fare in traditional rodeo events, but I know they're the most skilled rodeo royalty I've seen this year. All have been riding for almost as long as they have been able to walk. Darla Severe is also a track athlete who competes on the varsity squad at Utah Valley State College.

As the queen and her court race across the infield, Justin McKee intones, "They're beautiful on the TV cameras and—well, they're just beautiful to boot." It's hard to argue with him. They are wearing timeless Western outfits that would have been as appropriate in 1953 as they are in 2003. Farrah Fawcett hairdos are missing. Burbick writes, "The Pendleton Round-Up insisted that its rodeo royalty appear only in pageboy cuts, even if it meant wearing a wig to hide the teased hair or massive perms. Bouffant hairstyles beware." This year's court has eschewed wigs. The short hair is real and, like their outfits, timeless.

The rodeo begins with bareback riding. Indian relay racing follows—the first time I've seen an event quite like this. In the first heat, four teams compete, one from the Colville Nation in Washington, one from the Warm Springs Nation in Oregon, and two from the Okanagon Nation in British Columbia. Some of the horses are Appaloosas, the spotted breed of the Nez Percé. Some wear paint, just as their riders do. The horses are ridden bareback. Some of the riders wear nothing more than a breechcloth and moccasins. The race starts across the arena from me. The horses quickly round the end of the oval racetrack and thunder past the platform where I'm sitting.

"Have you ever seen this before?" a local reporter next to me asks.

"No, my first time here," I say.

"These guys are the best athletes in the whole rodeo," he says.

I believe him. I ponder my own limited skills as a rider, then try to imagine myself on the bare back of a spotted horse wearing war paint, galloping full blast around the racetrack. I'm certain I would fall off before the horse makes the first turn. And there's no way I could even begin to do what I see happening across the arena from me now. Once he's finished one lap of the track, the rider dismounts from his horse, scarcely slowing down to do so. One of his team members, waiting on the track at the start line, catches his horse. The rider rushes to his next mount, which is being held by another member of the three-person team. The rider leaps on board the fresh horse and takes off again, whipping the loose ends of the reins from side to side to encourage it to gallop faster.

The reporter says, "These races get pretty wild. They always have to haul some of these guys out of here on stretchers."

I believe him about that, too.

There will be three heats of Indian relay racing today, with more teams from the Colville and Warm Springs nations, as well as groups from the neighboring Umatilla Reservation and from the Crow Reservation in Montana. For me, watching these races would in itself be worth the fifteen-dollar price of admission.

During a break between events, Flint Rasmussen scolds a teenager who's talking on a cell phone during the rodeo. "If there's one thing that doesn't belong at a rodeo," Rasmussen says to McKee, "it's a cell phone. Leave 'em at home." McKee agrees. I find myself nodding. A cell phone is anathema to the whole spirit of the Pendleton Round-Up. Almost as bad as a handheld computer. I see the teenager Rasmussen scolded. She's still on her phone. I don't think she even heard him.

The rodeo continues through a full menu of saddle bronc riding, bulldogging, calf roping (which is still called calf roping at Pendleton, not tie-down roping), steer roping, team roping, barrel racing, and bull riding. The bull riding is split into two sections. Once the first section is over, dozens of the Native Americans encamped along the Umatilla River march onto the infield and begin dancing. The yellows, reds, blues, and greens of their outfits are vibrant in the afternoon sun. Some of the dancers look to be more than sixty years old. Some can be no older than two or three. After the dancing has gone on for a while, an announcer on the infield reads off a list of winners in the dance competition. The drumming and singing goes on for a few minutes longer. Then the dancers leave the field and the bull riding resumes.

The final event at the Pendleton Round-Up is something of a rarity in rodeo: wild-cow milking. Wild-cow milking turns the arena into mayhem as two-man teams of locals attempt to collect a squirt or two of milk from an anything-but-tame mother cow. There are fifteen teams down there now, each doing its best to separate a cow from the herd. The cows are having no part of it though. Eventually someone runs across a finish line holding a bottle with some milk in it. And the competition is over. But before that happens, the contestants' neighbors up in the stands get a lot of laughs out of watching them stumble, get kicked, and get stepped on.

I leave before the wild-cow milking is finished and head to the Let 'Er Buck Room.

I'M NOT SURE which is more dangerous, taking part in the wild cow–milking contest or trying to get to the bar in the Let 'Er Buck Room after the rodeo. The Let 'Er Buck Room is built into the side of the arena and is open for business during each rodeo performance and for a couple of hours afterward to serve rodeo contestants and fans alike. Then the management pulls the plug on the drinks and the crowd reluctantly ambles away to find another place for booze. There's no beer served in the Let 'Er Buck Room, just hard liquor. The whiskey-fueled high jinks in the Let 'Er Buck Room have taken on a mythology of their own, sometimes rivaling the feats that occur in the arena itself—or so I've heard. Things get wild enough in there that there's an unwritten rule at Pendleton: What happens in the Let 'Er Buck Room stays in the Let 'Er Buck Room. So, of course, I'm curious.

I buy drink tokens at a booth near the door, then worm my way through the crowd. As soon as I get my drink, I turn around—and immediately I feel a pair of hands slide into the back pockets of my Levi's and squeeze my ass. Behind me is a short woman with red hair. "It's all right, darlin'," she says. "I just need a big guy like you to plow through these people so I can get out of here." I oblige by shouldering my way through the all but impenetrable crush of bodies between us and the door, her hands in my back pockets the whole time. When we reach the door, she gives me a quick peck on the cheek and says, "Thanks, darlin'," before disappearing into the sunlight.

I hear some whooping coming from near the bar. In a small clearing near one of the posts supporting the ceiling, I see a young woman taking off her jeans. Now she's holding up the jeans and the people surrounding her—almost all men—whoop some more. She is wearing a straw hat, a Western shirt, a thong, and nothing else. I recognize the guy standing next to her as a bareback rider. She holds her jeans up again, the crowd hollers, and the bareback rider shrugs and starts pulling off his boots. Soon he has his jeans off, too. He gives his jeans to her; she gives hers to him. And they put on each other's jeans. The jeans seem to fit pretty well, although her Rockies might be just a tad snug on him.

"How's it feel?" someone asks the bareback rider.

"They feel pretty good."

The guy standing next to the bareback rider says, "And those Rockies *look* pretty damned good on you, too. Maybe you should wear them all the time."

The bareback rider turns to the guy and kisses him on the lips. Everyone around him hoots. The girl with the bareback rider blushes. Let 'er buck!

While I'm watching this, I feel a pair of arms encircle my waist. "What's goin' on over there?" a woman asks me.

I turn around. She is maybe thirty, wearing black jeans, a black knit top, and black sandals. She is as thin as an aerobics instructor, with short brown hair with a lot of highlights. She's wearing just a little too much makeup. "Just a guy and his honey trading their jeans," I say.

"And I missed it! Damn! Let me hear you say something again."

"What do you want to hear me say?" I ask.

"That's good enough," she says. "You're from Texas, aren't you, babe?"

I smile. "Yeah, I am."

"Do you know what hearing that accent does to us girls up here in Oregon? It makes us all—well, squirmy."

"That's nice to know," I say. I suppose I'm grinning like some middle-aged idiot. The wedding band I'm wearing doesn't seem to be an obstacle for her.

"So are you a roper? Let me see your hands." She takes my hand and examines it in the dim light. "Ooooo," she coos. "You have big, *strong* hands. I bet you *are* a roper. Let me see."

She tugs on the cord attached to my media credentials, which I have stuffed into the pocket of my Panhandle Slim shirt. She squints at it as I say, "No, I'm a writer."

"A rider?" she says, scrunching her face. "You ride saddle broncs?"

"No, no—a *writer*."

She still doesn't get it.

Just then, a mountain of a man in a black hat steps up behind her and reaches around to grasp her breasts. She twists her head around and says, "Well, hey there, honey. I wondered where you went." She moves backward and twitches her butt into his groin.

"I jes went to fetch me another drank of whiskey," he says drunkenly.

"This guy's a rider from Texas," she says, nodding toward me.

The guy removes his right paw from her breast and extends it toward me. His hand swallows mine as we shake. "Yeah, I seen you ride this afternoon. You drawed a good horse."

"No," I said, "I'm a *writer*." But it's as lost on him as it is on the woman in black. I have an urge to thank him for showing up. I do believe he's rescued me. I gulp down the last of my vodka and hold up my empty glass to the man-mountain and the woman in black. "I'm going to get another," I say and they nod.

I squeeze my way to the bar and order another vodka.

When it arrives, I gulp down half of it in one swallow. Then I head to the opposite end of the Let 'Er Buck Room, hoping to avoid the man-mountain and the woman in black. Along the way, about a half dozen women reach over to squeeze my ass as I move past them. I stop at a cluster of men who are shouting. I look over their shoulders to see a woman with her shirt unbuttoned, revealing her breasts. A man in front of her stoops to plaster a small sticker advertising Jack Daniels above her nipple. He delicately blows on the sticker once it's in place. When he straightens up, the men behind him slap his back and congratulate him for a job well done. *Let 'er buck!*

I turn and step into a man and a woman.

"Well, hello there," he says.

"I'm sorry," I say. "I didn't know you were behind me."

"Oh, hell, that's all right."

The woman has one arm around the man. She uses her free hand to reach around and pat me on the butt. Then she laughs. I laugh, too. Both the woman and the man appear to be in their fifties. Their faces are dark and heavily lined, so I know they both spend a lot of time outdoors. They turn out to be married. They have a place a few miles out of town where they live and raise horses. They also own a small business in Pendleton.

"Your first time here?" the woman asks.

"Yes it is."

"Kinda thought so," said her husband. "You're lookin' a little shell-shocked."

"Well, I've never been anywhere quite like this."

"But the important thing is," he says, "are you havin' a good time?"

"Oh yes," I say.

The woman says, "The Let 'Er Buck Room used to be even more fun. But the young people have hurt it a lot, especially on Fridays and Saturdays."

"That's right," says the man. "We don't even bother comin' in here after the Friday and Saturday rodeos."

"Oh, it's just gotten—" He's interrupted by squeals coming from behind him. We look to see yet another woman baring her breasts. The man raises his drink in her direction. He turns back to me. "You know how the young people are. It's just gotten out of hand."

And I'm thinking to myself, *This isn't out of hand?*

Before I can ask just *how* it's gotten out of hand on Fridays and Saturdays, the man and the woman start walking away from me. She looks over her shoulder and says, "You have a great time while you're in Pendleton." She winks. Then they're gone.

I'm walking back across the room when I feel a hand on my shoulder and hear a voice say, "Where'd you run off to?"

I pivot and see that it's the woman in black. Man-mountain is nowhere to be seen.

"Where's your friend?" I ask.

The woman in black says, "She's right here." I'd meant man-mountain when I asked about her friend, but she thought I was talking about someone else, I guess. She reaches behind her and grasps the hand of a woman about her age with brown eyes and long brown hair. She's shorter and chunkier than the woman in black. "Here's a guy from Texas," the woman in black says to her friend.

"Mmm," the friend says, "we just love to hear you guys from Texas talk."

"So I heard," I say.

"Ooo, you *do* sound like you live in Texas. You want to see my stickers?"

Before I can answer, she's raised her T-shirt and I see five stickers plastered on and around her breasts. She lowers her shirt and grins.

"Thank you," I say awkwardly. She grins bigger.

The woman in black steps between me and her friend and presses her back against my chest and pushes her butt against my crotch. She says to her friend, "I found him first."

"I thought you were with that big guy," I say.

"Him?" she says, looking up at me over her shoulder. "Oh, he's just a Pendleton asshole. Been trying to lose him all afternoon."

"Looks like you're fond of cowboys."

"Honey, I live and breathe cowboys—when I have the time to."

"What do you do the rest of the time?"

She sips her drink. "Surgical nurse. I spend a lot of long shifts with surgeons who think they're God's gift to the world—and especially God's gift to women. Assholes." She grimaces, hits her drink again. "You know, honey, you're about halfway cute."

"Uh, thanks." Now I hit my drink. "What makes cowboys better than doctors?"

She steps away from me and turns to face me. She puts her hand on my chest. "Ev-er-y-thing." She smiles and leans into me. "So what do you Texas guys think of us Oregon girls?"

"I think you're—nice," I say.

"You gonna come dancing with us tonight? A lot of the cowboys from the rodeo will be there."

"Where are you going to be?"

She gives me an incredulous look, as if she's wondering just how stupid I could be. "Well, Crabby's, of course."

"Crabby's?"

"Don't say you've never heard of it."

I shrug.

She says, "Well, it's the only place to dance in Pendleton." She turns to her friend. "Tell him how to get to Crabby's."

Her friend looks up at me, her face bright. "You gonna go dancing?"

"Sure, I'll be there."

She tells me how to get to Crabby's. I've driven around Pendleton enough to have a pretty good idea of how to follow her directions. "I'm glad you're coming," she says.

"I'll see y'all there," I say.

"God, we love how you Texans talk."

I walk to the back of the Let 'Er Buck Room. I stop and look back at the horde between me and the bar. The last call for drinks goes out and the throng presses closer to the besieged bartenders.

"Must be your first time here," someone says to me.

To my left is a woman I'd guess to be in her mid-thirties. She's maybe a couple of inches above five feet tall, with reddish brown hair and a spray of freckles across her cheeks and nose. She wears frameless glasses over her pale green eyes. She has a bookish air about her—maybe she's a librarian.

"It's that obvious, huh?" I say.

"You have that deer-in-the-headlights look going for you."

I nod. "Well, I just had my first-ever up-close and personal encounter with a couple of buckle bunnies."

She scrunches her nose as if she'd just smelled something bad. "Buckle bunnies?"

"Rodeo groupies."

She gives her head a couple of exaggerated shakes and says, "I see. If I had to guess, I'd have to say about half the people in this room would fall into that category, in one way or another."

"Think so?"

"Yes I do. Where are you from, anyway?"

"Austin, Texas."

"Really? You don't sound like it. You don't have an accent."

"Huh," I say. "Those two women were just telling me how much they liked my Texas accent."

"And you believed that bullshit?"

I laughed and said, "I'd like to say that I didn't believe a single word of it."

"And you'd be a liar, right?"

"Probably so."

She gives me an all-knowing nod. I tip my Resistol to her and step outside into the clean sunlight.

FOLLOWING the Territorial Indian Wars of 1855–58, Joe Crabb opened Crabb's Roadhouse in what's now Pendleton. The roadhouse served thirsty travelers on the road between Boise, Idaho, and Umatilla, Oregon—a town located at the confluence of the Umatilla and Columbia rivers. Crabby's Underground Saloon and Steakhouse was named in Joe Crabb's honor. I arrive a little after eight, pay a cover charge, and descend a flight of stairs to the basement restaurant and bar. It's crowded already, although nothing at all like the Let 'Er Buck Room. Not many rodeo cowboys are here yet, although the woman in black and her friend have found some men to dance with as the band plays a cover of a Merle Haggard song. I go to the bar to order a beer and I encounter a bull rider who'd taken a drilling earlier in the day.

"How you doing?" I ask.

"Oh, I'm okay," he says. "Just left the hospital and decided to come over here to see what was going on."

Just as his bull left the chute this afternoon, the rider failed to react to a twisting buck the bull made. The rider went flying over the bull's head, a disastrous way to take a spill. As he was falling, the bull caught him in the face with one of its horns. Two of the best bullfighters in the business, Lloyd Ketchum and Joe Baumgartner, are working the Round-Up this year, and they adroitly led the bull away from the fallen rider. I saw blood on the rider's face and neck as he was helped out of the arena.

"Glad you're feeling okay," I say.

"Yeah, well—" He touches a bandage on his cheek. "Damned ol' horn punched a hole clean through. I wanted the doctor to stitch it up, but he wouldn't do it. Said it would leave too bad a scar. I told him I didn't care about the scar, I just didn't want it to bleed all night. But, no, he stuck by his guns. All he'd do is butterfly it. So here I am. Can't get the thing to stop bleedin'. Oh well." And as if to emphasize the point, a droplet of blood dribbles down his cheek, off his jaw, and onto his shirt.

"You ready to go dance some?" he asks the woman he's hugging. She nods. He says to me, "Good talkin' to you."

"You too," I say. "Glad you came out of it not hurt too bad."

"You and me both, cowboy. Just wish that doctor woulda stitched it."

He and his lady friend step out onto the dance floor. I'll see them dancing throughout the night, blood dripping onto his shirt the whole time.

I carry my beer over to a bench against the wall and take a seat. Soon I'm introducing myself to some local couples about my age who are sitting nearby. It's hard to have much of a conversation over the band—all covers, "Margaritaville" to "Today I Started Loving You Again"—but they're friendly people, and I'm glad to meet them. Maybe feeling sorry for me because I'm there by myself, a woman or two invites me to take a turn on the dance floor. I do my best awkward attempt at a two-step—and have a great time doing it. I notice more and more rodeo cowboys are showing up. At one point, while I'm out dancing to "Silver Wings," I see the bareback rider and the woman with whom he traded jeans. I can't tell if he is still wearing her Rockies, but they are having a fine time tripping the light fantastic.

I leave with some of the locals and walk with them to the Rainbow Café, one of Pendleton's well-known landmarks. Café is a bit of a misnomer, although you can buy food at the Rainbow. The reason the place is a landmark is because it is a sure-enough damned fine bar. There's the bar on your right, a line of booths on your left. Not much to get between you and your shot and beer in here. The ceiling's high. The walls are covered with photos and other memorabilia documenting ninety years of Round-Up history—with a few racks of deer and elk antlers thrown in for good measure.

The problem with the Rainbow during Round-Up is getting in the place. It's by far more crowded than either Crabby's or the Let 'Er Buck Room. I drink a couple of beers while standing in the back of the building. I long ago lost count of how many drinks I've had today. I bring the beer can to my lips and think, *Here I am, eyeball deep in Cowboy Don's world.* He downed one or two beers in the Rainbow himself in his day. *"Salud,"* I say and lift my beer to him.

WHEN I GET back to the motel, I lie in the bed staring at the shadows on the ceiling and think about Cowboy Don. And that trip to Oregon five years earlier.

I spent the better part of a day near Turner, Oregon, with Frank Blair and his wife Jo-An. We sat in their well-worn Winnebago motor home, drank coffee, and talked. They gave me what few artifacts remained from Cowboy Don's life. His wallet, his address book—not much more. Frank regaled me with stories about Cowboy Don. I, in turn, filled in Frank and Jo-An on aspects of Cowboy Don's life they never knew about. "Don never talked about his past," Frank told me. "He mentioned that he had a sister in Denver and a half sister somewhere back East. He had a brother or half brother or something in California and Don *hated* him."

"Is that right?"

"Oh yeah, but I don't know what the problem was between them. I never figured it was my business. That's about all I knew. I do remember that years ago his mother died and he went off somewhere to take care of it—"

"Albuquerque," I said.

"Albuquerque you say? Well, he didn't say where. He'd leave every now and then and be gone for days at a time. He'd be checking up on something. Then he'd show back up and act like he'd never even been gone. He wouldn't say where he was going or what he was doing. But I know he kept track of a lot of things. He wouldn't talk about it or anything. Hmm, Albuquerque, huh?"

I nodded. Albuquerque.

After Cowboy Don's last wife divorced him, he lived out of the camper on his pickup, which he parked at Frank's place. He took up with a woman who had the same name as a famous actress and moved in with her. But when the symptoms of his cancer showed up, she didn't want to deal with it and threw him out. Cowboy Don was too ill to protest much when the woman and her relatives carted away the few belongings he had left. He retreated to Frank's place with little more than his pickup and the clothes on his back.

Frank and I walked out to the road and he showed me where Cowboy Don's pickup had been parked. It was now a thicket of blackberries.

"I sold his pickup after he died," Frank said. "I didn't know he had any relatives who might be interested—"

"That's okay, Frank," I said. "You deserved whatever money you made off it for taking care of him at the end."

"Well—," he said. "He was my friend."

"What was he like?" I asked. "What did he like to do?"

"He mostly liked to keep to himself. He always drank beer,

but as he got older, he didn't like to go to taverns or anything. He was always reading something. Mostly those detective magazines and paperback books. He liked to listen to country music."

"Merle Haggard?"

"Oh yeah, yeah. He liked him. I got him interested in going up into the mountains camping. And he got to where he liked to do that some. We'd go into Salem and eat out. He really liked Chinese food."

"But he never went to rodeos in his later years?"

"No, that was all behind him. He loved horses. He'd stop and look at 'em every chance he got. But, no, not the rodeo."

Frank and I stepped over to the rental car. I opened the trunk and showed him the box containing Cowboy Don's cremains. Frank didn't seem very interested in it.

"You know," Frank said after I shut the trunk, "Don sure coulda used you there at the end. He needed someone."

"Yeah, I wish I'd known how to get ahold of him."

Frank's short white hair flickered in the breeze. "Like I was telling you, Don kept track of people and stuff. I think he knew your mom married a man who could provide you with the kind of home he never could. I'd say he probably went to Oklahoma and drove right by the house where you lived to check it out. He could see how you were living, and he'd know he could never give you anything like that. Knowin' Don, it wouldn't surprise me if he didn't stick around long enough to see you playing in the front yard of your house there when you were a kid. I think he decided it was best if he just stayed away and let your mom and your stepdaddy raise you—that you'd turn out better that way." Frank was silent for a moment. Then he said, "He knew what he was. And he knew what he wasn't."

"You think so?"

"Yes—but he sure coulda used you when he was so sick."

Frank and I shook hands and I drove back to Salem. That evening I ate at Cowboy Don's favorite Chinese restaurant. The next day, I was up at dawn. While I ate breakfast, I decided I'd scatter half of the cremains in Oregon and bring the other half to Texas. I stopped by an Albertson's supermarket and bought an airtight plastic container. In the parking lot, I opened the sack inside the box containing the cremains. I poured about half of them into the container and sealed the lid—leaving some traces of Cowboy Don on the carpet in the trunk. I put the sack with the rest of the cremains back into the box and shut the trunk. I started driving, not really sure where to go.

I ended up on the highway that leads to Bend, Oregon. There was a motorcycle rally occurring in Bend that day, and it seemed that the only people on the highway were me in my rental car and about ten thousand bikers. The bikers and I navigated sharp turns and switchbacks as the fir-shaded highway climbed high into the Cascades.

Near Marion Forks, I pulled off the highway onto a short road that dipped down to a bend in the North Santiam River. A gravel bar topped by the bone gray trunk of a fallen spruce occupied the center of the stream. I killed the engine and eyed the scene. The swift water bubbled as it spread out over the gravel. Thick stands of trees sixty feet tall shuttered each side of the river. Here. This is the place.

I retrieved the bag of cremains from the box in the trunk and carried it down to the water. I walked into the river out on the gravel. The frigid water swept over my Stan Smith tennis sneakers and soaked my Levi's. I remembered the story about Cowboy Don's falling into the Columbia and how he was afraid of water ever after. But I figured whatever he knew of fear went up the smokestack at the crematorium. I'm sure he would have appreciated this bend in the river. I opened the bag and poured the mineral essence of him into the stream. I stood there, my feet numbed by the river, until the gray blossom formed by the cremains went away. "Adios," I said, my voice sounding as strange to me as Nick Adams's sounded to him in the darkening woods along the Big Two-Hearted River. Like Nick, I decided not to say anything else.

I wadded up the bag, stuffed it into the box, turned around, and walked out of the water. While I had been in the river, two bikers had pulled off the highway. They had parked their motorcycles next to my rental car. They leaned against their bikes and watched me while they smoked cigarettes. They were true bikers, not accountants pretending to be something they're not while mounted on Harleys on the weekends. Their arms, bare in the cool mountain air, bore a lot of ink. Over their T-shirts they wore Levi's jackets with the sleeves ripped off. I could tell there were colors of some sort on the backs of the jackets. Both men were bearded and wore their hair down to their shoulders.

I opened the rental car trunk and dropped the crumpled bag and box into it. As I closed the trunk, the biker closest to me raised his hand to give me a brief wave. He nodded at me— a sort of unspoken acknowledgment that we're all in *this*— whatever it is—together. I nodded back, climbed into the car, and wept for the first time in years, as a thirty-year-old Jerry Garcia song played on the radio.

MY NEIGHBORS at the motel have come down from Yakima, Washington, for the Round-Up. They've set up lawn chairs outside the doors to their motel rooms. Liquor bottles line the window frames of their rooms. They have charcoal grills in the parking lot between their pickups. *They know how to have a good time at Round-Up,* I tell myself. They're sipping Bloody Marys as I leave my room.

"There's a man who looks like he could use a drink," a shirtless man wearing shorts and a cowboy hat says to me. "Care for a Bloody Mary?"

My head already is throbbing. I'm too damned old to be hungover like this. The thought of drinking a Bloody Mary is enough to give me the dry heaves. "No, thanks," I say.

"Well, help yourself if you change your mind later."

"I will. Thanks."

There's a Denny's nearby and I head in that direction. Once inside, I force down some eggs and coffee, hoping I'll start feeling better. I don't. While I'm eating, Jesse Bail calls my cell phone. We agree to meet later that morning in the cowboys' ready area, which is nothing more than a patch of bare ground across from the Justin Sports Medicine trailer outside the arena.

Jesse's obviously had an easier night than I have. He's looking particularly spry and clear-eyed this morning. He has a new black felt hat on his head.

"I need to get this shaped," he says. "We can talk while I'm doing that."

"Sounds good."

I follow Jesse around the track. We exit the rodeo grounds and cross Court Street to the vast encampment of vendors opposite the arena. Jesse leads me to the Copenhagen trailer. Attached to the side of the trailer is a large canopy with wooden siding affixed to it to form a long narrow room. Inside is a casino setup—and music is blaring, each thud of the woofers driving spikes into my ravaged brain. The bare-bellied young women in charge of the room walk over to stop us. But when they recognize Jesse, they let us through, all of them smiling at him. Jesse steps up to a man, shakes his hand, and says something to him while pointing at me. The man eyes me, then nods. Jesse gestures for me to follow him. We climb into the trailer and go to a small room that's blessedly dim. With the door closed, I can barely hear the music from outside. It's good to be able to kick back with Jesse.

"Did you drive out here?" I ask.

"Oh yeah," he replies with that one-of-a-kind voice that resounds of wind through barbed wire, a coyote call on a winter midnight, the bark of a cattle auctioneer, and, more than anything else, the conversations you have with yourself when you're a long way from anyone else. "I parked the camper out at Severe's bunkhouse."

"Pretty good place?"

"Yeah, I like it out there."

The day before, a photographer and former rodeo princess named Sheila Addleman told me about Severe's bunkhouse. Addleman grew up "over the hill" in La Grande, Oregon. Though she's lived in Seattle for a long time, the Round-Up brings her back to eastern Oregon year after year. With her camera in hand, she's a regular on the arena floor. She has the scoop on what goes on during Round-Up, including at Severe's bunkhouse. The Severes are one of Pendleton's best-known families and have long had an association with the rodeo. This year's Round-Up queen is Darla Severe. Since 1955 the Severes have operated a high-quality saddlery, and they provide some of the Round-Up trophy saddles. For years, they've allowed cowboys in town for the Round-Up to stay at a bunkhouse near the saddlery. Addleman told me that she and a girlfriend once went out there to check it out. "They charged the cowboys about twenty dollars to flop there," she said. "There was a lotta drinking and a lotta bullshitting going on. No girls allowed, unless they were doin' one of the cowboys. Neither my friend or I were up to that, but we got in, anyway. I remember old Duff Severe playing his banjo out there—stopping every so often to signal someone to bring him a drink of whiskey."

I say to Jesse, "I've heard it's kind of fun out there."

"Yeah, I guess it is," he grins.

We talk about Jesse's early life. His dad, Wade, was a bull and saddle bronc rider. But Jesse's mother, Bunny, raised him and his sisters on her parents' ranch outside Camp Crook. "Not for dang sure just how big it is, probably ten thousand acres, but that's kind of a guess. We run—I don't know—maybe six, seven hundred head of cows and about a hundred head of horses up there. Camp Crook is right in the northwest corner of South Dakota. The ranch is mostly just rolling hills, but it's got a little of everything, some badlands. My mom, she rodeoed a lot, just amateur rodeoing—barrel racing and breakaway roping and little bit of everything, training barrel horses and stuff, which she still does. So I've always been around it. I guess you could say I kinda grew up on my grandpa's ranch riding young horses and stuff."

From the time he was barely able to walk, he was going to "all-girl" rodeos, where Bunny would participate. At other times, they'd go to rodeos where women competed only in barrel racing and breakaway roping while men took part in the other events. Jesse learned to rope when he was very young, and while his mother was busy in the arena, he'd be roping the dummy calves back by the pens, sometimes taking money off other kids in bets. But when it came time for the rough-stock events, Jesse put away his rope and paid careful attention. Bunny noticed that he studied every ride. These rodeos are burned into Jesse's memory. When I suggest to him that he's been to so many rodeos he probably can't remember the first one he went to, he corrects me: "Oh yeah, it was just up the road in Ekalaka, Montana."

Bunny eventually moved to Dupree, South Dakota, but Jesse stayed with his grandfather, Rex Burghduff, on his spread near Camp Crook. Jesse worked on the ranch, training horses, tending to mother cows and their calves, and taking part in the myriad other tasks necessary to keep a ranch going. He and his grandpa became inseparable buddies, Rex taking him to horse sales then into town for a prime rib dinner. Jesse got the lifestyle in his blood. He tells me: "I crawled power lines—you know, helped them put power lines up—when I was in high school. But that's about the only job I've had. I've really just worked on the ranch. I don't plan on ever punching the clock. When I finish rodeoing, I plan on going back and ranching. I bought me some land up near my grandpa's place and I bought some cattle, and that's what I'm planning on doing. Be tough for me to sit inside an office or something after I've always been outside."

Bucking horses and bulls is also in his blood. Even when he was small and riding his pony along the Little Missouri River, he tried to get it to buck. As soon as he was old enough to have dreams for the future, he let his family know that he wanted to ride someday in the National Finals Rodeo. He went to his first bull-riding school when he was twelve. He also went to saddle bronc riding school. World saddle bronc champion Billy Etbauer gave Jesse his first bucking saddle, and Jesse got the fundamentals of saddle bronc riding down by using that saddle on milk cows and on a bucking barrel. Things took off for him by the time he was in high school. "Yeah, I won the National High School Finals Rodeo in bronc riding one year, was runner-up the year before." But not everything about his story is rosy.

Jesse made a stab at the PRCA right out of high school—and wound up broke. "I thought it was going to be easier than heck. I thought I was gonna blow 'em away quick, but I went out on the circuit a year and couldn't win nothing. I had to go back home and work." Understanding that he needed more refinement, he accepted a scholarship to one of the country's best collegiate rodeo programs, Oklahoma Panhandle State

University in Goodwell.* In 2000 he won the College National Finals all-around cowboy championship. Jesse was ready for the PRCA.

He emerged in the PRCA as a stand-alone kind of cowboy, someone who harkens back to the glory of Jim Shoulders and Larry Mahan. Jesse can rope—he competed in roping through college. He is a good bulldogger: "I did steer wrestling in college and did all right, made the college finals both years, so it went pretty good, I guess. And I've done it out here on the PRCA circuit. But my knees have been bad the past couple of years, so I haven't bulldogged so much. I'm gonna get some knee braces and take a crack at it again next year." And he can ride saddle broncs and bulls with the best of them.

More important he possesses what now seems like an ancient spirit, one that goes back well beyond even Jim Shoulders—all the way back to the likes of Jackson Sundown and George Fletcher. Jesse is one of the last sure-enough natural men. He was formed by ranch land and herds of cattle and horses. He's happiest out in the sunshine and rain. His dream is to live out his life far away from fluorescent-lit cubicles in buildings adjacent to traffic-clogged freeways. For him, happiness is the whisper of wind through grass and the gurgle of water flowing down from the mountains. He's unencumbered by agents—he takes care of his own business, using what he learned in a class or two at Panhandle State, plus some savvy he picked up from his grandfather. He negotiates his own deals and so far has been successful at it.

He says, "I'm planning on rodeoing another eight, ten

---

*College rodeo competition began at Sul Ross State University in Alpine, Texas, shortly after World War II. Sixty years later, the National Intercollegiate Rodeo Association, the governing body of college rodeo, has accredited rodeo teams at 137 schools, most of them in the West. The NIRA sponsors an annual College National Finals Rodeo held in Casper, Wyoming.

years. My goal is winning the world all-around title at the finals. I'm dang sure chasin' that. Just go and win the world. But then I want to go back to South Dakota and ranch. It's home to me. I don't really want to be anywhere else." This sets him apart from many of the cowboys out on the circuit in the early twenty-first century, relatively few of whom share his connections with the land: "Anymore, a lot of 'em are just people who learned how to rodeo at rodeo schools and such. There still are some good all-around working cowboys who compete in rodeos, but not as many as there used to be. For me, it's a vacation to go home and work on the ranch."

Away from the ranch, he's racking up road miles in a way that would impress even Neal Cassady. A hundred thousand miles a year on the Dodge pickup, he'd guess. Sometimes traveling with two South Dakota natives who rank among his heroes, Billy Etbauer and Tom Reeves. "I hired a driver to help me this summer. He's a friend of mine from home, a ranch kid who wanted to see the country, so I took him on for the summer. I guess I've pretty much seen all of America over the last few years, at least from Ohio down to Florida and everything west. I haven't been up to the Northeast. Not yet, anyway."

Jesse checks his watch and says he better get his hat shaped so he can get ready for the rodeo.

"What are you going to do after the rodeo?" I ask.

"Oh, we're drivin' down to Albuquerque. I'll fly back up for the short-go on Saturday." He doesn't seem to have a doubt that he'll do well enough today to be back for the short-go.

"I'll catch up with you before you take off," I say.

"Okay. Enjoyed talking." And he's off to find someone to put some steam to his hat.

ANYONE WHO might doubt Jesse Bail's cowboy spirit will have all doubts quashed this afternoon. In the saddle bronc contest, he rides a mare named Dip'n Queeny for an 86, tying Billy Etbauer for the best score of the day. Jesse was right to be confident about returning from Albuquerque. The ride qualifies him for the short-go on Saturday.

But it's in the bull-riding competition that he shows his true mettle. He draws a bull named Sweet Pea. The bull proves to be as docile as its name. Sweet Pea takes a mild leap out of the chute—and then lies down on the track. Jesse tries spurring the bull, but for a few seconds it seems perfectly content to just relax in the dirt. The bull finally stands just as the buzzer sounds. Jesse receives a score of 52. Given Sweet Pea's performance, my guess is that at least fifty of those points were awarded to Jesse for his attempts to make a ride out of nothing.

There is a woman standing next to me on the press platform. Her long hair is iridescent in the sunlight. She's wearing well-scuffed boots with spurs. Her jeans are sun-bleached and frayed at the knees. I can tell by looking at her hands with their short, unpolished nails that she's the real thing, a ranch woman, a horsewoman. Strong, independent, resourceful. My guess is that she's lived her life free of the sort of self-absorbed neuroses epitomized by the *Sex and the City* characters, but maybe I'm wrong. But one thing I am sure of: She knows rodeo.

"I've never seen anything quite like that," she says to me.

"I haven't, either."

Jesse has the option of keeping his score of 52. Or he can opt to take a reride, since the bull's lying down qualifies as a foul. Under normal conditions, that would be a no-brainer. A 52 is too low to stand with it. But through the first two days of the Round-Up, the bulls have had a decided upper hand on the cowboys. Right now, that 52 would be enough to bring Jesse back for the short-go bull-riding contest on Saturday. But there are still a lot of riders left today plus a full field for Friday's rodeo. So, that 52 most likely won't hold up. Jesse opts for the reride.

On his second bull, Jesse hangs on for the full eight seconds and scores a 72. It is the third highest score of the day, certainly enough to get him into the short-go. But as the bull leaves the chute, it brushes Jesse's leg against the gate. A foul. Jesse can have another reride if he wants it. He can also stick with the 72 if he prefers. Most people would take the 72 and say, *See ya on Saturday.* But most people aren't cowboys cut from the makings of a Jesse Bail. I know what he will do—cowboys ride when they have the chance. He'll take the reride, hoping to best Mike Moore's 82 and Layne McCasland's 73 for the day money. You hear groans from the crowd when Justin McKee announces Jesse's decision.

His third bull of the afternoon charges through the gate. This time Jesse's drawn a hard bucker. He makes it through about four seconds of the ride before the bull drills him. As Joe Baumgartner leads the bull away, Jesse sits up and stares down at the grass between his chaps. Good-bye, third place. Good-bye for the short-go bull riding on Saturday. He stands up and walks to the gate. "Let's hear it for this cowboy who just rode three bulls for you today, ladies and gentlemen," McKee pleads. The audience responds with warm applause. Nice enough. But not exactly a paycheck.

"I knew he would do it," the woman standing next to me says.

"I did, too."

She shakes her head. "Cowboys—what are you gonna do with 'em?"

I shrug and leave the platform, hoping to shake Jesse's hand before he leaves. I find him packing his bag, looking crestfallen. "Helluva bronc ride," I tell him.

"Thanks," he says.

But I can tell he's replaying that last bull ride in his mind. I start to say something about it but then think better of it. "Be careful driving to Albuquerque." I can't imagine driving fifteen hundred miles in a Dodge pickup after what's just happened here.

"I will," he says. "You be here for the short-go?"

"Yeah."

"I'll see you then."

NICHOLAS RAY'S *The Lusty Men* ranks with *Junior Bonner* as one of the best rodeo movies ever filmed. Produced by RKO during the years Howard Hughes owned the studio, *The Lusty Men* suffers from an improbable story made even worse by the conventions of the studio system in force in Hollywood during the 1950s. Yet its merits outweigh its drawbacks. It has at once the look of a European art film and of John Ford's *The Grapes of Wrath*. The best parts of the script come from the contributions of Claude Stanush—the Texas writer whose reportage for *Life* forms the basis of the film—and Horace McCoy—a hard-boiled novelist (*They Shoot Horses, Don't They?*) and self-professed rodeo fan with his own Texas roots. To add verisimilitude, Ray shot exteriors at real rodeos, the Pendleton Round-Up chief among them. Stars Robert Mitchum and Arthur Kennedy as well as Ray himself got infected with the rodeo bug to the extent that they all tried riding bucking bulls and broncs themselves, violating their contracts with RKO's insurance companies in the process. After attempting to ride a bronc at Pendleton, Mitchum reported that he was "bleeding from [his] hair" by the time he dismounted. For his part, Ray said of the experience, "I guess we all have a little of that wildness in us."

I understand. Over the next two days, I feel that wildness infecting me as I hang out at the Round-Up. It's good that the rodeo comes to an end on Saturday. If I stay around Pendleton much longer, I decide, I just might succumb to some form of the wildness myself. My bags are packed and in the trunk of the rental car when I show up for the Round-Up finals.

The field of saddle bronc riders is peppered with former world champions. Two of them, Rod Hay and Dan Mortensen, have posted high numbers, an 85 and 84, respectively. Jesse Bail will have his work cut out for him. I'm standing at a rail, watching him adjust his saddle on a bronc named Turtle Dove. An old Native American man stands next to me, his braids forming silver stains down the back of his ribbon shirt.

Jesse exits the chute with his spurs high on Turtle Dove's shoulders. The horse bounds onto the grass infield, bucking high and rhythmically. Jesse has a long flowing lick going almost immediately. The crowd rises to its feet, cheering, as it senses this is an extraordinary ride. After the buzzer, the most enthusiastic applause of the day resounds from the old arena. Jesse gracefully leans into the pickup man who has ridden up to assist him. He lowers himself to the ground and gives his fist a quick triumph pump. The crowd cheers him again. "How 'bout that?" Justin McKee asks the audience. The applause continues. "The judges say Jesse's ridden Turtle Dove for an"—a pause, then—"*eight-tee-one.*"

You can hear the moans coming from the stands as McKee launches into an explanation of how the judges see things differently from the fans in the grandstand. It doesn't mollify anyone. The old man standing beside me shakes his head sadly. "That was the best ride of the whole Round-Up," he says softly. He leaves the platform.

But it's not exactly bad news for Jesse. Today's score combined with Thursday's gives Jesse a point total of 167. That ties him with Rod Hay for the lead, with only Billy Etbauer left to ride. Etbauer winds up being thrown by his draw, Dunne. That makes Jesse cochampion of the Pendleton Round-Up saddle bronc competition for 2003. Former University of Texas football coach Darrell K. Royal used to say that a tie was sort of like getting a kiss from your sister. But I guess that's better than no kiss at all. Jesse will take home his first trophy saddle from one of the three prestige rodeos (Pendleton, Cheyenne, and Calgary). He has to feel good about that. Jesse and Rod Hay take a victory lap around the track, waving their hats to the crowd, just as Jackson Sundown did all those years ago.

⊰ 6. CODA: THE LAST RODEO ⊱

Leakey, Texas—July 2004

The National Finals Rodeo
Las Vegas, Nevada—December 2003

IN THE DISTANCE, yellow, green, and blue fireworks smear an otherwise perfect July night. I look up at the black dome of sky, which is bejeweled with constellations. Not many lights of any kind to interfere with studying the stars in Leakey, Texas, tonight. The most brightly lit spot in the area is the rodeo arena on the outskirts of town, and I have to say those lights aren't exactly overwhelming. I have parked my rig in a grassy bar ditch and my old friend Jonathan "J.M." Roe and I are hiking up the road with a crowd of locals toward the gate that opens onto the rodeo grounds.

"Well, this is it," J.M. chuckles. "The Leak-eey Rodee-o. Probably pretty different from some of the other rodeos you've been to."

"Yeah, but that's okay. This is exactly what I'm looking for."

"Great."

There's a good reason why there aren't many lights to interfere with stargazing in Leakey, Texas. It's halfway to the middle of nowhere—and that's a good thing. It sits adjacent to the Frio Canyon in the most dramatically picturesque section of

Texas's fabled Hill Country—an expanse of juniper (mountain cedar) brakes, shinnery, and live oak and cypress groves on steep limestone-studded hills, which encompasses twenty-five counties in the central part of the state. None of the hills are particularly tall—thirteen hundred feet is the highest elevation in the Hill Country—but the air is considerably less humid than it is down on the plains leading to the Gulf of Mexico.

The relatively cooler, drier air; the abundance of shade; and the fast-flowing, spring-fed rivers and creeks in the canyons make the Hill Country an appealing getaway for a lot of Texans. This was true even before white settlers intruded into the region; Comanches in particular were fond of taking breaks from buffalo hunting on the plains to ride into the hills, where they'd splash around in blue holes of chilly canyon water. Some Hill Country towns, like Fredericksburg or Kerrville, are close enough to Austin and San Antonio to make for easy day-trips. But not Leakey (pronounced *lake-ee*): There's no direct route to Leakey from the cities. I've driven more than two hundred miles to get here today. After the rodeo tonight, J.M. and I'll drive more than forty miles to Uvalde to flop at the nearest Holiday Inn. Though it's the seat of Real (pronounced either *ree-all* or *ray-all*) County, Leakey is a hamlet with a population that falls short of 400. In 1990, 399 souls called it home. By 2000 that number had fallen to 387. In 1985 it was down to 385. Damn if I don't think everyone in town is at the rodeo tonight. And then some.

As an entertainment event, Leakey's Fourth of July Rodeo wouldn't interest many television producers. Not a hint of glitz around here. Not a single banner advertising Wrangler jeans or Jack Daniel's whiskey. Not a single big-time rodeo star here tonight. The best that I can tell, the rodeo is not even sanctioned by PRCA or any other governing body. But there's something authentic about the Leakey rodeo that's missing at many—

perhaps most—modern big-time rodeos and bull-riding events. And that's what matters to me tonight: authenticity.

J.M. and I hike to a set of rusted iron bleachers and have a seat. A lot of people aren't even bothering with bleachers. They're backing up their pickups to the arena fence, then setting up lawn chairs in the beds to view the rodeo. Cracking open the ice chest, leaning back, enjoying the show. I remember my mother's description of jackpot rodeos at the little arena on the Thedford Ranch nearly half a century ago, back when she was ribbon roping and enthralled by cowboys. It must have been something like what J.M. and I are viewing tonight. The cowboys and cowgirls mostly hail from the Hill Country, although one has driven all the way from a suburb of Houston, another from Georgetown, which is just up Interstate 35 from where I live.

There are only two bucking-horse rides. A handful of bull-doggers. A lot of ropers, both men and women—the women competing in breakaway roping. A lot of barrel racers, some of whom post times that would be respectable at any rodeo. The big event of the evening is mutton bustin'. You find this at a lot of rodeos and bull-riding events these days. It's a competition in which local kids compete to see who can ride a sheep the longest. The mutton bustin' ends in a tie tonight, so a footrace takes place among the finalists to determine the winner. There are a couple of other events for the local kids. In the mutton scramble, boys and girls under twelve chase after sheep, some of which have money tied to their tails. In the ensuing calf scramble, kids over twelve pursue *calves* with money tied to their tails. The screaming contestants raise a wall of dust as they rush after the bewildered calves.

"Well, at least they're not sackin' goats," J.M. says.

"Goat sackin'?" I say.

"Yep." He explains that it involves teams of kids who pursue goats in the arena with the intent of catching them and putting them into gunnysacks.

"No shit?" I say.

He nods. "It gets pretty wild."

"You ever do that?"

He laughs and nods again.

The Leakey rodeo concludes with—what else?—bull riding. J.M. and I walk down to the chutes to get a closer view. It seems to me that it's mostly a lot of area high school boys taking their shots on the back of bulls. Though there's no requirement for them to do so, all the riders wear padding and helmets even though these bulls don't seem particularly fearsome. The bulls mostly run when they come out of the gates, with a few bucks thrown in for good measure. I don't see a single one go into anything approximating the classic spin that topflight bulls execute. I doubt that any would ever qualify for a career as a PBR bull. Future Big Macs, I decide. As for the high school boys trying their luck on the bulls here tonight—who knows? Maybe we are seeing a future Justin McBride or Jesse Bail down there. Or maybe a future Cowboy Don.

After the rodeo, J.M. and I head to the street dance, which takes place adjacent to the Real County Courthouse, a handsome, if small, stone building—it hardly seems larger than my house. The band is mounted on a hay wagon and plays covers of country songs, even dusting off the old "Orange Blossom Special" at one point. The band lacks originality, but the musicianship of its members is not in question. They impress even J.M., a skilled multi-instrumentalist who has ties with Austin's fabled live music scene. "This band's a lot better than what they used to have here," he says admiringly.

After drinking a couple of beers, J.M. and I leave Leakey and head toward Uvalde. Even more fireworks shoot up into the sky, mostly from the myriad of campgrounds along the Rio Frio, east of us.

FOR SIX MONTHS before Leakey, I'd been on an attitudinal roller coaster about rodeo. Leakey did a lot to restore my faith in it.

I left Pendleton thinking I was a changed man. I felt as if I'd connected with something wild and free up there in eastern Oregon. Whatever that something was, it had taken charge of me. I came back to Austin thinking that I would no longer be able to tolerate traffic jams, cable TV, fast-food franchises, cramped suburban neighborhoods, or anything else that would diminish my soul.

I went back to my day job on the Monday after the Round-Up with the most reckless of attitudes. Maybe it wasn't just attitude. Something physically seemed changed, too. The fluorescent lights of my office building made my skin itch. My eyes couldn't focus on the endless rows of cubicles. Looking at a computer screen gave me a headache. I wore my Luccheses—which were caked with the gray mud I'd picked up behind the Round-Up arena—every day to work. I remember sitting in a conference room listening to an engineer surfeited with self-importance ramble on about virtual realities. I stared at the mud on my boots as he spoke. This virtual world he was going on about was a piss-poor substitute for the real world I sampled at Pendleton. How could I force myself to stay in the same room with some self-infatuated geek when I'd seen Jesse Bail ride those three bulls in one afternoon? In fact, I couldn't. I excused myself to go to the restroom and never went back to the meeting.

Reckless—that's exactly the word. I toyed with how I would write my resignation letter for an hour one day, unable to give any thought to what I would do without health insurance, without a retirement plan—hell, without a bimonthly direct deposit into my checking account. Not to mention how I would get along without a wife, for she surely would not stick around for long if I did something that irresponsible.

But none of those things mattered. I was possessed. I wanted to be back there on the banks of the Umatilla River. I wanted to sleep outside. I wanted to eat fry bread with boysenberry preserves. I wanted to ponder the wide waters of the Columbia. I wanted to sign up as Jesse Bail's driver. I wanted to work for Harry Vold as a hand in the pens behind the great rodeo arena. I wanted a life that was more real than the one I was living.

The fever broke after a week, when I had a conversation with a friend about his desperate search to find a job. He had been a freewheeler in many ways, proud to be able to live by his wits. But while he once regaled me with details of his most recent trip to France, he now told me he couldn't make an hour's drive to a boxing match outside San Antonio because he was carefully budgeting his gas money. I was glad not to be in his predicament. At home that night, I opened a statement from a health insurance company showing several hundred dollars of medical bills it had covered for my family. With that, practicality killed the wild impulse in me. I cleaned up my Luccheses, shined them, put them in their box, and stored them away in the back of my closet. I then washed my hands and went to my home office, where I fired up the computer and checked my stock portfolio.

Still, I felt more than a little ashamed of myself for surrendering.

TWO MONTHS after Pendleton, the championship of the PBR was decided in Las Vegas. Not surprisingly, it came down to a battle between Justin McBride and Chris Shivers. Or maybe it was surprising. In spite of his outstanding performance in 2003, McBride came close to missing the finale because of an injury.

A month before Vegas, a bull named Mission Pack stomped him, breaking a rib and collapsing one of his lungs—he had the sensation of a balloon exploding inside his chest and struggled to breathe for three hours after the accident. Nevertheless, by the time the finals rolled around, McBride had received the doctor's okay to compete. "I'd bet on me every time," McBride told a reporter. He was game, no doubt about it. He kept the pressure on Shivers throughout the finals, and in the short-go, McBride drew the best bull, Mudslinger. Shivers guessed McBride would be able to ride the bull pretty easily and that would be that. McBride thought he'd be able to ride Mudslinger, too. But he left the chute without ever really getting firmly seated, and 6.1 seconds into the ride, Mudslinger dumped McBride onto the dirt. McBride headed back to the gate realizing that he'd missed a million-dollar payday by 1.9 seconds. Shivers took home his second PBR championship—and a check for $1.2 million.

Not to mention a trophy as big as a birdbath.

In December I arrived in Vegas in a heavy rain. I drove down the Strip with the windshield wipers turned on full speed. It was also cold outside. In the foothills, the precipitation was coming down as snow. Yet the Strip was bumper-to-bumper, the sidewalks packed with pedestrians. Where else but Vegas?

It seemed to take an eternity, but I finally arrived at the Mirage—the host hotel for the PRCA's 2003 National Finals Rodeo. I surrendered the rental car to a valet, and as I made my way to the door, I scolded myself for my choice of hats. Because it was the cool season, protocol dictated that I wear a felt hat, so a couple of weeks earlier, I'd gone to a Western-wear store and bought a 4X beaver silver-belly. And in keeping with my contrarian nature, I'd eschewed Resistol—the de rigueur brand of hat for rodeos—in favor of good ol' John B. Stetson. The grayish silver-belly gave me a distinguished look, I decided, and set me apart from the multitude of black-hatted Garth Brooks wannabes at any rodeo. The only drawback to a silver-belly is that raindrops spot it—and you can't get the spots off once they've set in. So I had to tuck my hat under my corduroy jacket to protect it as I walked from the driveway to the entrance of the Mirage—just as I would do off and on for the next four days as the cold, gray, wet weather clamped down on the desert city.

This was the first time I'd been to a National Finals since it left Oklahoma City amid a great deal of acrimony twenty years earlier. As I started across the crowded, smoky casino to reach the elevators, I wondered how it would compare to those NFRs at the State Fairgrounds Arena I remembered so fondly. I stopped to adjust my Stetson and looked around, as the din from the slot machines rattled my brain. The Mirage may have been the host hotel for the NFR, but I didn't see a single cowboy in the place. I was the only person in the crowd wearing a Western hat. But this is not to say that anyone looked at me as if I were out of place. Vegas crowds would not be nonplussed if the pope himself shook the dice at a craps table. They've seen it all.

After I unpacked, I drove to the Thomas & Mack arena for that day's rodeo performance. The press was sequestered in a bunker deep in the ground beneath. Even at large rodeos I'd been to, like Cheyenne and Pendleton, press accommodations were informal at best. But here was a fully functioning press box, albeit one that gave you absolutely no view of the action. Except for the TV screens. If you wanted to see the action in person, you could do that. Sort of. A section of seats had been cordoned off for press use, high in the nosebleed zone of the Thomas & Mack. As is always the case at any rodeo, most of the people sitting in the press section seemed to have absolutely nothing to do with the media—never mind their press passes.

Friends in high places, I suppose. I tried sitting up there with them, but the view wasn't good. On top of that, I thought the sound system in the Thomas & Mack was horrid. Two Texans, Boyd Polhamus and Bob Tallman, were the announcers, and they're good enough at their trade to have a quarter of a century's worth of NFR appearances between them. But over the Thomas & Mack's distorted PA system, they harkened not at all back to the honeyed voices of Cy Taillon, Pete Logan, or Clem McSpadden. Instead, they sounded like hyperkinetic shock jocks working the drive-time shift on an FM rock station. A couple of days later, I happened on to the famed cowboy poet Baxter Black who was complaining that he couldn't make out what the announcers were saying because of the sound system. Here's to you, Baxter. I decided to escape the cacophony and descended into the Thomas & Mack catacombs to watch the rodeo on TV in the pressroom.

There I spotted a reporter who stood out from the others. She hustled a little harder, seemed to have more enthusiasm for her job. She darted from her seat out to the hall, clasping a tape recorder, where she caught up with the rodeo cowboys who'd left the locker room and were strolling past the media room. The cowboys seemed particularly happy to give her interviews, even though most if not all of them couldn't understand a word of the Navajo introduction with which she opened each interview.

Her name was L. A. Williams, and she had journeyed from Window Rock, Arizona, to Vegas to cover the NFR for radio station KTNN—the *K* is the call letter designating a station west of the Mississippi, the *TNN* stands for *the Navajo Nation*. It's a powerful AM station with a nighttime signal that allows its combined English and Navajo programming to be picked up as far south as Mexico and as far north as Canada. But its primary listeners are the citizens of the Navajo Nation, many of whom are too remotely located to have cable or to pick up broadcast TV signals. One of the most popular programs is the forty-five-minute rodeo report, which airs twice daily.

Williams was built like an athlete, and I found out she competed as a team roper and barrel racer in rodeos. She also served as coordinator of the Navajo Nation Fair Rodeo, the richest all-Indian rodeo in the world. I asked her about the importance of rodeo to the Navajos. She said the rodeo was the perfect complement for the Navajos' horsemanship traditions. "You come to our rodeo and you see things you don't find at many other rodeos," she said. Like cowhide racing. In it, a rider tows a tanned cowhide behind his or her horse, galloping toward the finish line, while a teammate attempts to ride the cowhide. "The way we do it reflects the old days, when the Navajos had all the good horses and the Hopis were horse poor." It's something I'd like to see someday.

After the rodeo, I was thinking about L. A. Williams's rodeo broadcasts in the Navajo language. I was thinking about my own rodeo roots. As I walked along the absurdity that is the Vegas Strip, I felt some pride swelling in me. Cowboy Don may have been just another rodeo bum, but he was tied to a wonderfully diverse tradition: Juan Leivas, a Chicano who won the first all-around title at Prescott Frontier Days. Ikua Purdy, the brilliant Hawaiian roper who stunned Cheyenne by proving himself to be the best cowboy at the world's largest rodeo. Lucille Mulhall, a woman who competed against men in roping and bulldogging events, and beat them. Bill Pickett, who virtually invented one rodeo event and who may have been the best cowboy ever. Not to mention the wonderful Jackson Sundown. That aspect of the tradition flourishes today. There was no bigger crowd favorite at 2003's NFR than Fred Whitfield, a powerful seven-time world champion calf roper from Hockley, Texas, who is African American. It's a tradition that has gifted a lot of people with the opportunity to prove themselves without regard to their background, including a screwed-up kid from a screwed-up family in Denver. In terms of rodeo history, Cowboy Don turned out to be a nobody. But it gave him a chance, and he took it and did the best he could with it.

THAT NIGHT at the Mirage I asked one of the casino's employees about how much difference the arrival of the NFR made to Las Vegas.

"You're one of the cowboys, right?" she asked.

I told her I was in town for the rodeo but wasn't connected to it. As we talked, I realized that when she said "the cowboys" she meant not only the cowboys participating in the rodeo but the fans and everyone else associated with the NFR.

She said, "Well, I don't want to be insulting or anything. But you can check it out in the newspaper and it will tell you the same thing. When the cowboys come to town, it's one of the slowest times of the year."

"Nothing out of the ordinary then?"

"No, it's just another convention to us. But—"

"Yeah?"

"Well, I hate to say it, but the cowboys have a reputation for not being very good tippers, and they don't spend that much gambling. And they don't go to shows while they're here. Just the rodeo, so that's it. So everything slows down. A lot of the shows take a week's hiatus when the cowboys are here. A lot of people take vacations."

"I see."

She seemed concerned that she was somehow insulting me by telling me this, even though I told her that I wasn't insulted. Before I left, she added, "Of course the cowboys are a lot better than the computer guys. What is that called? Comdex? They're the worst. They take up every room in town, but the computer guys don't gamble very much at all, and they don't know the meaning of the word *tip*. So the cowboys are better than Comdex."

She gave me a hopeful look before I left.

The fact is that the NFR doesn't seem to send much of a wave through Las Vegas. Vegas is still Vegas. It was different when it was in Oklahoma City. It was *the* big event of the year. The rodeo cowboys were viewed almost like movie stars. In Vegas, I saw world champions walk through casinos unrecognized. In Oklahoma City, they would have drawn autograph seekers. Oklahoma City partied as hard as Oklahoma City could when the NFR came to town. No one in a service business scheduled vacation then. The hotels were at their fullest. Rental cars became scarce. Restaurants did banner business. Waiters got their best tips of the year.

When Oklahoma City lost the NFR to Vegas, it was as if someone had chopped off one of The City's arms. Despite its best efforts, it never regained the character it had when it was home to the NFR. Shortly after losing the rodeo, Oklahoma City saw the collapse of the domestic oil and gas industry and the collapse of the agriculture industry—industries essential to The City's lifeblood. Everything changed. Early one morning in the late 1980s, I was driving in western Oklahoma City when I saw at least a dozen homeless people sleeping beneath an overpass on Interstate 40. Such a sight would have been unfathomable ten years earlier. My immediate thought was that everything had been tough in this town since the National Finals left for Vegas.

The next day at the Thomas & Mack, I watched the best rodeo cowboys and barrel racers in the world—well, not exactly the best: The best bull riders focus on the PBR these days and eschew qualifying for the NFR. Still, no doubt about it, this was *the* top rodeo. But I was overwhelmed with the feeling that this was nothing special. I had a vision of the work crew coming in on Monday after the NFR was finished and some cigar-chewing boss shouting, *Yeah, yeah, let's get this rodeo crap cleaned out here. We gotta get ready for the Eric Clapton concert on Tuesday.* Just another event coming to a close.

In terms of business, there's no question that moving the NFR to Vegas was the smart choice. The prize money nearly doubled the first year in Vegas. Twenty years after the fact, the prize money was six times greater than it was at its peak in Oklahoma City. Moreover, moving the event from a fly-over town like Oklahoma City to a major media outlet like Vegas increased the rodeo's visibility to the world beyond Kicker Culture—which had nourished it all those years in Oklahoma. Oklahomans chafed at the loss of the rodeo that they rightly believed they had built into a success. But business is business. Dollars and cents rule in rodeo as in every other aspect of American life. So good-bye Oklahoma City, hello Las Vegas. The money's a lot better, so don't feel bad if Mirage's white tigers get more attention than the rodeo does.

My mind drifted back to those rodeos I saw at the State Fairgrounds Arena, the NFR's home for fourteen of its twenty years in Oklahoma City. It was a singular place, steeped in rodeo tradition. It was where Larry Mahan worked his magic as a bareback, saddle bronc, and bull rider. It was where Donnie Gay proved himself to be the best bull rider in history. It was where Cy Taillon, Pete Logan, and Clem McSpadden sang out to all those kickers in the stands who knew and loved rodeo.

And it was where Freckles Brown rode Tornado.

On the JumboTron at the Thomas & Mack, a woman with long straight hair wearing a cropped top and low-slung jeans danced next to her seat. It was the same woman who repeatedly appeared on the screen the day before, and she would be up there again and again in the days to come. An Elvis impersonator worked the aisle and got his time on the JumboTron as well. An Elvis impersonator and rodeo? It's just not right.

I left the rodeo early.

THE NEXT DAY, Jesse Bail had left the locker room in the Thomas & Mack and was strolling down the walkway toward the pressroom when I ran into him. He smiled when he saw me.

"Hello, Kip," he said with that distinctive voice.

"Hey, Jesse," I said. I was glad to see him. "How you feeling?"

"Pretty good."

"You've made some money."

"Yeah, I've had a couple of good rides."

We agreed to try to get together the next day, but we never did.

Jesse had come into the 2003 NFR with a chance to win the all-around cowboy title, but he would have had to have put together a remarkable string of good rides to top Trevor Brazile, the roper from Decatur, Texas, who'd beaten Jesse in 2002 for the all-around crown. In 2002 it was nip and tuck through the finals as to who would come out on top. But by the time I talked to Jesse outside the pressroom, Brazile's lead had become all but insurmountable.

Jesse had a bad time with the horses and bulls he drew for the last two days of the NFR. In fact, I saw him drilled by a bull that pivoted and tried to get after him as he attempted to scramble up from the dirt. I thought Jesse was going to be seriously injured when, almost miraculously, bullfighter Joe Baumgartner squeezed into what seemed to be a nonexistent space between the bull's horns and Jesse's head. Baumgartner slapped the bull's head, then darted away from Jesse. The bull followed Baumgartner's lead, and Jesse was able to get away.

"Man," I said aloud. "Baumgartner just kept Jesse from getting hurt bad."

Cotton Yancey, a songwriting rodeo announcer from Pelahatchie, Mississippi, was working on the PRCA's crew in the pressroom. When he heard what I said, he shook his head at me. "Joe just saved his life. That's what he did."

I nodded. Cotton nailed it.

In the end, Brazile stood on the platform in the arena as the all-around cowboy for 2003, a victorious spider in a web of green laser beams. Not to take anything away from Brazile. I'd hung around him and some other ropers as they viewed their previous performances on video in the TV room, just down the hall from the pressroom. He's a brilliant roper, currently the best in what many observers believe is the most talented pool of ropers in the history of rodeo. And he seemed to be a good guy. But the laser show and hoopla at the end of the NFR was as out of place for a rodeo as the dancing girl on the JumboTron and the Elvis impersonator working the aisles.

It just wasn't right.

I took a night flight back to Austin. The cabin was packed with people who'd been to the NFR, many of whom dozed off as soon as the airliner hit cruising elevation. I found myself fretting about the future of rodeo as we flew over the darkened desert. The welding of rodeo to its roots is what makes it interesting. Cowboys like Jesse Bail make it compelling. But there are marketing forces at work that are only too willing to chop away rodeo tradition in order to get the best endorsement deals from the biggest corporate sponsors. Some of us who grew up in Kicker Culture are perplexed about the acceptance of bull riders wearing helmets with face guards and Nikes, instead of Western hats and boots. I kept coming across stories of young bull riders who don't know how to ride horses. If one of these guys wins a trophy saddle at an event, he is as likely to put it up for auction on eBay as he is to keep it. He never plans to get on the back of a horse for any reason, so what good is a saddle? TV audiences seem willing to accept bull riders who eschew a lot of rodeo tradition. NBC reports that the PBR events it airs are now drawing a larger viewing audience than some regular-season NBA games. And in 2003 magazines and newspapers carried stories about how rodeo in general and bull riding in particular stood poised to be the next breakout sport, the next NASCAR. If that is indeed the case, I fear that in the future, once the marketing minds have had their way and the sport has been remolded to appease demographic groups, rodeo will lose its soul.

Such were the troubling thoughts that kept me awake as I jetted back home to Texas.

WHICH BRINGS me back to Leakey.

Leakey showed me that the original spirit of rodeo is alive and well, out there in kicker country. People were riding bucking horses and bulls not for any sort of big financial reward or for an endorsement deal, but because they felt some sort of deep inner calling to do it. It is not like little league or a municipal softball tournament. Those are merely pastimes. No one *plays* rodeo the way he or she might *play* a mere game. Rodeo is more serious than that. It is ritual in places like Leakey. It defines the people who take part in it as well as the community in which it takes place. As long as that call continues to exist in Leakey and other communities across the West, rodeo will survive the onslaught of big money and big TV numbers.

J.M. and I arrived at the Holiday Inn at Uvalde after midnight. I stood in the hot, humid night air and reflected on the journeys I'd taken over the past twelve months. This was as good a place to end it as any. Leakey may be a Hill Country town, but Uvalde is South Texas, much flatter, with a lot of scrubby mesquite. It was down here in South Texas that it all began. It was in country like this that the original cowboys herded up wild longhorns and began heading them north. Long-forgotten cowboy contests took place here. *Betcha a dollar I can rope a steer and hog-tie it faster than you can. Oh yeah? Well, you're on!* Also, we were just an hour's drive from the Rio Grande, an hour's drive from vaqueros and the great tradition of the *charro*, the source of all things cowboy.

Yes, a good place to end it. At the beginning.

THE REMAINING portion of Cowboy Don's cremains sat in the plastic container in the closet for a long time. I had no particular plans for them. But one Sunday I was struck by a notion of what to do. I took the container from the closet and Luscaine and I climbed into our Nissan pickup. We drove north on Interstate 35 for a while before leaving the four-lane for a winding asphalt road in northern Williamson County that twists up into southern Bell County. The road eventually reaches a low-water crossing on Salado Creek. Long ago a weir to support a gristmill had been constructed across the creek, upstream from the crossing. Summer's Mill, as it was known, still stands, though these days the refurbished buildings function as a conference center. The grounds surrounding the mill are well landscaped. The Salado's water cascades over the weir, rushes under the crossing, and slices through a horse farm on the other side of the road. The farm is home to some thoroughbred stallions of some repute. On this day, as Luscaine and I pulled off the road, three horses were grazing peacefully along the creek.

"This is it," I said.

Luscaine nodded and we got out of the pickup. There was nothing ceremonious about it. As I opened the container, I said, "I thought this would be good because he never lost his love of horses. Years after he quit rodeoing, he'd still pull off the road and look at horses if they caught his eye."

Luscaine nodded silently again.

"So I thought this would be a good place," I said, as if I need to reassure myself about something. A scissor-tailed fly-catcher flitted down to a fence strand and perched for just a few seconds before taking flight again.

I poured the cremains into the Salado. Just as they had in Oregon, they bloomed gray in the water, but the stain seemed to hang against the current for a little longer. A couple of pick-ups roared past on the narrow road behind us. One of the horses flicked its tail at a pestiferous something on its flank. The scissor-tail flew to the fence again. The water cleared.

Cowboy Don was gone.

"IF YOU'VE seen one rodeo, you've seen 'em all."

That's one of the best-known sayings in all of rodeo. But after my excursions through the West with nearly two-dozen stops, I came to disagree with it. Each of the full-blown rodeos I attended had a character of its own, just as each community hosting the rodeo had a character of its own. The PBR events had more sameness to them than the rodeos did. But each ride was unpredictable, a compelling eight-second drama unto itself. I never got tired of watching riders and ropers. The rodeo and bull-rider circuits left me rejuvenated. But it was more than just the events themselves. The spirit of the cowboys and cowgirls, and that of the rodeo aficionados, stirred my passions.

Here's a final rodeo story for you.

Mel Lambert grew up on a reservation in Oregon, part white, part Indian. As a young man, he and his buddy Slim Pick-ens—who'd go on to become a great character actor—rodeoed up and down the West Coast. At one rodeo, an auctioneer had been hired as the announcer. He called the rodeo like an auction, and he was terrible. Lambert told officials *he* could do a better job, and they told him to have at it. Thus began an announcing career that wound up with Lambert's entry into the Rodeo Hall of Fame. Pickens started working in movies and he told his buddy Mel that money could be made in Hollywood as a stunt-man. Soon Lambert had a successful career performing danger-ous scenes in Westerns. He was good enough at it that he was inducted into the movie-stunt performers Hall of Fame as well. Meanwhile he opened Mel Lambert Motors in Salem, and estab-lished himself as one of the few car dealers in the Pacific North-west who refused to cheat Native American customers. Through these ventures, Lambert seemed to know just about everyone.

In the early 1970s, Lambert ran into actor and producer Michael Douglas. Douglas was in a dilemma. He was trying to produce a film version of *One Flew Over the Cuckoo's Nest*— his father, screen legend Kirk Douglas, had owned the film rights to Ken Kesey's novel for years. Jack Nicholson, Louise Fletcher, Danny DeVito, and most of the other members of that legendary cast had already been signed. But a key role re-mained to be filled, that of Chief Bromden. The actor who played the role had to be a Native American of huge stature, but Douglas and his director, Milos Forman, couldn't find any-one like this through traditional Hollywood casting resources. Douglas implored Lambert to let him know if he came across anyone fitting the bill.

Shortly thereafter, Will Sampson walked into Mel Lambert Motors to buy a pickup. Lambert knew Sampson through rodeo already, and he instantly realized that the huge Muscogee Creek bull rider–cum–forest ranger would be ideal in the part. As soon as he concluded business with Sampson, Lambert got on the phone to Douglas: "Michael, you should see this son of a bitch who was just in here. He's big. I mean, he's *big!*" Douglas said he wanted to meet Sampson as soon as possible. (It turned out there was a little delay. Lambert discovered Sampson had gone to jail for a few days for stealing a horse not long after his fateful stop at Mel Lambert Motors. "He didn't really steal the horse," Lambert told friends later. "It was a misunderstanding. He just sort of borrowed it.") Once Douglas, Forman, and Nicholson met Sampson, they knew they'd found their Chief Bromden. Sampson's performance in *One Flew Over the Cuckoo's Nest* was landmark, with many film scholars applauding it as the first time a contemporary Native American character was portrayed realistically in the movies. Lambert himself played a small but memorable part in the film as the harbormaster.

That yarn sums up the best part of rodeo—the sense of community. Actually, it's more than that. It's more like a sense of family. The family ties have had a profound effect on the shaping of American culture for more than a hundred years. By most standards, it's a family with an untamed lifestyle, maybe not as much so as it once was, but immeasurably so when compared to the lives of suburbanites on commuter trains or stuck in freeway congestion. Through Cowboy Don, I'm part of the family. I'm proud of that.

More than a year has passed since that night when I decided to hit the rodeo trail. This afternoon I step out onto my porch and I hear interstate traffic. The essential travel call remains, though I can't answer it, at least not right now. I think of Jesse Bail and that family of cowboys and cowgirls out there, *somewhere*, on the highway, headed to a rodeo, wild and free and set to ride.

May they keep riding forever.

⊰ AUTHOR'S NOTE ⊱

ONCERN FOR animal welfare has hit unprecedented heights in early twenty-first-century America, and all animal lovers, myself included, are grateful for this. In the realm of animal rights, rodeo is usually viewed as a dangerous anachronism. Without question, rodeo exploits animals for the entertainment of humans, causing injury and death to hundreds of horses and cattle each year. As many as a dozen head of rodeo stock—mostly calves and steers—will die annually at large rodeos like the Calgary Stampede. Horses, too, are at risk. The best rodeo in America, the Pendleton Round-Up, takes place on grass rather than dirt, and the slippery grass has led to the death of many valuable roping horses over the decades. Not surprisingly, humane organizations, including the American Society for the Prevention of Cruelty to Animals (ASPCA) and People for the Ethical Treatment of Animals (PETA), have targeted rodeo; PETA has dubbed rodeo "cruelty for a buck." PETA has gone so far as to demand that the town of Rodeo, California, change its name. Criticism is not limited to the political left. In his book *Dominion*, conservative Matthew Scully, a former spe-

cial assistant to and senior speechwriter for President George
W. Bush, brands rodeo as "gratuitous abuse of animals."

The Professional Rodeo Cowboys Association (PRCA)
and the Professional Bull Riders (PBR) argue that they are
committed to ensuring that rodeo animals are treated humanely.
The value of bucking stock (broncs, bareback horses, and
bulls) has escalated dramatically in recent years, so it is in the
best interest of rodeo stock contractors to make certain their investments are protected. These animals may not receive pam-
pering quite at the level of a racing thoroughbred, but their
lives are vastly better than that of most horses and cattle across
America. A top bucking horse or bull might have a rodeo career lasting as long as ten years (maybe more), then live the remainder of its life peacefully out to pasture. Unfortunately, the
same cannot be said for the calves and steers used in bulldogging and in roping events. After seeing use in a relatively few
rodeos, these animals end up at the slaughterhouse.

Animal-rights activists err when they target rodeo as something separate from the much larger beef-production industry.
Rodeo is an outgrowth of that industry and remains interlaced
with it. But nothing occurring in a rodeo arena is as bad as what
happens daily in the utter filth of a West Texas feedlot where
cattle are fattened out with hormone injections combined with
too much food and too little exercise, to prep them for slaughter. A bull with the innate inclination to buck and spin whenever a cowboy climbs on its back can escape a feedlot fate with
a "career" in rodeo. To a certain extent, the same is true for
horses. The saddle broncs and bareback horses seen in rodeos
are "outlaws"—that is, they cannot be broken for riding. Were
it not for rodeo, these horses would be killed and turned into
dog food or glue.

In writing *Chasing the Rodeo*, I approached rodeo as a cultural phenomenon, one that has been around for more than a

century. My purpose was not to determine whether it is a good or a bad thing in respect to animal rights. I think that debate is healthy, but it is not in the pages of my book. I went to more than twenty rodeos and bull-riding events to research *Chasing the Rodeo,* and I saw animals injured in the arena, some badly enough that they had to be destroyed. In all cases, the animals were treated as humanely as possible. Veterinarians were on hand at every rodeo. I never witnessed a single incident of abuse or neglect of the stock.

Another topic: Diversity in rodeo, through historical and modern times, fascinates me. In writing about native peoples, my preference has been to use the names of their particular nations (Lakota, Umatilla, etc.). In describing native peoples from multiple nations, I prefer the term *Native Americans.* Many Native Americans I met described themselves as *Indian.* The term also continues to be used within some rodeo-related events (all-Indian rodeos, for instance), and of course it frequently occurs in historical contexts. Because of this, I've used *Indian* interchangeably with *Native American,* in some areas. I describe Hispanic Americans with ethnic ties to Mexico as *Chicanos,* although on occasion I also employ the term *Mexican American.* I use the terms *black* and *African American* interchangeably. Women participating in rodeo refer to themselves as *cowgirls* and so have I. I mean no disrespect to anyone with these descriptions.

⊰ ACKNOWLEDGMENTS ⊱

I AM GRATEFUL to my wife, Luscaine, and to the rest of my family for putting up with me as I wrote *Chasing the Rodeo*. I was away from home quite a bit while gathering material. Although I was physically at home while writing, my mind usually was several states away, so in that sense I was just as absent as when I was traveling. Also, the book explores topics that I'm sure some of my relatives would just as soon I'd left unexplored. For enduring all that, I want to say a special thanks to my family. Paul Hemphill, John Schulian, Sarah Bird, Cyra McFadden, Tom Dodge, Robert Compton, Tara Elgin Holley, and Joe Holley were early supporters of this project. Their encouragement gave me the strength to take it on. My friend and former editor Pete Fornatale was extremely helpful as I wrote the proposal. My agent, David McCormick—the best in the business—found the right home for this project at Harcourt. My editor at Harcourt, Jenna Johnson, has been wonderful to work with. Her critical eye coupled with her enthusiasm for *Chasing the Rodeo* resulted in the book being much better than it otherwise would have been. Bill Wittliff and Bryan Woolley provided a much-needed sounding board as I wrote about the roots of rodeo. Callie Jones and Richard Zelade prevented me from moving into print with boneheaded mistakes still in the manuscript. My bull-riding friend, Louis "Bubba" Murphy, provided me with a lot of insight. Many, many people helped out with this project by providing information and suggesting avenues for exploration; in particular, I want to thank Ann Witham, Dorothy Burton, Lou-Jean Rehn (Denver's researcher extraordinaire), George Marshall, Peggy Hooper, Frank Blair, Bruce Stratton, Lisa Bradwell Goad, Robert Lockwood Mills, Tom Christopher, and Andrew Burnett. Thanks also to Ken Babbs and Mike Hagen for their help with Pendleton; long may the Pranksters run. The staffs at the Professional Rodeo Cowboys Association (PRCA) and the Professional Bull Riders (PBR) went out of their way to be helpful, as did officials at every rodeo and bull-riding event I attended; my thanks to them all. Sure-enough rodeo star Jesse Bail never failed to return a call and was accommodating in all ways; I owe you one, Jesse. Thanks to Larry McMurtry, who read the final manuscript shortly after it was complete and had kind things to say about it. Thanks to my longtime buddy J.M. Roe, who turned me on to the Leakey rodeo. My friend Mark Belanger was encouraging as always; he led me to Ross Miller, who had a significant effect on how this book turned out. My gratitude to them both. A nod of appreciation goes to my colleagues at National Instruments, who continue their support. A significant portion of this book is drawn from experiences I had during my ten years of working on newspapers; for those opportunities, a word of thanks to Susan Ellerbach, Foster Johnson, Thom Hunter, Dale Himes, and, especially, *el jefe*, Bill Lehmann. I would be remiss in not mentioning the passing of Robert "Punk" Ferris, who along with Kenny Walter first encouraged me to write. Finally, I would be considerably less sane than I am—a scary prospect— were it not for a group of Austin writer-friends who comprise what has been called with some irony the Manly Men Lunch Group—Jan Reid, Jesse Sublett, Christopher Cook (in absentia), and David Marion Wilkinson, all of whom helped with *Chasing the Rodeo*, especially David, who plowed into the manuscript when it was still in its embryonic state and helped put me on the right course. Two other Austin-based writers, Susie Kelly Flatau and Marsha Moyer, gave me suggestions for the book, although there's nothing manly about either of them.

I made use of a number of articles appearing in newspapers and magazines (both current and no longer existing), including *Arizona Highways, Men's Journal, Esquire, Texas Monthly, Pro Bull Rider, ProRodeo Sports News, Tulsa World, Dallas Morning News, Ponca City News, Daily Oklahoman, Austin American-Statesman, Fort Worth Star-Telegram, Oklahoma Today, Cheyenne Daily Leader, Wyoming Tribune-Eagle, Prescott Daily Courier, East Oregonian, Las Vegas Sun, Las Vegas Review Journal, Salem Statesman Journal, Guthrie Daily Leader, Logan County News,* and *Guthrie News Leader.* Also, Tom Christopher's *Neal Cassady* "fanzines" (volumes I and II cover the years 1926–46) provide a fascinating chronicle of the young Cassady in Denver. These were useful for the Denver material in *Chasing the Rodeo.*

Several Web sites provided essential material for me, including the excellent sites of the PBR (www.pbrnow.com) and the PRCA (www.prorodeo.com), both of which provide voluminous amounts of reliable information about the sport. As I mentioned in the text, the Lane Frost Web site (www.lanefrost.com) contains a complete account of that cowboy's life and tragic death. The Phippen and Sharlot Hall museums in Prescott, Arizona, were invaluable for the Arizona material. The Sharlot

Hall Museum is a researcher's dream, housing tons (literally) of documentation. Moreover, it hosts a terrific Web site (www. sharlot.org) that provides a wealth of information about Prescott and territorial Arizona. I also found myself using the online version of *The Handbook of Texas* frequently: www.tsha.utexas. edu/handbook/online. The best source of information about the paniolos who upset the rodeo world at the Cheyenne Frontier Days is found at the Paniolo Preservation Society's Web site: www.kamuela.com/pps/index.htm.

Junior Bonner is now available on DVD (from MGM), with insightful commentary from the three most important Peckinpah biographers/scholars: David Weddle, Garner Simmons, and Paul Seydor. *The Lusty Men,* alas, currently is not available either on VHS or DVD. Several years ago, VCI released it on videotape, and it turns up for sale at eBay and other online sources fairly often, as does a laser disc version. Both are somewhat collectable and can fetch a high price. Much of the Mel Lambert–Will Sampson material I took from Charles Kiselyak's *The Making of One Flew Over the Cuckoo's Nest,* which appears in the two-disc DVD version of *One Flew Over the Cuckoo's Nest* (Warner Brothers). This documentary is a truncation of Kiselyak's longer film, *Completely Cuckoo,* which, unfortunately, is currently not available. Cedric and Tonia Wildbill's award-winning documentary, *American Cowboys* (Wildbill Productions), is available in VHS format from several online sources. Narrated by William Hurt, it is the best rodeo documentary yet made and is essential viewing for anyone with an interest in the West. I relied on it for a good deal of my Pendleton material. Jeff Fraley and Harry Lynch's *Bull Riders: Chasing the Dream* is another documentary (Trinity Films/Gold Hill Home Media) that I found indispensable. A few quotes in *Chasing the Rodeo* are taken from it.

⚕BIBLIOGRAPHY⚕

FOR BACKGROUND research and for quoted material that appears in *Chasing the Rodeo,* I read all or parts of more than fifty books. Following is a partial bibliography of those works.

Abbott, E. C. "Teddy Blue," and Helena Huntington Smith. *We Pointed Them North.* New York: Farrar & Rinehart Inc., 1939. The classic memoir of a Texas cowboy who made the cattle drives.

Bridger, Bobby. *Buffalo Bill and Sitting Bull: Inventing the Wild West.* Austin, Texas: University of Texas Press, 2002.

Brown, Dee. *Bury My Heart at Wounded Knee.* New York: Holt, Rinehart & Winston, 1970.

———— *The American West.* New York: Simon & Schuster, 1995.

Burbick, Joan. *Rodeo Queens and the American Dream.* New York: Public Affairs, 2002.

Byers, Chester. *Cowboy Roping and Rope Tricks.* New York: G. P. Putnam's Sons, 1928.

Canutt, Yakima, and Oliver Drake. *Stunt Man: The Autobiography of Yakima Canutt.* New York: Walker, 1979. Foreword by Charlton Heston, afterword by John Wayne.

Cary, Diana Serra. *The Hollywood Posse: The Story of a Gallant Band of Horsemen Who Made Movie History.* Boston: Houghton Mifflin, 1975.

Cassady, Neal. *The First Third & Other Writings.* San Francisco: City Lights Books, 1971, 1981.

Dary, David. *Cowboy Culture: A Saga of Five Centuries.* New York: Alfred A. Knopf Inc., 1981, 1989.

Davidson, Sara. *Cowboy: A Love Story.* New York: HarperCollins, 1999.

Editors of *Esquire. The Soul of America.* New York: Charles Scribner's Sons, 1985. Includes Ken Kesey and Ken Babb's first published writing about the Pendleton Round-Up.

Eisenschitz, Bernard. *Nicholas Ray: An American Journey.* London: Faber and Faber Ltd., 1993.

Flynn, Shirley E. *Let's Go, Let's Show, Let's Rodeo: The History of Cheyenne Frontier Days.* Cheyenne, Wyoming: Wigwam Publishing Company, 1996.

Freeman, Danny. *World's Oldest Rodeo.* Prescott, Arizona: Prescott Frontier Days Inc./Classic Printers, 1988.

Furlong, Charles Wellington. *Let 'Er Buck.* New York: G. P. Putnam's Sons, 1921. Highly recommended, something like reading Stephen Crane on rodeo.

Gray, Robert N. *Mr. Rodeo Himself: Cecil Cornish, His Life and Times.* Waukomis, Oklahoma: The Rodeo Press, 1990.

Hanes, Colonel Bailey C. *Bill Pickett, Bulldogger.* Norman, Oklahoma: The University of Oklahoma Press, 1977.

Heinz, W. C. *Once They Heard the Cheers.* Garden City, New York: Doubleday & Company Inc., 1979.

Hinsdale, Harriet. *Born to Rope: The Sam Garrett Story,* Fallbrook, California: Aero Publishers Inc., 1971.

Jones, Allen, and Jeff Wetmore, eds. *The Big Sky Reader.* New York: Thomas Dunne Books/St. Martin's Griffin, 1997.

Jory, Doug and Cathy. *From Pendleton to Calgary.* Bend, Oregon: Maverick Publications Inc., 2002.

Kerouac, Jack. *On the Road.* New York: Viking, 1957.

———— *Visions of Cody.* New York: McGraw Hill, 1972.

Kesey, Ken. *Last Go Round: A Real Western*. New York: Viking, 1994. Written with Ken Babbs.

———— *One Flew Over the Cuckoo's Nest*. New York: Viking, 1962.

Lawrence, Elizabeth Atwood. *Rodeo: An Anthropologist Looks at the Wild and the Tame*. Chicago: The University of Chicago Press, 1984. The best scholarly treatment of rodeo.

Lesley, Craig. *Winterkill*. Boston: Houghton Mifflin, 1984. Moving story of a Native American rough-stock rider in eastern Oregon, maybe the best rodeo novel.

McFadden, Cyra. *Rain or Shine: A Family Memoir*. New York: Alfred A. Knopf Inc., 1986. A portrait of McFadden's life with her father, Cy Taillon, it is the best rodeo-related memoir.

McKinney, Grange B. *Art Acord and the Movies*. Raleigh, North Carolina: Wyatt Classics Inc., 2000.

McMurtry, Larry. *It's Always We Rambled: An Essay on Rodeo*. New York: Frank Hallman, 1974. Difficult to find small-press book containing astute observations on rodeo.

———— *Moving On*. New York: Simon & Schuster, 1970. McMurtry's big rodeo novel.

———— *In a Narrow Grave: Essays on Texas*. Austin, Texas: Encino Press, 1968.

Moses, L. G. *Wild West Shows and the Images of American Indians, 1883–1933*. Albuquerque, New Mexico: University of New Mexico Press, 1996.

Rendon, Al. *Charreada: Mexican Rodeo in Texas*. Denton, Texas: Texas Folklore Society, University of North Texas Press, 2002. Includes insightful essays by Julia Hambric, Bryan Woolley, and Francis Edward Abernathy.

Roosevelt, Theodore. *The Rough Riders*. New York: Charles Scribner's Sons, 1899.

Rupp, Virgil. *Let 'Er Buck: A History of the Pendleton Round-Up*. Pendleton, Oregon: Pendleton Round-Up Association/Master Printers, 1985.

Scully, Matthew. *Dominion: The Power of Man, the Suffering of Animals, and the Call to Mercy*. New York: St. Martin's Press, 2002.

Serpa, Louise L. *Rodeo*. New York: Aperture, 1994. With notes by Larry McMurtry.

Server, Lee. *Robert Mitchum: "Baby, I Don't Care."* New York: St. Martin's Press, 2001. Definitive Robert Mitchum biography, with excellent material on the making of *The Lusty Men*.

Stansbury, Kathryn B. *Lucille Mulhall: Her Family, Her Life, Her Times*. Mulhall, Oklahoma: privately printed, 1985. Remains the most complete and accurate work on Lucille Mulhall; also valuable because Kay reprinted much of her excellent collection of Lucille Mulhall postcards in it.

Tippette, Giles. *The Brave Men*. New York: Macmillan, 1972.

————— *Donkey Baseball & Other Delights*. Dallas, Texas: Taylor Publishing Company, 1989.

————— *I'll Try Anything Once: Misadventures of a Sports Guy*. Dallas, Texas: Taylor Publishing Company, 1991. The late Giles Tippette was a professional rodeo cowboy in the 1950s and '60s who went on to become a regular contributor to *Sports Illustrated* and *Texas Monthly* as well as a prolific novelist. His rodeo journalism, collected in these three books, represents some of the best writing about the sport.

Wallis, Michael. *The Real Wild West: The 101 Ranch and the Creation of the American West*. New York: St. Martin's Press, 1999.

————— *Way Down Yonder in the Indian Nation: Writing from America's Heartland*. New York: St. Martin's Press, 1993.

Wooden, Wayne S., and Gavin Ehringer. *Rodeo in America: Wranglers, Roughstock & Paydirt*. Lawrence, Kansas: University of Kansas Press, 1996. A good introduction to rodeo.

⚜ INDEX ⚜

Abbott, Denise, 200
Abbott, E. C., 51
Abernathy, Francis Edward, 32
Acord, Art, 174, 232
Addleman, Sheila, 270
African Americans, 42, 170–79, 187, 201, 217–18, 226, 232, 235–36, 239–43, 244, 246, 248, 289–90
Akin, Lee, 148
Alexander, Moses, 245
Allen, Grady, 113
Allen, Guy, 134
Allen, Kathryn E. (Kappy), 113–15
alternative metal bands, 138
"Amazing Grace," 140
American Cowboys (film), 239
American Society for the Prevention of Cruelty to Animals (ASPCA), 300–301
analgesic creams, 78, 123
Anderson, Broncho Billy, 174–75
Angel (bronc), 243–45
Angier, Frederick, 97–98
animal-rights' activists, 70, 71, 133, 163, 300–302

Applebome, Peter, 29
Arizona High School Rodeo, 7
Arizona Rough Riders, 24–25
Arnold, Justin, 80
Austin, Texas, 171–72, 248–49
Autry, Gene, 206

Babbs, Ken, 217
Baca, Avelino, 73
"Bad to the Bone," 62
Bail, Bunny, 271–72
Bail, Jesse
    all-round titles of, 46, 144
    in collegiate rodeo program, 272–73
    family background of, 271–72
    at Frontier Days (Cheyenne, Wyoming), 144–45, 148–49, 151
    at National Finals Rodeo (Las Vegas, Nevada), 293–94
    at Navajo Nation Fourth of July Rodeo (Window Rock, Arizona), 46, 47, 79, 144
    at Pendleton Round-Up (Pendleton, Oregon), 269–77

Bail, Jesse (*continued*)
  at Prescott Frontier Days (Prescott, Arizona), 45–47, 78–79, 80
Bail, Wade, 271–72
Baker, Joe Don, 42
Baldrige, Malcolm, 67
Ballard, Lucien, 42
bareback riding, 9, 134, 135
  described, 60–61
  scoring in, 61n
barrel clowns, 54, 61–62, 143–44, 250–51
barrel racing, 9, 271
  described, 67–68
  injuries in, 181
  top riders, 113–15
Bates, Ben Jr., 59–60
Baumgartner, Joe, 262–63, 276, 293–94
BBC, 146, 198
Beasley, Fred, 102
Beat Generation, 85, 86, 108, 109, 136
beef-production industry, 301
Bell, Jim (great-grandfather), 155
Belle Fourche, South Dakota, 36, 208, 212
Ben-Hur (film), 209
Berline, Byron, 185–86
Beutler, Lynn, 206
Bigfoot, 227
Bill Pickett, Bulldogger (Hanes), 170–72, 174, 175–77, 178–79
Black, Baxter, 288
Black Hills Roundup (Belle Fourche, South Dakota), 36, 212
blacks. *See* African Americans
Black Smoke (bull), 13
Blair, Frank, 221–23, 228, 250, 264–67
Blair, Jo-An, 264
Blue, Teddy (E. C. Abbott), 51
Bodacious (bull), 14, 44
body boards, 141
Bogdanovich, Peter, 246
Bogue, Marcus, 101–2

Bonfil, Frederick, 178
boots, 27, 107, 131, 185, 284, 285
Borglum, Solon H., 25
"Born in the U.S.A.," 69
branding, 31, 132, 133, 160, 172
Bray, Rance, 80
Brazile, Trevor, 293, 294
Brazilian bull riders, 31, 70, 151
breakaway roping, 271
broncs. *See* saddle bronc riding
Brooks, Garth, 52, 138, 287
Brooks & Dunn (shirts), 106
Brown, Dee, 32
Brown, Edith, 10, 11, 194–97
Brown, Freckles, 10–19, 120, 135, 193–97, 232
  approach to bull riding, 11–12, 14, 15, 36
  Bullnanza as tribute to, 192
  death of, 130, 192, 197
  early career of, 10–11
  financial hardships of, 202–3
  illness of, 130, 196, 197
  injuries of, 12–13
  in National Finals Rodeo (1967; Oklahoma City), 13–19, 190, 192, 194, 196–97, 292
bucking horse contests, 30–31
bucking strap, in bull riding, 71–72
buckle bunnies, 74, 261
Buck Owens and His Buckaroos, 185
Budweiser Clydesdales, 116, 117
Buell, Don Carlos, 82
buffalo, 63–64, 84, 174, 281
Built Ford Tough Series, 146, 192, 199
bull baiting, 70
Bull-Dogger, The (film), 175–76
bulldogging. *See* steer wrestling (bulldogging)
bullfighters (clowns), 14–15, 16–17, 128–29, 143
bullfighting, 69–70
Bullmania, 192

Bullnanza
  Oklahoma City, Oklahoma, 153–54,
    188–92, 197–204
  roots in Lazy E Arena (Guthrie,
    Oklahoma), 190–92
bull riding, 10–19, 31, 42–43, 68–73,
  126, 135
  body type for, 36–37
  Brazilian bull riders, 31, 70, 151
  Freckles Brown/Tornado (1967),
    13–19, 190, 192, 194, 196–97, 292
  clowns (bullfighters) in, 14–15,
    16–17, 128–29, 143
  described, 70–73
  Lane Frost/Takin' Care of Business
    (1989), 127–30
  Charles Wellington
    Furlong/Sharkey, 218–20
  history of, 69–70
  injuries in, 12–13, 44, 127–30
  kicker culture and, 187–88
  most famous fatality in, 127–30
  nature of bulls in, 110–11
  as next breakout sport, 145–51,
    201–4, 295
  rider safety and, 130–31, 283, 294
  scoring in, 15–16, 61n
  Don Carlos Stratton Jr. and, 6,
    35–37, 205–6
  top riders, 10–19, 45–47, 53, 73,
    78–79, 80, 127–30, 144–51, 192,
    193–97, 198–203, 275–77, 285–86,
    293–94
  See also Professional Bull Riders
    (PBR)
bull rope, in bull riding, 70, 71, 72, 78,
  123, 200
bull running, 70
bull vaulting, 69
Burbick, Joan, 55, 251–52
Burghduff, Rex, 271–72
Burk, Barry, 140–41, 149
Burlington Northern, 86

Burnett, Burk, 164–65
Burnett, Tom, 164–65
Bush, George W., 197, 300–301
Byers, Chester "Chet," 181, 232

Caldwell, Lee, 243
calf roping. See tie-down roping (calf
  roping)
calf scramble, 282
Calgary Stampede, 112, 164, 174, 300
Canutt, Yakima, 162, 164, 226, 232
Carillo, Adam, 203
Carillo, Gilbert, 203
Cassady, Neal, 108–9, 274
Cayuse tribe, 233, 243
Central State College, 184, 188
Central State University, 184
Chaney, Lon, 168
Chapman-Barnard Ranch, 187, 201
chaps, 49, 106, 214–15, 238, 243
chariot racing, 134
Charlie Brown (bull), 73
charreadas (contests for charros), 32, 65
charrería (Grand Mexican horseman
  tradition), 33
charro (man on horseback), 32
Chatman, Rick, 128–29
Cherokee Outlet, 206
Cherokee Strip Cowpunchers
  Association, 171, 177
Cherokee Strip Land Run, 206
Cheyenne, Wyoming, 30, 81–151
  cattle barons and, 91–95
  described, 85–88, 103–4
  history of, 91–98
  Old Red Barn/Great Western
    Corral, 95, 96, 98
  See also Frontier Days (Cheyenne,
    Wyoming)
Chief Joseph, 234–35, 237
Chief Joseph's War, 234–35, 237–38,
  244
Chief Many Horses. See Vold, Harry

Chinese Americans, 235n, 244
Chisholm Trail, 206
Choctaw Nation, 10, 193
Cinch jeans, 51, 52–53
Civil War, 25, 31, 82, 91, 193
Clark, Hugh, 122
"Classical Gas," 152
Clay, Henry, 177
Clift, Montgomery, 193–94
clowns
  barrel clowns, 54, 61–62, 143–44,
    250–51
  bullfighters, 14–15, 16–17, 128–29,
    143
Cody, Buffalo Bill, 96–97, 98, 158, 204
Cody, Wyoming, 10
Colisseum (Rome), 69–70
College National Finals Rodeo, 272–73,
  273n
Colville Nation, 252–53
Comanche, 164, 281
Confucius, 179
Congress of Rough Riders and Ropers,
  158–64, 166, 204
Conway, John, 101–2
Conway-Bogue Realty Investment
  Company, 101–2
Cooper, Roy, 120
Corley, Randy, 53, 56, 61–62, 63
Cornish, Cecil "Mr. Rodeo," 12,
  206–12, 221–22, 225
Cornish, Dick, 206
Cornish, Wayne, 210, 212–14, 221–22
corporate sponsorships, 46, 51, 54–55,
  78, 116, 117, 146, 189, 192, 197,
  199–203
"Courtesy of the Red, White, and Blue
  (The Angry American)," 138, 146,
  197–98
Court's Saddlery Company, 119
cowbell, in bull riding, 70–71, 198,
  199
Cowboy: A Love Story (Davidson), 49

cowboy attire, 4–5, 27, 48–53, 77–78,
  103–7, 130–31, 185, 210, 214–15,
  238, 243, 283, 286–87, 294
Cowboy Christmas, 36, 44–45, 47, 79
Cowboy Culture (Dary), 93
Cowboy Don. See Stratton, Don
  Carlos Jr. (father)
Cowboy Sports Agents, 200
cow dogs, 172
cowhide racing, 289
Crabb, Joe, 262
Creek Nation, 233–34
Crimber, Paolo, 151
Crimson Skull, The (film), 175, 176
Crosby, Bob, 120
Crossfire Hurricane (bull), 148, 203
Crow tribe, 253
Croy, Homer, 178

Daddy of 'Em All. See Frontier Days
  (Cheyenne, Wyoming)
Dallas, Texas, 8–9
dallying, 67
Danger (Brahma bull), 207–8, 210
Danks, William, 102
daredevil riding, 135
Dary, David, 93
Davidson, Sara, 49
Davis, Miles, 109
day money, 44–45, 80
day sheets, 36, 44, 104
"dead spots," 144
Deadwood Days of '47 Rodeo (South
  Dakota), 46
Declaration of Independence, 30
Deer Trail, Colorado, 30–31
Dell (bronc), 241
DeMoss, Cody "Hot Sauce," 79–80
Denver, Colorado, 81–85, 89–91,
  98–103
DeVito, Danny, 298
D&H Cattle Company, 148
Dillinger (film), 206–7

Dip'n Queeny (bronc), 274–75
Dodge, Grenville M., 91–92
Dominion (Scully), 300–301
Donnelly, John, 66
Donovan, Wild Bill, 10
Doolin, Bill, 170
Douglas, Kirk, 298
Douglas, Michael, 298–99
drugstore cowboys, 48
Duncan, Mary, 251–52
Dust Bowl image, 2
Duvall, Robert, 130

Earp, Virgil, 26, 40
Earp, Wyatt, 26
Eastwood, Clint, 186
Ebeling, Harry, 184, 188
Ehringer, Gavin, 72
Eighty-Niners' Day Rodeo (Guthrie, Oklahoma), 5, 6, 168–69, 185, 187, 205, 210
Electric Horseman, The (film), 194
Ellison, Flipper, 187
End of the Trail, The (statue), 208, 210
Estes Park, Colorado, 213–14
Etbauer, Billy, 272, 274–75, 278

face guards, 294
Fairbanks, Douglas Sr., 119
Fawcett, Farah, 54–55
Fellowship of Christian Athletes, 140
Ferguson, Thompson B., 162
Fey, Paul, 1
Fey, Vic, 170
Five Civilized Tribes, 31
flak jackets, 130–31
flanking, 33
flank strap, in bull riding, 71–72
Flatheads, 238
Flavors (Williams), 153
Fletcher, George
    described, 235–36, 239–40, 244

in Fletcher/Sundown/Spain competition (1911), 217–18, 240–43
Fletcher, Louise, 298
Flynn, Shirley E., 95, 98
Ford, John, 277
Ford Center (Oklahoma City), 152–54, 188–92, 197–204
Forman, Milos, 298, 299
Fort Worth (Texas) Fat Stock Show, 164
Freeman, Danny, 29, 33
Frisco Railroad, 158, 161
Frizzell, Lefty, 109
Frontier Days (Cheyenne, Wyoming), 85–88, 96–98, 103–7, 110–51
    arena, 125–26, 139–43
    cowboy attire and, 103–7
    Cowboy Church, 139–42, 149
    cowboy ready room, 123–25, 145
    events in, 126–36, 142–43, 164, 167, 173, 174
    Frontier Park, 104, 110–12, 115–18, 151
    history of, 99–100
    museum, 118–23
    nighttime concerts, 137–39
    origins of, 97–98
    paniolo tradition and, 120–23
    post-rodeo events, 136–39, 145–51
    size of, 111–15, 125–26, 135–36
Frontier Days (Prescott, Arizona), 27–36, 38–39, 42–50, 53–80, 69
    cowboy ready area, 77–79
    events in, 56–73, 173, 174
    history of, 23, 28–32
    Junior Bonner (film) and, 40–43, 74–75, 76, 168, 277
    post-rodeo events, 75–77
Frost, Kellie, 129
Frost, Lane, 127–30, 232
Furlong, Charles Wellington, 214–16, 218–20, 228–29, 233
Future Farmers of America (FFA), 185

gambling, 92, 290–91
Gap, The, 52
Gardenshire, Emilne, 30–31
Garrett, Marvin, 53
Garrett, Sammy, 158, 166–67, 174, 181,
    232
Gateway to the Sahara (Furlong), 215
Gay, Donnie, 73, 120, 187–88, 292
Gaylord, E. K., 190–91
Gaylord, Ed, 190–91
Gaylord, Edward L., 191
George Thorogood and the Destroyers,
    62
Geronimo, 161, 174
Gibson, Hoot, 164, 232
Ginsberg, Allen, 108
goat sackin', 282–83
Goldberg, Isaac, 26
Goldwater, Barry, 24
Goldwater, Morris, 24
"good hand," 47
grand entry, 53–55, 125–26, 251
Grand Ole Opry, 191
Grapes of Wrath, The (book;
    Steinbeck), 2
Grapes of Wrath, The (film), 277
Grateful Dead, 109, 125, 185
Graves Dougherty Hearon & Moody,
    114–15
Gray, Robert, 206–11
Great Land Run (1889), 155, 156–58,
    162–63, 167–68
Great Train Robbery, The (film), 174–75
Great White Hope, 240
Guthrie, Oklahoma, 167–71
    carnival, 169–70
    described, 167–68
    Eighty-Niners' Day Rodeo, 5, 6,
        168–69, 185, 187, 205, 210
    Guthrie Roundup Club, 5, 181, 185
    as hometown of author, 1–6, 40,
        76–77, 168–70, 179–84, 204, 266
    kicker culture and, 184–88

Lazy E Arena, 52, 190–92
    rodeo parades, 76–77
    roots of Bullnanza in, 190–92
Guts (Johnson), 178–79

Hacky Sack, 125
Haggard, Merle, 246, 262, 266
Hall, Bronco Bob, 243–45
Halsey, Hump, 166–67, 181
Hanes, Bailey C., 170–72, 174, 175–77,
    178–79
Hanger (bronc), 61
Harrison, John, 135
Harry Vold Rodeo Company, 55–57
Harter, Bradley, 80
"Hawaiian Rough Riders," 123
Hawaiian steer ropers, 120–23
Hawks, Howard, 193–94
Hay, Rod, 278–79
Hays, Jack, 31
hazers, 57–58
header, 66–67
Heath, Chris, 149–50
Hedeman, Tuff, 44, 53, 127
heeler, 66–67
Heinz, W. C., 12, 19
helmets, 131, 283, 294
Heston, Charlton, 209, 226
Hickok, Wild Bill, 92, 95
Hillside Strangler (bull), 148
hippie movement, 108
Hogue, Calvery, 59–60
Holliday, Doc, 26, 40
Holmes, John Clellon, 108
Honey, Jace, 59
Honey, Keo, 59
hoolihans, 58, 245
hotshot, 57
Howard, Robert, 153
Hubbard, Ray Wylie, 151
Hud (film), 186
Hughes, Howard, 277
hung up, 59

Independence Day, 30, 36, 77, 96–98, 123
Indian cowboys, 217–18, 233–34, 237–45, 279, 289, 298–99
Indian relay racing, 252–53

jackpotting, 182
Jackson, Michael, 143
James, Charmayne, 114–15
Jamestown Exposition (Virginia; 1907), 174
Jauregui, Andy, 120
Jaycee Bootheel Rodeo (Sikeston, Missouri), 46
jeans, 50–53, 106, 107, 168, 185, 210
Jeffries, Jim, 240
John, Elton, 148
Johnson, Ben, 42, 187, 201, 226, 232, 246, 248
Johnson, Ben O., 187, 201, 232
Johnson, Cecil, 178–79
Johnson, Jack, 240, 241
Johnson, Scott, 80
Jones, Tommy Lee, 130
Jory, Cathy, 236–37
Jory, Doug, 236–37
JumboTron, 18, 292–93, 294
"Jumping Jack Flash," 148
Junior Bonner (film), 40–43, 74–75, 76, 168, 277

Ka'au'a, Archie, 121–23
Kamehameha, King, 120
Keith, Toby, 138–39, 142–43, 146, 197–98
Kelly, Bert, 240
Kennedy, Arthur, 277
Kerouac, Jack, 85, 86, 108, 109, 136
Kesey, Ken, 108, 109, 216–18, 230, 233–34, 298–99
Ketchum, Lloyd, 262–63
kicker culture, 184–88, 280–84, 295–96
Kiff, Martin, 54, 61–62, 66

Kimball, George D., 102
King, Carole, 141
kipuka roping, 121
Koyle, Dustin, 62

Lakota, 238
Lambert, Cody, 129
Lambert, Mel, 297–99
Lane, Phil, 244
Last Go Round (Kesey and Babbs), 217–18
Last Picture Show, The (film), 246
Las Vegas, Nevada
    conventions and, 290–91
    gambling and, 290–91
    Thomas & Mack arena, 287–90, 292–93
    See also National Finals Rodeo
Lawrence, Elizabeth Atwood, 96–97
Lawrence Welk and his orchestra, 138
Lazy E Arena (Guthrie, Oklahoma), 52, 190–92
Leakey (Texas) Fourth of July Rodeo, 280–84, 295–96
leather handgrip, in bull riding, 71
Lee (jeans), 50
Leivas, Juan, 33, 40, 289
Leone, Sergio, 186
Lesniak, Ray, 39, 44, 47, 56–57, 79
Let 'Er Buck (Furlong), 214–16, 218–20, 228–29
Levi Strauss & Co., 50–53, 107, 168, 185, 210
Lewis, Walton, 177
Lightfoot (bronc), 240
Limas, Alfonso "Poncho," 144–45
Lincoln, Abraham, 25
Little Egypt, 26
Littlefield Cattle Company, 172
Locke, Mary Agnes, 156, 157
Lockwood, Anna. See Stratton, Anna Lockwood Newell (grandmother)
Lockwood, Jacob W., 88–89

Logan, Pete, 8–9, 15, 197, 288, 292
Lonesome Dove (film), 130
Long Quiet, 31
Long Tom (bronc), 241
Low, Eben, 121–23
Lucchese (boots), 107, 188, 284, 285
Lucchese, Sam, 107
Luchsinger, E. P., 140
Luchsinger, Paul, 140–42
Luchsinger, Susie, 140–42
Lupino, Ida, 42
Lusty Men, The (film), 41, 277

MacMurray, Fred, 137–38
Madison Square Garden, 162–63, 237
Mahan, Larry, 7–8, 10, 15, 46, 120, 232, 273, 292
Manifest Destiny, 30
Man with No Name (film), 188
marking out, 60, 65
Marx, Harpo, 143
Massachusetts Bay Commonwealth, 88
matched horse racing, 134–35
McBride, Justin, 36n, 47, 146, 148, 149–50, 151, 198, 203, 285–86
McCasland, Layne, 276
McClary, Ty, 113
McClure, Dave "Mr. Cowboy," 173
McCoy, Horace, 277
McEntire, Clark, 140
McEntire, John, 140
McEntire, Pake, 140
McEntire, Reba, 140
McKee, Justin, 125–26, 132, 134, 135, 143, 250–51, 252, 255, 276, 278
McKinley, William, 161
McKinney, Alexis, 99
McKinney, Bill, 42
McMullin, John, 31
McMurtry, Larry, 23, 64, 66, 130
McQueen, Steve, 41, 75
McSpadden, Clem, 8–9, 17–19, 129–30, 196–97, 202, 288, 292

Meyers, A. G., 191–92
Midnight (bronc), 100
Mighty Duck, The (film), 113
Miles, Nelson "Bear Coat," 237
Milius, John, 206–7
Miller, Scott, 80
Miller, Zack, 177–78
Miller Brothers' 101 Ranch, 174–77, 204
Miller Brothers' 101 Ranch Show, 164, 174–75
Minthorn, Gilbert, 233
Mission Pack (bull), 286
Mr. Rodeo, Himself (Gray), 206–11
Mr. T (bull), 14
Mitchum, Robert, 277
Mix, Tom, 27, 40, 161–62, 164, 168, 174, 175
Molalla (Oregon) Buckaroo Rodeo, 221
Montana Blizzard (bronc), 30–31
Moore, Mike, 276
Mortensen, Dan, 79, 278
Mr. T (bull), 128
Mudslinger (bull), 286
Mulhall, Lucille, 159–66
    death of, 165–66
    as first well-known cowgirl, 155–56, 159–64, 168, 174, 177, 204, 232, 289
    marries Tom Burnett, 164–65
    in National Cowboy Hall of Fame, 181
Mulhall, Zack, 155–66
    Congress of Rough Riders and Ropers, 158–64, 166, 204
    family background of, 155
    financial hardships of, 165
    as railroad livestock agent, 156–58
Murphy, Louis "Bubba," 78, 201, 202
Murray, Terry, 232–33
Murray, Ty, 46, 79, 127, 189, 200
Musil, Denis, 182–83
mutton bustin', 282
mutton scramble, 282

Napolitano, Janet, 75, 76
NASCAR, 54, 146, 295
Nation, Carry, 168
National Cowboy Hall of Fame
    (Oklahoma City), 19, 123, 170, 181
National Editors Association
    convention, 174
National Finals Rodeo
    awards, 119
    as big-money event, 112, 292
    Dallas, 1960, 8–9
    events in, 112–15, 134, 144, 190, 272
    Las Vegas, 1995, 44
    Las Vegas, 2003, 286–93
    move from Oklahoma City to Las
        Vegas, 140–41, 287, 291
    Oklahoma City, 1967, 1–3, 6–19,
        190, 192, 194, 196–97, 292
National Finals Steer Roping, 134n,
    190–92
National High School Finals Rodeo, 272
National Intercollegiate Rodeo
    Association, 273n
nationalism, 30
National Western Stock Show, 100, 100n
Native Americans. See Indian cowboys;
    names of specific tribes and nations
Native dance competition, 254
Navajo Nation, 288–90
Navajo Nation Fourth of July Rodeo
    (Window Rock, Arizona), 46, 47,
    79, 144, 289
NBC, 199–200, 295
Nelson, Willie, 193–96, 218
Newell, Anna Lockwood. See Stratton,
    Anna Lockwood Newell
    (grandmother)
Newell, Mary Lockwood (great-
    grandmother), 89
Newell, William (great-grandfather), 89
New Journalism, 218–20
Newman, Paul, 186
New Spain, 31–32

Nez Percé, 218, 234–35, 237–39,
    243–44
Nicholson, Jack, 298, 299
Nike sneakers, 131, 294
Nixon, Richard, 9
Norman Film Manufacturing Company,
    175
North Platte, Nebraska
    Cowboy Fun, 96–97
    Old Glory Blowout, 96–97
Nunnemaker, Jaron, 80

Oates, Warren, 206–7
Ohl, Cody, 53
Okanagon Nation, 252–53
Oklahoma A&M, 5
Oklahoma A&M Entertainers, 167
Oklahoma City, Oklahoma, 152–204
    described, 152–54
    Ford Center, 152–54, 188–92,
        197–204
    Professional Bull Riders Bullnanza,
        153–54, 188–92, 197–204
    Roselawn Cemetery, 154–56, 177
    See also National Finals Rodeo
Oklahoma City Blazers, 190
Oklahoma Historical Society, 31–32
Oklahoma Panhandle State University,
    272–73
Oklahoma State University, 5, 167
Old Joseph, 234–35, 244
Once They Heard the Cheers (Heinz), 19
One Flew Over the Cuckoo's Nest (film),
    233–34, 298–99
O'Neill, William Owen "Buckey,"
    24–25, 82, 158
On the Road (Kerouac), 85, 86, 136
Oral History of Rodeo, An (Jory and
    Jory), 236–37
Oregon Health Sciences University
    (Portland), 247–48, 250
Osage Nation, 35, 105, 187, 201
Owens, Buck, 185

Palace Saloon, Prescott, Arizona, 26–27, 38–39, 40–41, 74–75
Palance, Jack, 4
Palmer, Joe, 19
pancake breakfasts, 75, 137
Panhandle Slims (shirts), 106–7, 210
paniolo tradition, 120–23
parades, 75–77, 137
Parker, Charlie, 109
Parker, Quannah, 164
Parkison, Chuck, 9
Parsons, Gram, 185–86
Pawnee Bill, 204
Payne, John, 62–64, 207
Peacock, Gene, 205
Peck, Schuyler, 102
Peckinpah, Sam, 40–43, 74–75, 76, 246
Pecos, Texas, West of the Pecos Rodeo, 28–31, 46, 69
Pendleton, Oregon
    Crabby's Underground Saloon, 260–64
    described, 228–34
    Happy Canyon pageant, 251
    Rainbow Café, 264
    "underground Pendleton," 235n, 244
    See also Pendleton Round-Up (Pendleton, Oregon)
Pendleton Round-Up (Pendleton, Oregon), 216–20, 228–34, 235–45, 250–79, 300
    events in, 164, 166–67, 174, 232, 250–55, 274–79
    finals, 277–79
    Fletcher/Sundown/Spain competition (1911), 217–18, 235–45
    Last Go Round (Kesey and Babbs), 217–18
    Let 'Er Buck (Furlong), 214–16, 218–20, 228–29
    Let 'Er Buck Room, 255–62
    origins of, 232, 233

post-rodeo events, 255–64, 268–69
preliminary activities, 231–32, 233, 245
Round-Up grounds and arena, 229
    size and importance of, 229–30, 232–33
Sundown/Rollens/Hall competition (1916), 243–45, 279
Pendleton Woolen Mills, 229
People for the Ethical Treatment of Animals (PETA), 300–301
Peterson, Wiley, 146, 198, 203
Petty, James, 183
Phillips, Terrell, 113
Pickens, Slim, 297–98
Pickett, Bill, 170–79, 232, 289
pickup men, 113, 143
pigging string, 133
Pletcher, K. J., 148
Plimpton, George, 218
Polhamus, Boyd, 288
Ponca City, Oklahoma, 34–35
Poncas, 105
Porter, Willard, 201
Poseidon, 69
Prescott, Arizona, 22–80
    as "Cowboy Capital of the World," 39
    described, 23–27, 40–41
    in history of rodeo, 23, 28–32
    Palace Saloon, 26–27, 38–39, 40–41, 74–75
    Vendome Hotel, 27, 40, 75–77
    Whiskey Row, 25–27, 40–41
    See also Frontier Days (Prescott, Arizona)
Preston, Robert, 42
Pritchett, Eddie Lou, 167
Proctor, Alexander Phimister, 243
Professional Bull Riders (PBR), 47, 53, 71–72, 126, 180
    animal rights and, 301
    Built Ford Tough Series, 146, 192, 199

Challenger Tour, 146
championship, 285–86
in Cheyenne, Wyoming, 145–51
formation of, 130
in Las Vegas, Nevada, 291
in Oklahoma City Bullnanza,
    153–54, 188–92, 197–204
open events, 200
safety attire of, 130–31
Professional Rodeo Cowboys
    Association (PRCA)
animal rights and, 301
awards of, 63
corporate sponsors of, 51, 53
members of, 7, 36, 45, 46, 112, 140
National Finals Steer Roping and,
    134n, 190–92
National Western Stock Show and,
    100n
origins of, 196
rodeos sanctioned by, 169, 251,
    272–73, 281
steer roping sanctioned by, 134n
"world's oldest rodeo" and, 30
See also National Finals Rodeo
Purdy, Ikua, 120–23, 289
Putnam, G. P., 214–16
"Pu'u Huluhulu," 123
Puyallup (Washington) Fair and Rodeo,
    46, 221

racism, 175–79, 218, 235–36, 240–45
raking, 60, 65, 73, 241
Ranch Rodeo (Ponca City, Oklahoma),
    34–35
Randall, Glenn Sr., 209
rank, 14, 14n
Rasmussen, Flint, 143–44, 148, 250–51,
    254
Ray, Nicholas, 41, 277
Reagan, Ronald, 67
Redding, Seth, 126
Redford, Robert, 194

Red River, 193–94
Red River (film), 193–96
Reeves, Tom, 46, 274
Resistol (hat), 105–6, 107, 286–87
ribbon roping, 182–83
Ricky and the Raiders, 185
"Ride Me Down Easy," 37, 37n
riding glove, in bull riding, 70, 200
ringmaster, 55–57
Risky Chris (quarter horse), 114–15
Ritter, Tex, 206
Rocky Mountain Clothing Company,
    52–53
rodeo (general)
big-money events in, 46, 100n, 112,
    199–202, 292
corporate sponsorships of, 46, 51,
    54–55, 78, 116, 117, 146, 189, 192,
    197, 199–203
cowboy attire and, 4–5, 27, 48–53,
    77–78, 103–7, 130–31, 185, 210,
    214–15, 238, 243, 283, 286–87, 294
dances following, 73–75, 260–64
events in, 56–73, 126–36
films about, 41–43, 74–75, 76, 168, 277
grand entry, 53–55, 125–26, 251
history of, 23, 28–32, 69, 96–100,
    295–96
kicker culture and, 184–88, 280–84,
    295–96
origins of, 28–32, 295–96, 301
pancake breakfasts, 75, 137
parades, 75–77, 137
prototypes for, 155–60
racism and, 175–79, 218, 235–36,
    240–45
ringmaster, 55–57
rodeo queens, 54–55, 76, 251–52
trophy saddles, 118–19, 294–95
See also Wild West shows
Rodeo Cowboys Association (RCA), 7,
    36, 51
rodeo dances, 73–75, 260–64

rodeo del Ganado, 32
rodeo groupies, 74, 261
Rodeo Hall of Fame, 298
Rodeo in America (Wooden and
    Ehringer), 72
rodeo queens, 54–55, 76, 251–52
Rodeo Queens and the American Dream
    (Burbick), 55, 251–52
Rodewald, Roy, 112–13
Rodewald, Ryan, 112–13
Roe, Jonathan, "J. M," 280–84, 295–96
Rogers, Roy, 206, 209
Rogers, Will, 3–4, 19, 160–66, 177, 181
Rollens, Rufus, 243–45
Roller, Bob, 114
Roman riding, 135, 207
Romer, Bobby, 128–29
Rooftop Rodeo (Estes Park, Colorado),
    213–14
Roosevelt, Theodore, 24–25, 94, 98,
    158, 159, 161, 162, 174
roping. *See* ribbon roping; steer roping;
    team roping; tie-down roping (calf
    roping); trick roping
Rosebrook, Jeb, 42–43
Roselawn Cemetery (Oklahoma),
    154–56, 177
rosin, 71, 78
Rough Riders, 24–25, 82, 158, 161, 162
rough-stock events. *See* bareback
    riding; bull riding; saddle bronc
    riding
Rowley, Dennis, 28, 32–35
Royal, Darrell K., 278–79
Rude, Ike, 119–20, 134, 232
Rupp, Virgil, 240, 241, 242
Rusty (horse), 63–64

Sackmann, Charles C., 101–3
saddle bronc riding, 9, 29, 45–47, 134
    described, 64–66
    Fletcher/Sundown/Spain
        competition (1911), 217–18, 235–45

scoring in, 61n
Sundown/Rollens/Hall competition
    (1916), 243–45
top riders, 45–47, 78–80, 112–13,
    122, 145, 148, 240–45, 272,
    274–75, 278–79
Sagers, Stormy, 54
St. Paul (Oregon) Rodeo, 221
Sampson, Will, 233–34, 298–99
San Angelo (Texas) Stock Show and
    Rodeo, 46
San Antonio (Texas) Livestock
    Exposition, 46
Santa Fe, New Mexico, 31
Santa Fe railroad, 156–58
Savery, C. W., 83, 84
Savery Savory Mushrooms Company,
    83, 84–85
"Screw You, We're From Texas," 151
Scully, Matthew, 300–301
Sedgwick, Josie, 251–52
Sedona, Arizona, 39
Serpa, Louise L., 58–59
Severe, Darla, 251, 252, 270
Severe, Duff, 270
Shane (film), 4
Sharkey (bull), 218–20
Sharlot Hall Museum (Prescott,
    Arizona), 26, 35–36, 39
Shaver, Billy Joe, 37, 37n, 213
Sheppard, Chuck, 67
shiny brights, 74, 261
Shivers, Chris, 53, 198, 200, 202, 285–86
short-go (finals), 127
Shoulders, Jim
    as owner of Tornado (bull), 14, 17,
        196
    rodeo career of, 7, 11, 13, 120, 127,
        232, 273
Sikeston, Missouri, Jaycee Bootheel
    Rodeo, 46
"Silent Majority," 9
silent Westerns, 163–64

Silkwood, Karen, 182
Sinor-Estrada, Sheri, 68
Sitting Bull, 238
slack (elimination rounds), 32–33, 33n, 231–32, 233, 245
Slack, Henry, 28–29, 29
Sleeping Good, David, 218
Smith, Phil, 61
Smith, Red, 19
Smokey (bronc), 104
Smokey the Wonder Horse, 208–10
snuff, 78
Snyder, Emily (Peggy), 90–91, 98–99
Social Security Death Index, 249
Sooners, 157
Spain, John
    described, 236–37
    in Fletcher/Sundown/Spain competition (1911), 217–18, 240–43
Spain, King, 236, 239
Spanish-American War, 24–25, 82–83, 100, 119–20
Speckled Bird (bull), 148
Spradley (horse), 175, 177
Springboard (bronc), 80
Springsteen, Bruce, 69
Sproat, Clyde Kindy, 120–21
Stampede (Cody, Wyoming), 10
Staneart, Marty, 128
Stanley, Dick, 122
Stanley, Henry M., 216
Stansbury, Kathryn B. (Kay), 156–57, 160–61, 165
Stanush, Claude, 277
Stapleton, Ben, 102
"Star-Spangled Banner, The," 126, 198
State Fairgrounds Arena (Oklahoma City)
    described, 6–7
    and National Finals Rodeo (1967; Oklahoma City), 1–3, 6–19, 190, 192, 194, 196–97, 292

Steagall, Red, 19, 194
steer roping, 29, 127, 131–34
    described, 131–32
    history of, 132–34
    as illegal activity, 133
    Lucille Mulhall, 159–64
    National Finals Steer Roping, 134n, 190–92
    as sanctioned by PRCA, 134n
    top ropers, 120–23, 134, 159–64, 187, 201
steer wrestling (bulldogging), 9, 134, 135, 245
    described, 57–60
    injuries in, 58–60
    origins of, 170–74
    scoring in, 59–60
    top wrestlers, 166–67, 170–79
Stetson, John B., 286–87
Stills, Stephen, 191–92
stock contracting business, 55–57, 66, 80, 126, 148, 182
Storm Barn Snuff (bronc), 66
Strait, George, 51–52
Stratton, Anna Lockwood Newell (grandmother), 88–91
    carnival business of, 110, 118
    children of, 88, 89–91, 98–99, 107–10
    family background of, 88–89
    first marriage of, 89–90
    identities of, 89
    imprisonment of husband and, 102–3, 107–9
    marries Don Carlos Stratton Sr., 98–99
    meets Don Carlos Stratton Sr., 85, 90–91
    moves to Denver, 89–91
Stratton, Don Carlos Jr. (father), 6, 20–21
    artifacts of life, 264
    Bigfoot and, 227
    birth of, 88, 99, 227

Stratton, Don Carlos Jr. (father)
(*continued*)
  birth of son, Kip, 6, 38
  Frank Blair and, 221–23, 228, 250,
    264–67
  carnivals and, 110, 211–12
  charm of, 37–38, 49
  as construction worker, 221–24
  Cornishes and, 206, 208–14, 221–22,
    225
  cremains of, 247–48, 250, 266,
    267–68, 296–97
  death of, 248, 249–50, 265
  described, 265–66
  drinking and, 213, 222, 223–25,
    226–27, 265–66
  family background of, 82–83,
    107–10, 151
  imprisonment of father, 102–3, 107–9
  in Oklahoma City, 153
  in Oregon, 220–25
  as petty criminal, 109, 224–25
  photographs of, 51, 208, 210
  as rodeo bum, 36–38, 49, 82, 100,
    109, 110, 151, 213–14, 221–22, 289
  as rodeo competitor, 6, 35–38, 45, 51,
    205–6, 223
  smoking and, 222
  son's search for, 20–21, 210–14,
    245–50
  as truck driver, 225
  womanizing of, 213, 214, 220–24,
    227–28
Stratton, Don Carlos Sr. (grandfather)
  in Canon City penitentiary, 102–3,
    107–9
  Cheyenne Frontier Days and, 99–100
  death of, 109–10
  death of first wife, 85
  early career, 82–85
  embezzlement and, 83, 84–85,
    100–103
  family background of, 82–83

  marries Anna Lockwood Newell,
    98–99
  meets Anna Lockwood Newell, 85,
    90–91
  personal references of, 102
Stratton, Gib, 35–36
Stratton, W. K. (Kip)
  birth of, 3–4, 6, 38
  career in journalism, 20, 34–35, 62,
    168, 176, 191–92, 193–97, 210–11
  career in politics, 34
  childhood illnesses of, 183
  college years of, 184, 188
  early love of cowboy clothes, 4–5,
    183
  family background of, 1–6, 20–21, 38
  Guthrie, Oklahoma as hometown,
    1–6, 40, 76–77, 168–70, 179–84,
    204, 266
  kicker culture and, 184–88, 280–84,
    295–96
  at National Finals Rodeo (1967;
    Oklahoma City), 1–3, 6–19
  rodeo parades during childhood,
    76–77
  search for father, Don Carlos Stratton
    Jr., 20–21, 210–14, 245–50
Stratton, Luscaine (wife), 23, 27, 28,
    32–40, 75, 296–97
Stratton, Mary (grandmother), 85
Stratton, Winfield Scott, 82–83
Strickland, Mabel, 251–52
stunt riding, 130, 135, 162
suertes (events), 32
suicide wrap, in bull riding, 70
Sul Ross State University, 273n
Sundown, Jackson
  described, 237–39
  in Fletcher/Sundown/Spain
    competition (1911), 217–18,
    240–43, 289
  in Sundown/Rollens/Hall
    competition (1916), 243–45, 279

sunfishing, 66
Swanson, Juliana, 181
Sweek, Jack, 242
Sweeney (bronc), 241
Sweet Pea (bull), 275
Synder, Luke, 53

Taft, William Howard, 229
tail, in bull riding, 70
Taillon, Cy, 8–9, 197, 288, 292
Takin' Care of Business (bull),
    128–29
Tallman, Bob, 288
Tar Baby (bull), 148–49
Taupin, Bernie, 148
Tauromaquia, 70
Taylor, Dub, 42
Taylor, Tillman, "Til," 218, 242
team bronc riding, 56–57, 79, 80
team roping, 9, 52, 135, 144
    described, 66–67
    injuries in, 67
    top ropers, 187
Texas Rangers, 31
Texas State Fairgrounds (Dallas), 8–9
Thedford, Darrell, 182
Thedford Ranch, 181–83, 282
They Shoot Horses, Don't They?
    (McCoy), 277
Thomas & Mack arena (Las Vegas),
    287–90, 292–93
Thompson, Hunter S., 218
Thorogood, George, 62
Thurston, Ray, 126
Tibbs, Casey, 11, 45, 79, 106, 120
tie-down roping (calf roping), 9, 113,
    134
    described, 33–34, 62
    top ropers, 119–20
Tony Lama (belt), 107
Tony Lama (boots), 185
Tooyalaket, Heinmot (Chief Joseph),
    234–35, 237

Tornado (bull)
    burial at National Cowboy Hall of
        Fame, 19
    described, 13–15
    in National Finals Rodeo (1967;
        Oklahoma City), 13–19, 190, 192,
        194, 196–97, 204, 292
Trapnell, Fred, 183–84
Trapnell, Myrtle, 183–84
"Trashy Women," 142
Travis County Livestock Show
    (Texas), 38
trick riding, 62–64, 207–12
trick roping, 135, 166–67, 181
Trigger (horse), 209
trophy saddles, 118–19, 294–95
Truitt, Dick, 120
Tuekakas (Old Joseph), 234–35, 244
turn-out, 44–45, 104
Turtle Dove (bronc), 278

Umatilla tribe, 218, 230, 233, 239–40,
    243, 253
Unassigned Lands, 156–58
Union Pacific Railroad, 86, 91–92, 96,
    97–98, 103, 119
U.S. Marshals Posse, 76
U.S. Smokeless Tobacco Cup
    Challenger Series, 46, 189, 199
U.S. Team Roping Championship, 52
University of Central Oklahoma, 184
University of Oregon, 217–18
Urban Cowboy (film), 48

Van Bergen, Martin, 164
Vandeveer, Zachariah P. See Mulhall,
    Zack
Vold, Harry, 55–57, 66, 80, 126
Vold, Kirstin, 56
Voyles, Lee, 208

Waaya-Tonah-Toesits-Kahn. See
    Sundown, Jackson

"Waiomina," 123
Wakeley, Jimmy, 206–7
Walker, Jerry Jeff, 142–43
Wall, Chris, 142
Walla Walla tribe, 233, 243
Wallis, Michael, 94, 157
Ware Bros., 102
Warm Springs Nation, 252–53
Washburn, Owen, 36n, 53
Watts, Curtis, 187
Wayne, John, 193–94
Welk, Lawrence, 138
well, the, 16, 16n, 144–45
We Pointed Them North (Blue), 51
West, Clay, 58–59
West, Terry Don, 36n
West of the Pecos Rodeo (Pecos, Texas), 28–31, 46, 69
Wettengel, Earl, 101
White, Mike, 53
White Bird, 237–38
White Eagle, 177
Whitfield, Fred, 53, 289–90
Whitman, Spud, 203
Wildbill, Cedric, 239, 240, 244
Wildbill, Tania, 240, 244
wild-cow milking, 254–55
wild-horse racing, 135
wild steer riding, 30
Wild West shows, 51, 55, 96–97, 98, 158–64, 166, 174–75, 177–78, 204
Wilkins, Lewis, Jr., 206
Willert, Jeffrey, 80

Williams, George P., 102
Williams, Hank, 109
Williams, Hank Jr., 138
Williams, L. A., 288–90
Williams, Mason, 152–53
Wills, Bob, 206
Wills, Johnnie Lee, 206
Wilson, Woodrow, 215
Windham, Trav, 29
Window Rock, Arizona, Navajo Nation Fourth of July Rodeo, 46, 47, 79, 144, 289
Winthrop Fleet, 88
Wolfe, Tom, 219
Women's Professional Rodeo Association, 114
Wooden, Wayne S., 72
World's Oldest Rodeo (Freeman), 29
World War I, 215, 236, 243
World War II, 216, 273n
Wrangler (jeans), 50, 51–53, 54, 106

X1 (bull), 80

Yancey, Cotton, 294
Yard Dawgz, 190
Young, Edmund, 102
Young, Neil, 185
youth culture, 6–7, 9, 108–9, 136, 138–39, 146–47, 148, 185–86
"You've Got a Friend," 141

Ziegfeld Follies, 163